T0211013

Lecture Notes in Artificial Intelligence　　10238

Subseries of Lecture Notes in Computer Science

LNAI Series Editors

Randy Goebel
　University of Alberta, Edmonton, Canada
Yuzuru Tanaka
　Hokkaido University, Sapporo, Japan
Wolfgang Wahlster
　DFKI and Saarland University, Saarbrücken, Germany

LNAI Founding Series Editor

Joerg Siekmann
　DFKI and Saarland University, Saarbrücken, Germany

More information about this series at http://www.springer.com/series/1244

Reyhan Aydoğan · Tim Baarslag
Enrico Gerding · Catholijn M. Jonker
Vicente Julian · Victor Sanchez-Anguix (Eds.)

Conflict Resolution in Decision Making

Second International Workshop, COREDEMA 2016
The Hague, The Netherlands, August 29–30, 2016
Revised Selected Papers

 Springer

Editors
Reyhan Aydoğan ⓘ
Özyeğin University
Istanbul
Turkey

Tim Baarslag ⓘ
Centrum Wiskunde and Informatica (CWI)
Amsterdam
The Netherlands

Enrico Gerding ⓘ
University of Southampton
Southampton
UK

Catholijn M. Jonker ⓘ
Interactive Intelligence
Delft University of Technology
Delft, Zuid-Holland
The Netherlands

Vicente Julian ⓘ
Department of Computer Systems and
  Computation
Technical University of Valencia
Valencia
Spain

Victor Sanchez-Anguix ⓘ
Coventry University
West Midlands
UK

ISSN 0302-9743   ISSN 1611-3349 (electronic)
Lecture Notes in Artificial Intelligence
ISBN 978-3-319-57284-0   ISBN 978-3-319-57285-7   (eBook)
DOI 10.1007/978-3-319-57285-7

Library of Congress Control Number: 2017938167

LNCS Sublibrary: SL7 – Artificial Intelligence

Printed on acid-free paper

This Springer imprint is published by Springer Nature
The registered company is Springer International Publishing AG
The registered company address is: Gewerbestrasse 11, 6330 Cham, Switzerland

Preface

Today's world is social and complex in nature. Societies have evolved and many problems faced by individuals can no longer be solved in solitude. We require cooperation with others to pursue our own goals, in many complex scenarios like politics and businesses, as well as in our day-to-day life. As we all hold different goals and interests, conflict emerges as a natural part of our lives. Successful cooperation requires solving conflicts among interested parties. The importance of conflict resolution has driven research in many fields like anthropology, psychology, mathematics, biology, and recently, in artificial intelligence. Despite their diametrically different approaches, the goal of these disciplines has always revolved around either solving conflict or helping us to understand conflicts. This can be explained not only by our need to cooperate, but also by the global importance of avoiding escalation and, therefore, striving for a better world.

The Second International Workshop on Conflict Resolution in Decision Making (COREDEMA 2016) focused on theoretical and practical computational approaches for solving and understanding conflict resolution. These computational approaches may be inspired by a wide variety of disciplines such as anthropology, psychology, economy, biology, mathematics, and computer science itself. Indeed, one of the goals of this workshop is to allow researchers from different disciplines to discuss their perspectives on conflict resolution.

This book gathers the proceedings of COREDEMA 2016, which was held in conjunction with the 22nd European Conference on Artificial Intelligence (ECAI 2016), The Hague, The Netherlands, on August 29. A total of 13 submissions were sent to the workshop, four of them being short papers from ECAI 2016 invited to submit a full version to the workshop, and nine of them being direct submissions to the workshop. All the invited contributions from ECAI 2016 were accepted as full papers, while 55% of direct submissions were accepted as full papers. All of the contributions were reviewed by at least three experts in the area.

We would like to thank all of the authors that contributed to the workshop, as well as the fantastic Program Committee that helped to ensure and check the scientific quality of the articles. Finally, we also want to thank the reader, and we hope that this book helps you in advancing the current state of the art in computational approaches for conflict resolution.

January 2017

Reyhan Aydoğan
Tim Baarslag
Enrico Gerding
Catholijn M. Jonker
Vicente Julian
Victor Sanchez-Anguix

Organization

The Second International Workshop on Conflict Resolution in Decision Making (COREDEMA 2016) was organized in conjunction with the 22nd European Conference on Artificial Intelligence (ECAI 2016) in The Hague, The Netherlands, on August 29, 2016.

Organizing Committee

Reyhan Aydogan	Ozyegin University, Turkey
Tim Baarslag	CWI, The Netherlands
Enrico Gerding	University of Southampton, UK
Catholijn M. Jonker	TU Delft, The Netherlands
Vicente Julian	Polytechnic University of Valencia, Spain
Victor Sanchez-Anguix	Coventry University, UK

Program Committee

Javier Bajo	Polytechnic University of Madrid, Spain
Vicente Botti	Polytechnic University of Valencia, Spain
Tung Bui	University of Hawaii, USA
Natalia Criado	King's College London, UK
Scott Cunningham	TU Delft, The Netherlands
Stella Heras	Polytechnic University of Valencia, Spain
Koen Hindriks	TU Delft, The Netherlands
Gert Jan Hofstede	Wageningen University, The Netherlands
Gregory Kersten	Concordia University, Canada
Jerome Lang	LAMSADE, France
Paulo Novais	University of Minho, Portugal
Nir Oren	University of Aberdeen, UK
Valentine Robu	Heriot-Watt University, UK
Avi Rosenfeld	JCT, Israel
Samy Sa	Federal University of Ceara, Brazil
Zhaleh Semnani-Azad	Clarkson University, USA
Carles Sierra	CSIC-IIIA, Spain
Bauke Steenhuisen	TU Delft, The Netherlands
Jose Such	King's College London, UK
Katia Sycara	CMU, USA
Alejandro Torreño	UPV, Spain
Laurent Vercouter	INSA de Rouen, France

Contents

Boolean Negotiation Games

Nils Bulling and Koen V. Hindriks[✉]

TU Delft, Delft, The Netherlands
{n.bulling,k.v.hindriks}@tudelft.nl

Abstract. We propose Boolean Negotiation Games, a computationally grounded model to investigate strategic aspects of negotiations. Our model is inspired by the popular Boolean Game framework and Rubinstein's bargaining model of alternating offers. We analyse restrictions on negotiation protocols and investigate properties of agreements. We propose and investigate protocols that do not allow repeating offers. In the context of Boolean Games we then naturally obtain finite games, which arise in many practical negotiation contexts. We show that Boolean negotiation games (BNGs) can yield agreements which are more beneficial than the stable solutions (i.e. Nash equilibria) of the underlying Boolean game, and propose an algorithm to compute stable negotiation strategies.

1 Introduction

In [20, p. 2] automated negotiation is said to be "perhaps the most fundamental and powerful mechanism for managing inter-agent dependencies at run-time". Given the need for collaborative and interoperable autonomous systems, automated negotiation has attracted a lot of attention in the multi-agent community ever since, and in economics and game theory for even longer. There are at least two prominent methodologies to analyse negotiation settings: off-line using game theoretic techniques [4,20,24], and online using heuristic and evolutionary models [2,15]. In particular, in the game theoretic approach a lot of work uses Rubinstein's bargaining model of alternating offers [5,23], often making the assumptions of perfect rationality and perfect information. We are interested in studying partial knowledge. Although a lot of research has already looked at negotiation under incomplete information [3,14] where the knowledge parties have about the opposing party is incomplete, analysing this setting theoretically has been a challenge. Boolean Games, moreover, allow us to study aspects of control and power in a negotiation that can occur in multi-agent domains.

In this paper our focus is on providing a compact model that allows to investigate strategic aspects of protocols for negotiating. The model we propose is inspired by Boolean games [8,19] (BG) which have become a popular model in the multi-agent domain. The many variants and extensions of BGs related to knowledge [1], cooperative teams [12], control and manipulation [13,17], secret goals [10], iterated execution [18], dependencies [7], and pre-play negotiations about payoffs [25] just to name a few, make them an ideal starting point for our purposes. Our model can naturally be extended to incomplete information settings in future work.

© Springer International Publishing AG 2017
R. Aydoğan et al. (Eds.): COREDEMA 2016, LNAI 10238, pp. 1–18, 2017.
DOI: 10.1007/978-3-319-57285-7_1

The main *contributions* of this paper are a model of negotiation called *Boolean Negotiation Games* (BNG) and a formal analysis of this model in a setting where offers cannot be repeated. In the context of BGs the non-repetition of offers naturally yields finite games, which arise in many practical contexts. We present an algorithm to compute stable strategies called *negotiation equilibria*. We show that negotiation equilibria always exist and illustrate that BNGs can yield agreements which are more beneficial than the Nash equilibria of the underlying BG. In this context, the negotiation protocol plays a crucial role. A negotiation protocol gives rise to a specific unfolding of a BG with similarities to extensive games, but this unfolding is more general as it may not result in a complete agreement on all outcomes resulting in a smaller BG being played after the negotiation phase. As such, different properties of negotiation protocols greatly affect the game being played.

Outline of the paper. In Sect. 2 we introduce preliminaries including the Boolean game (BG) model. Then, in Sect. 3 we introduce our model called generalised extensive BG that constitutes in combination with a negotiation protocol, a Boolean negotiation game (BNG). Properties of BNGs are studied in Sect. 4, where we also present an algorithm to compute negotiation equilibria. We show that these equilibria always exist. Finally, we sketch related work and conclude. Due to space limitation we omit proofs.

2   Preliminaries

Throughout the paper we assume a fixed set of agents, also referred to as players, $\mathsf{Agt} = \{1, \ldots, k\}$. We use bold font to denote a vector $\boldsymbol{x} = (x_1, \ldots, x_k)$ of length k if not said otherwise; $\boldsymbol{x}_i$ refers to element x_i in $\boldsymbol{x}$. We denote by $\boldsymbol{x}_\cup$ the union $\bigcup_{i=1}^{k}\{\boldsymbol{x}_i\}$. Note that we impose no restrictions on the type of the $\boldsymbol{x}_i$'s; it can be a number, a set or a function.

Propositional Logic. For the remainder of this paper we also assume a finite set of (propositional) variables Π. We use PL to refer to the set of propositional formulae where propositional variables are drawn from Π. The formulae $\top$ and $\bot$ denote truth and falsum, respectively. An X-*valuation*, where $X \subseteq \Pi$, is a function $\xi : X \to \{\mathsf{t}, \mathsf{f}\}$ where $\{\mathsf{t}, \mathsf{f}\}$ is the set of Boolean truth values. It defines which variables from X are true and false, respectively. We often represent ξ by the indexed set $\{x \in X \mid \xi(x) = \mathsf{t}\}_X$, explicitly specifying only the variables set true. By slight abuse of notation we simply write $\xi_X \subseteq X$. $\xi_\emptyset$ denotes the special valuation with the empty domain. The set of all X-valuations is Val_X. We often omit the index X in ξ_X and Val_X whenever $X = \Pi$. An *extension* of ξ_Y is any valuation ξ_X with $Y \subseteq X$ such that $\xi_X \cap Y = \xi_Y$. We use $\mathsf{Val}_Y^{\subseteq} = \bigcup_{X \subseteq Y} \mathsf{Val}_X$ to denote the union of all X-valuations where X is a subset of $Y \subseteq \Pi$. Sometimes it is more convenient to represent ξ_X, with $X = \{x_1, \ldots, x_n\}$, as a sequence of the form $x_1 \ldots \bar{x}_i \ldots x_n$ where each $x_i \in \xi_X$ and $\bar{x}_i \notin \xi_X$. For example, $\bar{p}q\bar{r}$ denotes the valuation $\{q\}_{\{p,q,r\}}$. We assume that the reader is familiar with standard propositional logic and write $\xi \models_{\mathsf{PL}} \varphi$ to denote that Π-valuation ξ

makes φ true. Finally, given a valuation ξ_X and a formula φ, we write $\varphi[\xi_X]$ for the formula that equals φ but where each variable $x \in X$ is replaced by $\top$ and $\bot$ if $x \in \xi_X$ and $x \notin \xi_X$, respectively.

Boolean Games (BGs). We consider BGs without costs similar to [6] but replace, for the ease of presentation, prioritized goal bases with simpler preference lists. Preference lists are used by several authors to model agents' preferences. A *preference list* $\Gamma_i = (\gamma_1^i, \ldots, \gamma_{p_i}^i)$ of player i, $p_i \in \mathbb{N}$, is a sequence of formulae of PL where γ_1^i is the tautology $\top$. Formula γ_j^i represents the goal of rank j. The agent prefers formulae to be true with a rank as high as possible. We assume that each agent i has its own preference list Γ_i. A preference list gives a natural way to define a payoff function $\mu_i : \mathsf{Val}_\Pi \to \mathbb{N}_0$ for each agent: $\mu_i(\xi) = \max\{j \mid \xi \models \gamma_j^i\}$. Often, it is convenient to use a preference relation $\preceq_i$ where $\xi \preceq_i \xi'$ iff $\mu_i(\xi) \leq \mu_i(\xi')$. A *Boolean game* is a tuple $\mathcal{B} = (\mathsf{Agt}, \Pi, \boldsymbol{\Pi}, \boldsymbol{\Gamma})$ with $\mathsf{Agt} = \{1, \ldots, k\}$ a non-empty set of agents, Π a finite, non-empty set of variables, $\boldsymbol{\Pi}_i \subseteq \Pi$ a set of variables *controlled* by i such that $\boldsymbol{\Pi}$ forms a partition of Π, and each $\boldsymbol{\Gamma}_i$ is a preference list of formulae of PL. We require that $\boldsymbol{\Pi}$ forms a partition because the control of variables should be exclusively assigned to a single agent. Note that agents can usually not ensure the truth of their goal formulae on their own, which is for examples the case for $x \wedge y$ if x and y are controlled by different agents. A *strategy profile* is a vector $\boldsymbol{\xi}$ consisting of $\boldsymbol{\Pi}_i$-valuations $\boldsymbol{\xi}_i \in \mathsf{Val}_{\Pi_i}$ for $i \in \mathsf{Agt}$. A strategy profile $\boldsymbol{\xi}$ can be naturally identified with the Π-valuation $\boldsymbol{\xi}_\cup$. We shall lift the preference relation to Boolean games and strategy profiles[1]: $\boldsymbol{\xi} \succeq_i^\mathcal{B} \boldsymbol{\xi}'$ iff $\boldsymbol{\xi}_\cup \succeq_i^\mathcal{B} \boldsymbol{\xi}'_\cup$. We write $\boldsymbol{\xi} =_{-i} \boldsymbol{\xi}'$ whenever $\boldsymbol{\xi}_j = \boldsymbol{\xi}'_j$ for all players $j \in \mathsf{Agt}\backslash\{i\}$. A strategy profile $\boldsymbol{\xi}$ is a *Nash equilibrium* if no agent can unilaterally deviate from $\boldsymbol{\xi}$ to improve its payoff, i.e. there is no $\boldsymbol{\xi}'$ with $\boldsymbol{\xi} =_{-i} \boldsymbol{\xi}'$ such that $\boldsymbol{\xi}' \succ_i \boldsymbol{\xi}$. The set of all Nash equilibria in $\mathcal{B}$ is denoted by $\mathsf{NE}(\mathcal{B})$. Finally, we define a modified version of a BG in which the truth values of some variables according to a valuation $\xi_X \in \mathsf{Val}_X$ have been fixed. The ξ_X-*reduced BG of* $\mathcal{B}$ is the BG $\mathcal{B}[\xi_X] = (\mathsf{Agt}, \Pi', \boldsymbol{\Pi}', \boldsymbol{\Gamma}')$ where $\Pi' = \Pi\backslash X$, $\boldsymbol{\Pi}'_i = \boldsymbol{\Pi}_i\backslash X$ and $\boldsymbol{\Gamma}'_i = (\gamma_1^i[\xi_X], \ldots, \gamma_{p_i}^i[\xi_X])$; in words, all variables fixed by ξ_X are removed from the game and in the goal formulae these variables are replaced by $\bot$ and $\top$ according to ξ_X.

Example 1 (Prisoners Dilemma). Let us consider the classical Prisoners Dilemma normal form game [21]:

Prisoners Dilemma		Pris. 2	
		don't c. ($\neg c_2$)	confess (c_2)
Pris. 1	don't c. ($\neg c_1$)	(2,2)	(0,3)
	confess (c_1)	(3,0)	(1,1)

The propositions c_i play the role of actions: setting c_i true means that Prisoner i confesses; otherwise, the prisoner defects/does not confess. Each full valuation gives a payoff for both players, e.g. $c_1 \bar{c}_2$ gives Prisoner 1 a payoff of 3 and Prisoner 2 a payoff of 0. We can model the game as a BG[2]

---

[1] We omit the superscript $\mathcal{B}$ whenever clear from context.

[2] As $\mathsf{Agt} = \{1, 2\}$, $\boldsymbol{x}$ refers to vectors of length 2.

$\mathcal{B} = (\{1,2\}, \{c_1, c_2\}, (\{c_1\}, \{c_2\}), \boldsymbol{\Gamma})$ with $\boldsymbol{\Gamma}_i = (\top, c_i \wedge c_{-i}, \neg c_i \wedge \neg c_{-i}, c_i \wedge \neg c_{-i})$ for $i \in \{1,2\}$ and $-i$ equals $3 - i$. As in the normal form setting, the unique Nash equilibrium is the strategy profile $\boldsymbol{\xi}$ with $\boldsymbol{\xi}_i = \{c_i\}$ for $i = 1, 2$.

3   Negotiations in Boolean Games Settings

In this section we introduce Boolean negotiation games (BNGs) which allow players to interact in BGs by exchanging proposals sequentially. Therefore, we first define generalised extensive Boolean games (GBGs) which are then instantiated with negotiation protocols. A negotiation protocol is imposed on a given BG affecting the possible actions of agents. Such a protocol adds a new layer of strategic interaction as not just the plain selection of a specific proposal is important but also the timing is of crucial significance, for example in the setting in which proposals cannot repeat.

3.1   Generalized Extensive Boolean Game

Like a BG, a *generalized extensive Boolean game* (GBG) consist of agents that try to obtain an outcome which gives them maximal payoff. GBGs generalise the standard game theoretical notion of an extensive (Boolean) game [21] as well as that proposed in [19]: (i) agents' actions are not limited to setting a single variable at a time but may *propose settings for multiple variables*, in principle including those which they *do not control*, (ii) at terminal histories, not all variables must be assigned a truth assignment. Throughout this paper we assume a vector **Act** consisting of sets of actions. Agent i draws its actions from the set **Act**$_i$. Possible choices are, e.g., **Act**$_i = \mathsf{Val}\!\subseteq_{\overline{\Pi}_i}$ and **Act**$_i = \mathsf{Val}_{\Pi_i}$, but it is important to note that we do not restrict ourselves to these cases and allow actions differently from variable valuations, as we shall discuss in the next section. We denote actions by act and use the notation act$_X$ to indicate that the action corresponds to a valuation from Val_X. We also denote by act$_i$ a variable ranging over actions, in contrast to that note that act$_X$ is a specific action. An action act$_X$ is said to *conflict* with action act$_Y$ performed earlier during the game if act$_X \cap Y \neq$ act$_Y \cap X$; or in words, if there is an $z \in X \cap Y$ that is assigned opposite truth values by act$_X$ and act$_Y$. As in extensive form games, a protocol determines which agent's turn it is as well as the enabled actions at the current situation. A *history* is a possibly empty sequence $h \in \mathbf{Act}_\cup^*$ of actions. ϵ is the empty sequence. $\ell(h)$ is the length of h with $\ell(\epsilon) = 0$, and if $\ell(h) = n$, $h \cdot$act is the $n+1$-length history with the last action being act. The operator $\cdot$ represents the concatenation of two sequences; $h^{\leq n}$ denotes the subsequence of h that consists of the first n actions of h, if $\ell(h) \geq n$. Finally, we write act $\in h$ to denote that act is an element on h.

Definition 1 (Protocol, P-history, P-run). *A protocol (over **Act**) is a (partial) function $P : \mathbf{Act}_\cup^* \to \mathsf{Agt} \times 2^{\mathbf{Act}_\cup}$ such that if $P(h) = (i, V)$ then $V \subseteq \mathbf{Act}_i$. A history $h = (\mathsf{act}_1, \ldots, \mathsf{act}_n)$ is P-consistent, P-history for short, if for all m with $0 \leq m < \ell(h)$ we have $\mathsf{act}_{m+1} \in V$ with $P(h^{\leq m}) = (i, V)$, $i \in \mathsf{Agt}$. A P-run* *is a finite or infinite sequence* $\rho \in \mathbf{Act}_\cup^* \cup \mathbf{Act}_\cup^\omega$, *where* $\mathbf{Act}_\cup^\omega$ *denotes the set of all infinite sequences over* $\mathbf{Act}_\cup$, *such that each finite prefix of* ρ *is a P-history, and if* ρ *is finite then it cannot be extended; we also say that it is* terminal. *We use* $\mathcal{R}_P$ *to refer to the set of all P-runs.*

Whenever $P(h) = (i, V)$ we write $P^{agt}(h)$ to refer to agent i, and $P^{act}(h)$ to refer to the set of actions V. We use the same notation introduced for histories also for runs where $\ell(\rho) = \infty$ for an infinite run ρ. Given a protocol P, a P-*strategy* for agent i for that game is a (partial) function $\pi_i : \mathbf{Act}_\cup^* \to \mathbf{Act}_i$ the domain of which consists of all non-terminal P-histories h with $P^{agt}(h) = i$ such that $\pi_i(h) \in P^{act}(h)$. A *profile* of P-strategies $\boldsymbol{\pi}$ yields a unique P-run $\rho_{\boldsymbol{\pi}}$. Moreover, we denote by $\rho_{\boldsymbol{\pi},h}$ the P-run which results if $\boldsymbol{\pi}$ is followed from P-history h on.

Example 2. Consider the Prisoners Dilemma from Example 1 and the protocol P over $\mathbf{Act} = (\{c_1, \bar{c}_1\}, \{c_2, \bar{c}_2\})$ with the set of runs being $\mathcal{R}_P = \{\bar{c}_1, c_1 c_2, c_1 \bar{c}_2\}$ and $P^{agt}(\varepsilon) = 1$ and $P^{agt}(c_1) = 2$. A P-strategy π_1 of player 1 can e.g. assign $\{\bar{c}_1\}$ to ϵ, and π_2 be defined arbitrarily, then $\rho_{\boldsymbol{\pi}} = \bar{c}_1$.

Definition 2 (Generalized Extensive BG). *A* generalised extensive Boolean game *(GBG) is a tuple* $\mathcal{G} = (\mathrm{Agt}, \Pi, \boldsymbol{\Pi}, \boldsymbol{\Gamma}, \mathbf{Act}, P)$ *where* $\mathrm{BG}(\mathcal{G}) = (\mathrm{Agt}, \Pi, \boldsymbol{\Pi}, \boldsymbol{\Gamma})$ *is a BG and* P *a protocol over* $\mathbf{Act}$. *We often write* $P_\mathcal{G}$ *to refer to* P. *The BG* $\mathrm{BG}(\mathcal{G})$ *is called the* underlying BG *of* $\mathcal{G}$.

Outcomes and Strategies. Let us now consider how players interact in a GBG. First, we note that the unique P-run $\rho_{\boldsymbol{\pi}}$ yielded by strategy profile $\boldsymbol{\pi}$ may not set the truth of all variables as is the case in Example 2. In addition to that, some of the performed actions might be conflicting, e.g. a player may set a variable true and the same variable false later during the game. The general rule used to determine the outcome is that any action that conflicts with an action performed later during the game is reverted and ignored in the computation of the outcome. We present a formal treatment in the context of BNGs in Sect. 3.2. At this moment the intuition that the P-*outcome of a P-strategy profile* $\boldsymbol{\pi}$ at P-history h, denoted by $out_P(\boldsymbol{\pi}, h)$, is a (partial) valuation from $\mathrm{Val}|_{\Pi}^\subseteq$ which results if all players follow $\boldsymbol{\pi}$ from h on, is sufficient. If the P-outcome is not a Π-valuation, then the agents need to settle on the remaining variables in some way or another. For this purpose the agents interact in the $out_P(\boldsymbol{\pi}, \varepsilon)$-reduced BG of $\mathrm{BG}(\mathcal{G})$, $\mathrm{BG}(\mathcal{G})[out_P(\boldsymbol{\pi}, \varepsilon)]$. In that game agents have to select a strategy to define a truth value for the variables which not yet have a truth value. Therefore, a *strategy profile of a GBG* $\mathcal{G}$, $\mathcal{G}$-*strategy profile* for short, is a tuple $\boldsymbol{\sigma} = (\boldsymbol{\pi}, \boldsymbol{s})$ consisting of a $P_\mathcal{G}$-strategy profile $\boldsymbol{\pi}$ and functions $s_i : \mathrm{Val}|_{\overline{\Pi}}^\subseteq \to \mathrm{Val}|_{\Pi_i}^\subseteq$ such that $s_i(\xi_X) \in \mathrm{Val}|_{\Pi_i \setminus X}$, defining actions in the possible ξ_X-reduced BG, for each $i \in \mathrm{Agt}$. This gives us a natural way to define the outcome of a GBG, combining the valuation obtained from following the P-strategy and the outcome of the reduced BG. The $\mathcal{G}$-*outcome of a* $\mathcal{G}$-*strategy profile* $\boldsymbol{\sigma} = (\boldsymbol{\pi}, \boldsymbol{s})$ at $P_\mathcal{G}$-history h is defined as $out_\mathcal{G}(\boldsymbol{\sigma}, h) = out_{P_\mathcal{G}}(\boldsymbol{\pi}, h) \cup \bigcup_{i \in \mathrm{Agt}} s_i(out_{P_\mathcal{G}}(\boldsymbol{\pi}, h))$. Note that the

$\mathcal{G}$-outcome is always a full Π-valuation. Next, we lift preference relations to $\mathcal{G}$-strategy profiles: $\boldsymbol{\sigma} \preceq_i^{\mathcal{G},h} \boldsymbol{\sigma}'$ iff $out_{\mathcal{G}}(\boldsymbol{\sigma}, h) \preceq_i^{\mathsf{BG}(\mathcal{G})} out_{\mathcal{G}}(\boldsymbol{\sigma}', h)$; we write $\preceq_i^{\mathcal{G}}$ for $\preceq_i^{\mathcal{G},\epsilon}$. As a solution concept, we introduce the concept of *generalised equilibrium*, a combination of a Nash equilibrium and subgame perfect Nash equilibrium. A $\mathcal{G}$-strategy profile $\boldsymbol{\sigma} = (\boldsymbol{\pi}, \boldsymbol{s})$ is a *generalized equilibrium* if for all $P_{\mathcal{G}}$-histories h, all players i and all other $\mathcal{G}$-strategy profiles $\boldsymbol{\sigma}' = (\boldsymbol{\pi}', \boldsymbol{s}')$ with $\boldsymbol{\sigma}'_{-i} = \boldsymbol{\sigma}_{-i}$ we have that $\boldsymbol{\sigma}' \preceq_i^{\mathcal{G},h} \boldsymbol{\sigma}$. We observe that a generalised equilibrium does not have to exist as some reduced BGs may not have a stable outcome. To see this, consider the trivial case in which the GBG consists of a single root node after which normal form games not having any Nash equilibria are played. In that case there is no generalised equilibrium either.

Example 3. The unique generalised equilibrium in the GBG given by the Prisoners Dilemma BG from Example 1 and the protocol from Example 2 is the strategy profile $(\boldsymbol{\pi}', \boldsymbol{s}')$ with $\boldsymbol{\pi}'_1(\epsilon) = c_1$, $\boldsymbol{\pi}'_2(c_1) = c_2$, and $\boldsymbol{s}'_2(\bar{c}_1) = c_2$. In particular, note that if Player 1 played $\bar{c}_1$ then Player 2 would ensure outcome $(0, 3)$ in the $\bar{c}_1$-reduced BG of BG($\mathcal{G}$).

3.2   Negotiation Protocols and Negotiation Game

It is well accepted that there are at least two minimal requirements most negotiations should satisfy: (i) agents can make proposals and are able to respond to them; (ii) agents need to approve a possible agreement before it is concluded [20,22]. The latter point also implies that taking part in a negotiation should be individually rational for each agent. Based on these two properties we now introduce negotiation protocols and Boolean Negotiation games (BNGs).

Proposals, Accepting and Agreeing. In contrast to GBGs we give a slightly different reading to actions from $\mathbf{Act}_{\cup}$. In the negotiation setting, actions should be thought of as *proposals* made to the other players. As a consequence, a proposal conflicting with a proposal made earlier implicitly *rejects* the earlier proposal and serves the purpose of a *counter-proposal*. To implement point (ii) above, we identify a sub-class of protocols that requires all agents except for the agent who made the last proposal to explicitly approve the agreement that is on the table. Therefore, players which are happy with the current proposals can accept. Players have to be cautious, though, because if a proposal is made all other players could accept it which concludes the negotiation. To this end, we slightly modify the interpretation of the empty valuation $\mathsf{act}_\emptyset$ which now serves as an accept action and is identified with the special action accept. In order to allow agents to accept, the protocol needs to support this. Formally, a protocol over $\mathbf{Act}$ *supports agreeing* iff accept $\in \mathbf{Act}_i$ for all $i \in \mathsf{Agt}$ and accept is enabled after each non-terminal history. We say that a P-history $(\ldots, \mathsf{act}^{n-k}, \mathsf{act}^{n-k+1}, \ldots, \mathsf{act}^n)$ is *agreeing* iff all but one agent accept the proposal act^{n-k} made by the remaining agent. Formally, we state this as:

(i) the agents that performed the last $|\mathsf{Agt}| = k$ actions are all mutually disjoint, i.e. $\mathsf{Agt} = \{P^{agt}(\ldots, \mathsf{act}^{n-l}) \mid l = 0, \ldots, k-1\}$,

(ii) the $(n - k + 1)$th action was a proposal, i.e. $\mathsf{act}^{n-k+1} \in \mathsf{Val}_{\overline{H}}^{\subseteq}$, and

(iii) the last $k - 1$ actions were accepts, i.e. $\mathsf{act}^{n-l} = \mathsf{accept}$ for $l = 0, \ldots, k - 2$.

Leaving the Negotiation: Quitting and Closed Runs. So far we have discussed two types of actions for an agent: an agent can either make a (counter-)proposal or accept the current proposals on the table. But agreeing is only one side of the coin. In some negotiation settings, a proposal may be unacceptable for a party and their may be no way an acceptable agreement can be reached. Therefore, the protocol must provide a mechanism which allows agents to leave a negotiation (i.e. a way to explicitly express that the agent does not accept). To do so, agents execute the action quit which leads, in terms of [4], to 'no deal'. Once an agent quits, the negotiation terminates[3]. A protocol over **Act** *supports quitting* iff quit $\in \mathbf{Act}_i$ for all $i \in \mathsf{Agt}$ and quit is enabled after each non-terminal history. Then, a run is *closing* iff its final action is quit and it does not contain any further quit actions.

Negotiation Protocols. Exchanging proposals, accepting and quitting are the essential ingredients of any negotiation; however, it is also important to organise a negotiation. A sensible assumption we make is that the negotiation is run in a turn-based way, as in Rubinstein's alternating offers protocol [23]. A protocol

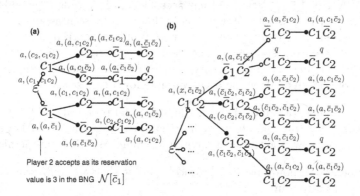

Fig. 1. Prisoner dilemma negotiation protocol. Open circles represent Player 1 actions whereas closed ones represent Player 2 actions. The labels show the computation of Algorithm 1, i.e. the labels are assigned to nodes. We simply write q for $(q, \{(\mathsf{quit}, \emptyset)\})$ and $x, (y, z)$ for $(x, \{(y, z)\})$. In Fig. (b), we have $x \in \{\bar{c}_1\bar{c}_2, \bar{c}_1c_2, c_1\bar{c}_2\}$. Moreover, we use a when used as an action as shortcut for accept. We also omitted accept as well as quit actions in the figure (due to the two player setting).

---

[3] We note that quitting is treated in a very specific way: the whole negotiation ends. Other alternatives include the setting where only the quitting agent leaves the negotiation (as e.g. in [12]) and the other players go on negotiating, where proposals no longer including any variable controlled by the players which quit.

P over agents $\mathsf{Agt} = \{1, \ldots, k\}$ is *turn-taking* if agent 1 is the first to act, then player 2,...then k, then 1 again etc. until the negotiation ends. Formally stated, P is turn-taking if for every P-history h with $\ell(h) \geq n \geq 2$ we have that[4] $P^{agt}(h^{\leq n}) - 1 \equiv P^{agt}(h^{\leq n-1}) + 1 \mod k$; moreover, we shall assume that Player 1 always starts, $P^{agt}(\varepsilon) = 1$. We are ready to give our formal definition of a negotiation protocol.

Definition 3 (Negotiation protocol). *A negotiation protocol (NP) is a protocol P which is turn-taking, supports agreeing as well as quitting and in which each P-run ρ is either agreeing containing no quit action, or is closing.*

The definition of NPs is very general. It often makes sense to put a restrictions on the proposals that can be made. For example, it is usually not helpful to make the same proposal again and again. If a proposal has not resulted in an agreement it will, under reasonable assumptions, also not do so if it is made over again, only if the proposer counts on wearing out his/her opposite. The assumption is also reasonable in terms of real negotiations where it is often difficult to get back to a previously rejected proposal [9]. Therefore, we focus on non-repeating protocols. A negotiation protocol P is *non-repeating* if no proposal can be made twice with the exception of $\xi_\emptyset$ playing the role of the accept action. Furthermore, in order to investigate agents' interactions we focus on two types of protocols: one in which agents make proposals concerning their own variables only; and one where agents propose full valuations only. A negotiation protocol P is called *(single) individual proposal* if $\mathsf{Act}_i = \bigcup_{p \in \Pi_i} \mathsf{Val}_{\{p\}} \cup \{\mathsf{quit}, \mathsf{accept}\}$, and it is called *full proposal* if $\mathsf{Act}_i = \mathsf{Val}_\Pi \cup \{\mathsf{quit}, \mathsf{accept}\}$. These assumptions can be seen as an abstraction of many negotiation settings. Consider for example the marked of second-hand items. Variables encode specific package deals (e.g. the red car with extra winter tires). Moreover, in such negotiations it is also a reasonable assumption that offers are not repeated. We leave other variants for future study.

Example 4. Figure 1(a) and (b) shows the individual proposal and full proposal non-repeating NP corresponding to the Prisoners Dilemma BG of Example 2, respectively. For now, the reader is advised to ignore the labels on the histories.

A key benefit of non-repeating protocols is that they are finite which allows to solve them bottom-up.

Proposition 1. *All runs in a non-repeating individual or full proposal NP are finite.*

Outcome and Strategies. We are ready to give the, previously postponed, formal definition of the P-outcome of a negotiation protocol. For this purpose, we first define an auxiliary function $\mathsf{rh} : \mathsf{Act}_\cup^* \cup \mathsf{Act}_\cup^\omega \to \mathsf{Act}_\cup^* \cup \mathsf{Act}_\cup^\omega$ that helps us to obtain a *reduced history* in which proposals that are rejected by later

---

[4] We need the -1 on the left-hand-side of the equation to accommodate the fact the agents are numbered starting from 1.

proposals are removed from that history. Afterwards, the remaining proposals are combined into a single valuation. The function rh is defined as follows: $\mathsf{rh}(h) = \epsilon$ if $\mathsf{quit} \in h$; else $\mathsf{rh}(\epsilon) = \epsilon$; and $\mathsf{rh}(\mathsf{act}_X \cdot h) = \mathsf{act}_X \cdot \mathsf{rh}(h)$ if there is no $\mathsf{act}_Y \in h$ such that act_Y conflicts with act_X, and $\mathsf{rh}(\mathsf{act}_X \cdot h) = \mathsf{rh}(h)$ otherwise. Now, given a non-conflicting history $\mathsf{rh}(h)$ we define $\mathsf{val}(\mathsf{rh}(h))$ as the X-valuation ξ_X where $\xi_X = \bigcup \{\mathsf{act}_Y \mid \mathsf{act}_Y \in \mathsf{rh}(\rho)\}$ with $X = \bigcup \{Y \mid \mathsf{act}_Y \in \mathsf{rh}(\rho)\}$.

Definition 4 (Protocol outcome). *The P-outcome of a P-strategy profile $\boldsymbol{\pi}$ at P-history h, $out_P(\boldsymbol{\pi}, h)$ is given by $\mathsf{val}(\mathsf{rh}(\rho_{\boldsymbol{\pi}, h}))$.*

We are ready to define Boolean negotiation games (BNGs) which are GBGs equipped with a negotiation protocol.

Definition 5 (Boolean negotiation game). *A Boolean negotiation game (BNG) is a GBG $\mathcal{N} = (\mathsf{Agt}, \Pi, \boldsymbol{\Pi}, \boldsymbol{\Gamma}, \mathbf{Act}, P)$ where P is a negotiation protocol over* **Act***.*

As for Boolean games we also use the notation $\mathcal{N}[\xi_X]$ to refer to the BNG in which some actions are removed and truth values of variables are fixed (cf. Sect. 2) according to ξ_X. We also lift the properties of NPs (e.g. full proposal) to BNGs.

3.3 Preferences and Reservation Values

In the following let $\mathcal{N}$ be a BNG. We are especially interested in the question whether agents have an $\mathcal{N}$-strategy profile $\boldsymbol{\sigma}$ which yields an agreement which is acceptable for all agents, given the possible outcomes of the underlying BG $\mathsf{BG}(\mathcal{N})$. The strategic reasoning of agents is rather involved, especially if the protocol is non-repeating, because by proposing some valuation it can never be proposed again if rejected by a player. If a player quits the negotiation, we assume that the outcome could be any Nash equilibrium in the underlying BG, if one exists. Thus, the specific outcome can be uncertain. As usual in negotiation settings agents have a reservation value [5] which corresponds to the payoff below which a player would refuse any proposal. A rather strict notion of reservation value would be a player's maxmin-strategy defining an outcome which the player can guarantee on its own. We call the corresponding reservation value the *maxmin $\mathcal{N}$-reservation value*. In the strategic setting we consider here, it makes good sense to relate the reservation value to outcomes of Nash equilibria, as they give a payoff at least as good as the maxmin reservation value. In general, there can be more than one Nash equilibrium, therefore, we define a weak and a strong notion. The *greedy $\mathcal{N}$-reservation value* (resp. *modest $\mathcal{N}$-reservation value*) is the player's maximal (resp. minimal) payoff received by any Nash equilibrium in $\mathsf{NE}(\mathsf{BG}(\mathcal{N}))$. If a game does not have any Nash equilibria both reservation values are defined as the player's maxmin $\mathcal{N}$-reservation value. We refer to *greedy* (resp. *modest*) agents as such which use as baseline their greedy (resp. modest) reservation values.

Proposition 2. *The greedy reservation value is at least as high as the modest reservation value which is at least as high as the maxmin reservation value.*

Payoff of Partial Valuations. Later in the paper, we need to be able to compare partial valuations. Given a partial valuation ξ_X we define $\mu_i^{\mathcal{N}}(\xi_X)$ as i's modest[5] $\mathcal{N}[\xi_X]$-reservation value, i.e. $\mu_i^{\mathcal{N}}(\xi_X)$ returns the reservation value in the reduced BG obtained with respect to valuation ξ_X. Note that $\mu_i^{\mathcal{N}}(\emptyset)$ is i's $\mathcal{N}$-reservation value. For two partial valuations ξ_X and ξ_Y we write $\xi_X \preceq_i^{\mathcal{N}} \xi_Y$ iff $\mu_i^{\mathcal{N}}(\xi_X) \leq \mu_i^{\mathcal{N}}(\xi_Y)$. Consequently, for two $P_{\mathcal{N}}$-strategy profiles π and π' we define $\pi \preceq_i^{\mathcal{N},h} \pi'$ iff $out_{P_{\mathcal{N}}}(\pi, h) \preceq_i^{\mathcal{N}} out_{P_{\mathcal{N}}}(\pi', h)$.

4   Analysis of Boolean Negotiation Games

In the following we analyses how rational agents in BNGs interact. We first present an algorithm to compute strategies of negotiating agents. Then, we investigate properties of the algorithm. Our analysis differs from a standard game theoretical analysis (of BGs) in several ways. First, the negotiation settings offers agents to quit a game which results in the play of BGs. As such our models merge one-shot games with extensive form games. Second, all characteristics of the game are clearly motivated from a negotiation point of view, which makes it specific on one hand, but, on the other hand, gives a flexible framework resulting in different unfolding of an input BG (one shot game) which allows to compare the effects of various negotiation protocols. As such, our framework allows to compare structural properties of games induced by different choices made in the underlying negotiation protocol.

Table 1. Postulates about the negotiation behavior of a *rational agent*. The postulate **Social** is needed to allow players to anticipate the result of their proposal; otherwise, the outcome would be non-deterministic which would require a more technical and less intuitive treatment. Also compare Footnote 6.

(Propose) A player chooses the best available proposal if it guarantees an outcome at least as high as its reservation value
(Accept) A player i accepts after h iff $\mu_i(\mathsf{val}(\mathsf{rh}(h)))$ is *better* than the outcome obtained by any other action if the negotiation was continued
(Quit) A player quits iff the continuation of the negotiation would yield an outcome below its reservation value
(Social) If an agent is indifferent between a set of proposals it chooses one which is most beneficial for its predecessors, where closest predecessors have higher priority than ones farther away

---

[5] Modest, because the agent cannot be sure that any better Nash equilibrium will be realised.

4.1   Computation of Strategies of Rational Agents

Before we can analyse BNGs we need to make weak assumptions about play-ers' behavior wrt. accepting proposals, making counter-proposals and quitting a negotiation. We list four postulates in Table 1 and define a *rational agent* as one which satisfies these postulates[6].

Thanks to Proposition 1 we can use Algorithm 1 to solve a non-repeating BNG by backward reasoning similar to the computation of subgame perfect Nash equilibria [21]. We present the main idea of the algorithm below and give a concrete illustration of how the algorithm is applied in Example 5. The input is provided by a BNG $\mathcal{N}$ the negotiation protocol of which is denoted by P. Each P-history h is labelled with $\mathsf{Lab}(h) \in \{a, q\} \times 2^{\mathsf{Act} \cup \mathsf{Val}_{\bar{n}}^{\subseteq}} \setminus \{\emptyset\}$. A label $\mathsf{Lab}(h) = (x, \{(\mathsf{act}_1, \xi_1), \ldots, (\mathsf{act}_h, \xi_h)\})$, $x \in \{a, q\}$ has the following meaning:

– if all agents act rationally then the negotiation continuing from h results in an agreement if $x = a$ and results in quitting the negotiation if $x = q$, respectively; and
– the agent whose turn it is performs some (optimal) action act_i, $i \in \{1, \ldots, h\}$ which results in a (final) outcome from $\{\xi_k \mid (\mathsf{act}_k, \xi_k), \mathsf{act}_k = \mathsf{act}_i, k = 1, \ldots, h\}$. All the outcomes in the set are equally good for the very agent.

The algorithm computes the labels starting from the terminal histories, fol-lowing the three main steps:

1. The first case considers a terminal history h. That is, either all truth values are settled after h or the BG $\mathcal{N}[\mathsf{val}(\mathsf{rh}(h))]$ is played. If the utility after h for i is less than its reservation value the agent quits in which case h is labelled $(q, \{(\mathsf{quit}, \emptyset)\})$. The first q indicates that the whole negotiation is quit; quit denotes the action of the very agent, and $\emptyset$ indicates that no (partial) agreement is reached. Otherwise, the agent accepts and the outcome is defined as the valuation induced by the reduced history of h. Consequently, h is labelled $(a, \{(\mathsf{accept}, \mathsf{val}(\mathsf{rh}(h)))\})$. Note that h must be agreeing, for otherwise the other agents could still perform an accept action themselves rendering h not to be terminal.
2. The algorithm continues recursively. Therefore, we consider a history h all successors of which have already been labelled. Case 2.1 describes the setting in which the agent quits as all continuations would result in an outcome worse than its reservation value. Case 2.2. computes an optimal action guaranteeing the best possible outcome. Therefore, the possible outcomes of all successor nodes, each labelled by $\lambda_i = (a, L_i)$, $i = 1, \ldots, l$, are considered and h itself is labelled by an action which maximises the outcome of the agent, i.e. leads to the best outcome in $\bigcup_{r=1}^{l} L_r$. However, there is one caveat: a label L_j at history $h' = h \circ \mathsf{act}$ may contain two elements, say (act_1, ξ_1) and (act_2, ξ_2),

---

[6] We include **Social** as the aim of negotiating parties is often not to demoralise others, if the agent itself does not benefit from it. However, other postulates would also be interesting to study in the future, e.g. *envious* agents.

such that the agent whose turn it is (at h) is indifferent between ξ_1 and ξ_2. In that case, we assume that the agent is social and chooses the alternative which is more beneficial for the precedent agents according to postulate **Social**. For this purpose the function *social* is applied to $\bigcup_{r=1}^{l} L_r$ before the optimal action for the agent is computed.

3. If all histories are labelled an action is picked form each label resulting in a P-strategy. If after each such P-strategy not all variables have a truth assignment the remaining variables are fixed by picking a Nash equilibrium strategy in the induced Boolean game. The combination of a P-strategy, together with a selection of a Nash equilibrium in the induced BG results in a $\mathcal{N}$-strategy profile.

Some subtleties of the algorithm to ensure the properties of Table 1 have been neglected in the informal description above and are captured in the following proposition.

Proposition 3. *Given a non-repeating, full or individual proposal BNG $\mathcal{N}$, Algorithm 1 computes a set of $\mathcal{N}$-strategy profiles for rational agents, i.e. postulates* **Propose, Accept, Quit** *and* **Social** *are obeyed.*

4.2   Properties of the Algorithm

To better understand how the algorithm works, we consider two examples before studying some properties more formally.

Example 5. (Prisoners Dilemma cont.). Let us first consider the individual proposal non-repeating NP shown in Fig. 1(a). Histories are labelled according to Algorithm 1. For example, the history $h = c_1 c_2 \bar{c}_1 \bar{c}_2$. which is labelled by $(a, \{(\text{accept}, \bar{c}_1 \bar{c}_2)\})$. To induced valuation is $\xi = \text{val}(\text{rh}(h)) = \bar{c}_1 \bar{c}_2$. This valuation gives Player 1 a utility of $\mu_1(\xi) = 2$ which is at least as high as the agents $\mathcal{N}$-reservation value. Thus, by Case 1 the agents accepts, yielding the valuation ξ which renders the whole history accepting (thus the label a).

For further illustration let us consider history $h = \bar{c}_1$. The two successor histories $\bar{c}_1 c_2$ and $\bar{c}_1 \bar{c}_2$ are labelled by $(a, \{(c_1, c_1 c_2)\})$ and $(a, \{(\text{accept}, \bar{c}_1 \bar{c}_2)\})$, respectively. The former indicates that if Player 2 proposes c_2, then Player 1 would propose c_1 which would result in an agreeing run yielding the valuation $c_1 c_2$. At h, Player 2 has to decide which of its four actions to take: quit, accept, propose c_2, or propose $\bar{c}_2$. The latter two actions would yield utility 1 ($c_1 c_2$) and 2 ($\bar{c}_1 \bar{c}_2$), respectively. Quitting the negotiation would guarantee the player's $\mathcal{N}$-reservation value. Accepting, however, would result in the BG $\mathcal{N}[\bar{c}_1]$ where Player 2 has a reservation value of 3 as the unique Nash equilibrium in the BG $\mathcal{N}[\bar{c}_1]$ is c_2. Thus, being rational Player 2 would accept after h; therefore, the history h is labelled $(a, \{(\text{accept}, \bar{c}_1)\})$ (Table 2).

Finally, we consider the initial history where Player 1 has to decide whether to quit, to propose c_1 or to propose $\bar{c}_1$. Quitting would result in the original game being played. Playing c_1 would result in the valuation $c_1 c_2$ and thus in a

Table 2. Variant of Backward Induction algorithm for BNGs for rational agents. Histories are labelled with tuples (x, L), having the following reading. The current history leads to acceptance (resp. quit) if $x = a$ (resp. $x = q$). An element $(\mathsf{act}, \xi) \in L$ means that act is an optimal action at the current history yielding outcome ξ (or ξ' if there is some other $(\mathsf{act}, \xi') \in L$ with the same action).

Algorithm 1
Input: a non-repeating BNG $\mathcal{N}$ with negotiation protocol $P = P_{\mathcal{N}}$.
Output: set of $\mathcal{N}$-strategy profiles for rational agents.

We recursively label each P-history h with a label $\mathsf{Lab}(h) \in \{a, q\} \times 2^{\mathsf{Act} \cup \times \mathsf{Val}_{\overline{\Pi}}^{\subseteq}} \setminus \{\emptyset\}$. Let h be a P-history and $P^{agt}(h) = i$.

1. If $h \in \mathcal{R}_P$: $\mathsf{Lab}(h) \leftarrow (q, \{(\mathsf{quit}, \emptyset)\})$ if $\mu_i(\mathsf{val}(\mathsf{rh}(h)))$ is worse than i's reservation value; and, $\mathsf{Lab}(h) \leftarrow (a, \{(\mathsf{accept}, \mathsf{val}(\mathsf{rh}(h)))\})$ otherwise.
2. If each $h \cdot \mathsf{act}_j$ with $\mathsf{act}_j \in P(h)$ is labelled with $\lambda_j = \mathsf{Lab}(h \cdot \mathsf{act}_j)$ and h is not yet labelled:
   2.1. If for all these labels $\lambda_j = (q, L_j)$ then: $\mathsf{Lab}(h) \leftarrow (q, \{(\mathsf{quit}, \emptyset)\})$ if $\mu_i(\mathsf{val}(\mathsf{rh}(h)))$ is worse than i's $\mathcal{N}$-reservation value; and, $\mathsf{Lab} \leftarrow (q, \{(\mathsf{accept}, \emptyset)\})$ otherwise.
   2.2. Otherwise, suppose $\lambda_1, \ldots, \lambda_l$ are all the labels with $\lambda_j = (a, L_j)$ and $L_j = \{(\mathsf{act}_1^j, \xi_1^j), \ldots, (\mathsf{act}_{h_j}^j, \varsigma_{h_j}^j)\}$. Let $L' = social(i, \bigcup_{r=1}^{l} L_r)$. Note that all these valuations necessarily result in the same payoff p for i.
      (i) If p is worse than i's $\mathcal{N}$-reservation value then $\mathsf{Lab}(h) \leftarrow (q, \{(\mathsf{quit}, \emptyset)\})$;
      (ii) else, $\mathsf{Lab}(h) \leftarrow (a, \{(\mathsf{act}_s^j, \xi_s^j) \mid (\mathsf{act}_s^j, \xi_s^j) \in L' \cap L_j, j = 1, \ldots, l\})$.
3. If ε is labelled, then selecting an action from each label of each P-history gives rise to a P-strategy profile, where accept is only chosen if no proposal is possible (to ensure **Accept**). All possible combinations of these selections yield a set of P-strategy profiles $\{\pi^1, \ldots, \pi^l\}$ (note that at each history there might be several "equally good" actions to follow). Now, let $s^1, \ldots, s^h$ be a sequence of functions $\mathsf{Val}_{\overline{\Pi}}^{\subseteq} \to \mathsf{Val}_{\overline{\Pi}}^{\subseteq}$ such that for all $n = 1, \ldots, h$ and all $\xi_X \in \mathsf{Val}_{\overline{\Pi}}^{\subseteq}$, $(s_1^n(\xi_X), \ldots, s_k^n(\xi_X)) \in \mathsf{NE}(\mathsf{BG}(\mathcal{N})[\xi_X]$ if $\mathsf{NE}(\mathsf{BG}(\mathcal{N})[\xi_X]) \neq \emptyset$, and $s_i^n(\xi_X)$ is i's maxmin strategy in $\mathsf{BG}(\mathcal{N})[\xi_X]$ otherwise. Finally, the algorithm returns the set $S = \{(\pi^r, s^i) \mid r = 1, \ldots l \text{ and } i = 1, \ldots, n\}$.

function $social(i, L)$
Input: an agent i and a set $L = \{(\mathsf{act}_1, \xi_1), \ldots, (\mathsf{act}_j, \xi_j)\}$
Output: a subset of L
The function is defined by recursion: If $i = 0$ return L. Otherwise, remove from L all elements (act, ξ) for which $\mu_i(\xi)$ is not the maximum in L. Return $social(i - 1, L)$.

---

payoff of 1. The action $\bar{c}_1$ would result in the Boolean Game $\mathcal{N}[\bar{c}_1]$ being played where Player 1 has a reservation value of 0. Thus, Player 1 would play action c_1, independent of whether it is greedy or modest.

The computed $\mathcal{N}$-strategy profile yields the outcome $(1, 1)$ for both greedy and modest players. Thus, it coincides with the Nash equilibrium of the standard Prisoners Dilemma BG. The full proposal variant is shown in Fig. 1(b). Here, the computed $\mathcal{N}$-strategy profile results in the (Pareto optimal[7]) outcome $(2, 2)$.

---

[7] A strategy profiles $\boldsymbol{\xi}$ is *Pareto optimal* if there is no other $\boldsymbol{\xi}'$ such that $\boldsymbol{\xi}' \succeq_i \boldsymbol{\xi}$ for all $i \in \mathsf{Agt}$ and $\boldsymbol{\xi}' \succ_i \boldsymbol{\xi}$ for some $i \in \mathsf{Agt}$.

Note that an additional alternative c_3 which is not part of any goal does not affect the outcome. In particular, if Player 2 plays c_3 after Player 1 played c_1, Player 1 accepts $c_1 c_3$: the outcome of $\mathsf{BG}(\mathcal{N})[c_1 c_3]$ is $(1,1)$ as well.

Example 6 (Bach and Stravinsky). We consider the classical Bach and Stravinsky normal form game represented as BG. The game has two Nash equilibria ($c_1 \bar{c}_2$ and $\bar{c}_1 c_2$):

Bach and Stravinsky		Player 2	
		Bach ($\neg c_2$)	Stravinsky (c_2)
Player 1	Bach ($\neg c_1$)	(2,1)	(0,0)
	Stravinsky (c_1)	(0,0)	(1,2)

We first analyse the game as a individual proposal, non-repeating BNG. The outcome depends on whether the players are greedy or modest. In the former case no agreement is reached and the BG version of Bach and Stravinsky is played. If, however, the players are modest the players agree on the outcome $(1,2)$. That is, Player 2 is better off. In contrast to the Prisoners Dilemma game, adding additional choices makes a difference. If Player 1 is given an additional action c_3 the outcome is either 'no agreement' (in the greedy case) or $(2,1)$ (in the modest case). The same pattern is true for the non-repeating, full proposal BNG.

Example 6 shows that in contrast to the bargaining setting of [21], there is in general no *First Mover Advantage* in BNGs; rather the contrary: it seems more beneficial to react to proposals as late as possible. The example also suggests that the number of choices is important. In general, agents with more options seem to have more negotiation power. A formal study is out of the scope of this paper and left for future research. Before we turn to the existence of specific strategies we give the following result.

Proposition 4. *Suppose π is a $\mathcal{N}$-strategy profile of the non-repeating, full choice or individual proposal BNG $\mathcal{N}$ computed by Algorithm 1.*

1. *If all players follow π and some player quits, then the players are greedy and $\mathsf{NE}(\mathsf{BG}(\mathcal{N})) \neq \emptyset$.*
2. *In the case of modest players, if a proposal ξ is accepted by all players then ξ is a full Π-valuation.*
3. *In the case of greedy players, if a proposal ξ is accepted by all players, then either ξ is a full Π-valuation or $\mathsf{NE}(\mathsf{BG}(\mathcal{N})[\xi]) \neq \emptyset$.*

Whereas the existence of a subgame perfect equilibrium in finite extensive form games is guaranteed by Kuhn's theorem (cf. [21]) this is not obvious in our setting. Indeed, it does not hold for the notion of generalised equilibrium put forward in the context of GBGs. The reason is that agents can quit the negotiation which results in a Boolean game over the not yet fixed variables. Thus, this Boolean game may not have any Nash equilibria which is the reason that a generalised equilibrium may not exist. In general the solution concept of generalised equilibrium is too strong as players base their decision on reservation values. Therefore, we define a weaker solution concept more appropriate for BNGs.

Definition 6 (Negotiation equilibrium). *An $\mathcal{N}$-strategy profile $\sigma = (\pi, s)$ is a negotiation equilibrium if for all $P_\mathcal{N}$-histories h, all players i and all other strategy profiles $\sigma' = (\pi', s')$ with $\pi'_{-i} = \pi_{-i}$ we have that $\pi' \preceq_i^{g,h} \pi$.*

That is, a $\mathcal{N}$-strategy profile $\sigma = (\pi, s)$ is a negotiation equilibrium if for all other P-strategies π' and from each history h the received payoff for each player if π' is followed is at most as high as the payoff received if π is followed from h one, if the induced outcome is complete; or the modest reservation value in the induced game after following π' is at least as high as the modest reservation value after following π. (The notation as been introduced at the end of Sect. 3.3.) Thus, this solution concept makes no further assumption about the players' behavior if a (complete) agreement is not reached apart from assuming that each player can be ensured to receive a payoff at least as good as its modest reservation value in the resulting reduced BG.

Theorem 1. *Algorithm 1 returns only negotiation equilibria. All computed $\mathcal{N}$-strategy profiles give each player a payoff which is at least as high as its reservation value with the exception of greedy players if $\mathsf{NE}(\mathsf{BG}(\mathcal{N})) \neq \emptyset$. Moreover, if for all $P_\mathcal{N}$-strategy profiles π we have that $\mathsf{NE}(\mathsf{BG}(\mathcal{N})[out_{P_\mathcal{N}}(\pi, \varepsilon)]) \neq \emptyset$ then all computed negotiation equilibria are generalised equilibria.*

From this it follows that a BNG always has (at least) a negotiation equilibrium.

Corollary 1. *All non-repeating BNGs have a negotiation equilibrium (for greedy as well as modest players).*

A study of further properties of negotiation protocols is left for future research. It would for instance be interesting when Pareto optimal outcomes are guaranteed. Example 5 shows that this is dependent on the protocol used; for example, the individual-proposal NP does not lead to a Pareto optimal outcome, where the full-proposal variant does.

5   Related and Future Work

A great body of work has analysed negotiations using game theorical models and in particular Rubinstein's bargaining model, see [11,15,20,22] for an overview. Much work in the game theoretic context deals with bilateral negotiations or specific setting like one-to-many negotiations [5]; in contrast, we admit multiple agents without further restrictions apart from turn taking. Also characteristic to our setting is that the negotiation is not about objects per se, but about actions and power. This is also a key difference to the BG model proposed in [25] where players can transfer some of their payoff to other players in order to incentivize them to change their strategies in specific ways. In future work it would be interesting to relate these approaches. We believe, however, that there are key differences as the negotiation protocol in our setting can be used to force players to accept specific outcomes which may not be achievable by transferring parts of an agent's payoff. A similar direction is followed in [16] where players can transfer utility before a binary voting game is played. The work presented in [12] is most closely related to our setting. The authors proposed a negotiation protocol for cooperative Boolean games. Using our terms their negotiation protocol is complete-offer and turn-based. Moreover, an agent the offer of which is refused leave the negotiation. The remaining agents continue the negotiation process. Another key difference is that agents cannot make any of their available offers but have to ensure that agents who made previous offers will not be worse off by the new offer. In this sense, the protocol is cooperative, in contrast to our setting where agents are completely self-interested. This property indicates another property of negotiation protocols which can be studied in our framework. Also, the protocol of [12] leads to a Pareto optimal outcome; here, it would be interesting to mirror the assumptions to our setting to obtain an analogous result.

BNGs inherent attractive properties of Boolean games such as being computationally grounded and we believe that BNGs have the potential to play a role similar to that BGs play for the analysis of strategic interactions in multi-agent systems. We are currently studying incomplete information extensions of BNGs where agents not only negotiate about 'control' but can also underpin their proposals with information and thus influence the behavior of others. We are also interested in heuristic approaches; in general, BNGs offer many interesting aspects which remain to be studied analytically as well as empirically, e.g. in which settings an agreement reached in BNGs is strictly better than the outcomes of the underlying BG. Related to our notion of reduced BG is also the work presented in [26] which interprets the last step of a negotiation as a normal form game, where mixed strategies are allowed. As they always guarantee a Nash equilibrium, a generalization to mixed strategies would also ensure the existence of a generalised equilibrium in BNGs according to Theorem 1. This provides an interesting direction for future investigations. At the moment we do also not consider explicit deadline of agents, only those imposed by the protocol. Individual agent deadline could be another aspect to include in the analysis of BNGs. Those deadlines could also be used to ensure that the resulting negotiation will always terminate.

6   Conclusions

In this paper we proposed Boolean negotiation games (BNGs) as compact and computational models, based on Boolean games (BGs), for studying strategic aspects in negotiations. We interpreted fundamental aspects of negotiations and presented an algorithm to compute stable negotiation strategies. We showed that such strategies always exist and that they give modest agents at least their reservation value which is defined based on the concept of Nash equilibrium.

The main contribution of this paper is the formal framework which allows to study interesting aspects related to negotiation settings in which agents have incomplete knowledge.

References

1. Ågotnes, T., Harrenstein, P., Hoek, W., Wooldridge, M.: Boolean games with epistemic goals. In: Grossi, D., Roy, O., Huang, H. (eds.) LORI 2013. LNCS, vol. 8196, pp. 1–14. Springer, Heidelberg (2013). doi:10.1007/978-3-642-40948-6_1
2. Baarslag, T., Hendrikx, M.J., Hindriks, K.V., Jonker, C.M.: Learning about the opponent in automated bilateral negotiation: a comprehensive survey of opponent modeling techniques. Auton. Agents Multi-agent Syst. 1–50 (2015)
3. Baarslag, T., Hindriks, K.V.: Accepting optimally in automated negotiation with incomplete information. In: Proceedings of the International Conference on Autonomous Agents And Multi-agent Systems, pp. 715–722. International Foundation for Autonomous Agents and Multiagent Systems (2013)
4. Beam, C., Segev, A.: Automated negotiations: a survey of the state of the art. Wirtschaftsinformatik 39(3), 263–268 (1997)
5. Binmore, K., Vulkan, N.: Applying game theory to automated negotiation. Netnomics 1(1), 1–9 (1999)
6. Bonzon, E., Lagasquie-Schiex, M.-C., Lang, J.: Compact preference representation for boolean games. In: Yang, Q., Webb, G. (eds.) PRICAI 2006. LNCS (LNAI), vol. 4099, pp. 41–50. Springer, Heidelberg (2006). doi:10.1007/978-3-540-36668-3_7
7. Bonzon, E., Lagasquie-Schiex, M.-C., Lang, J.: Dependencies between players in boolean games. Int. J. Approx. Reason. 50(6), 899–914 (2009)
8. Bonzon, E., Lagasquie-Schiex, M.-C., Lang, J., Zanuttini, B.: Boolean games revisited. In: ECAI, pp. 265–269 (2006)
9. Broekens, J., Jonker, C.M., Meyer, J.-J.C.: Affective negotiation support systems. J. Ambient Intell. Smart Environ. 2(2), 121–144 (2010)
10. Bulling, N., Ghosh, S., Verbrugge, R.: Reaching your goals without spilling the beans: boolean secrecy games. In: Boella, G., Elkind, E., Savarimuthu, B.T.R., Dignum, F., Purvis, M.K. (eds.) PRIMA 2013. LNCS (LNAI), vol. 8291, pp. 37–53. Springer, Heidelberg (2013). doi:10.1007/978-3-642-44927-7_4
11. Chatterjee, K.: Game theory and the practice of bargaining. In: Chatterjee, K., Samuelson, W. (eds.) Game Theory and Business Applications, vol. 194, pp. 189–206. Springer, USA (2014)
12. Dunne, P.E., van der Hoek, W., Kraus, S., Wooldridge, M.: Cooperative boolean games. In: AAMAS, vol. 2, pp. 1015–1022 (2008)
13. Endriss, U., Kraus, S., Lang, J., Wooldridge, M.: Designing incentives for boolean games. In: AAMAS, pp. 79–86 (2011)
14. Fatima, S.S., Wooldridge, M., Jennings, N.R.: Optimal negotiation strategies for agents with incomplete information. In: Meyer, J.-J.C., Tambe, M. (eds.) ATAL 2001. LNCS (LNAI), vol. 2333, pp. 377–392. Springer, Heidelberg (2002). doi:10.1007/3-540-45448-9_28
15. Fatima, S.S., Wooldridge, M., Jennings, N.R.: A comparative study of game theoretic and evolutionary models of bargaining for software agents. Artif. Intell. Rev. 23(2), 187–205 (2005)
16. Grandi, U., Grossi, D., Turrini, P.: Equilibrium refinement through negotiation in binary voting. In: Proceedings of the 24th International Conference on Artificial Intelligence, pp. 540–546. AAAI Press (2015)

17. Grant, J., Kraus, S., Wooldridge, M., Zuckerman, I.: Manipulating boolean games through communication. In: IJCAI, pp. 210–215 (2011)
18. Gutierrez, J., Harrenstein, P., Wooldridge, M.: Iterated boolean games. Inf. Comput. **242**, 53–79 (2015)
19. Harrenstein, P., van der Hoek, W., Meyer, J.-J., Witteveen, C.: Boolean games. In: Proceedings of the 8th Conference on Theoretical Aspects of Rationality and Knowledge, pp. 287–298. Morgan Kaufmann Publishers Inc. (2001)
20. Jennings, N.R., Faratin, P., Lomuscio, A.R., Parsons, S., Wooldridge, M.J., Sierra, C.: Automated negotiation: prospects, methods and challenges. Group Decis. Negot. **10**(2), 199–215 (2001)
21. Osborne, M., Rubinstein, A.: A Course in Game Theory. MIT Press, Cambridge (1994)
22. Osborne, M.J., Rubinstein, A.: Bargaining and Markets. Academic Press Inc., New York (2005)
23. Rubinstein, A.: A bargaining model with incomplete information about time preferences. Econometrica J. Econometric Soc. **53**(5), 1151–1172 (1985)
24. Sarit, K.: Strategic negotiation in multiagent environments. In: Strategic Negotiation in Multi-agent Environments (2001)
25. Turrini, P.: Endogenous boolean games. In: Proceedings of the Twenty-Third International Joint Conference on Artificial Intelligence, pp. 390–396. AAAI Press (2013)
26. Zlotkin, G., Rosenschein, J.S.: Negotiation and task sharing among autonomous agents in cooperative domains. In: IJCAI, vol. 11, pp. 912–917. Citeseer (1989)

Can We Reach Pareto Optimal Outcomes Using Bottom-Up Approaches?

Victor Sanchez-Anguix[1]([✉]) [iD], Reyhan Aydoğan[2,4] [iD], Tim Baarslag[3] [iD], and Catholijn M. Jonker[4] [iD]

[1] Coventry University, Coventry, UK
ac0872@coventry.ac.uk
[2] Özyeğin University, Istanbul, Turkey
reyhan.aydogan@ozyegin.edu.tr
[3] Centrum Wiskunde and Informatica, Amsterdam, Netherlands
T.Baarslag@cwi.nl
[4] Technical University of Delft, Delft, Netherlands
C.M.Jonker@tudelft.nl

Abstract. Classically, disciplines like negotiation and decision making have focused on reaching Pareto optimal solutions due to its stability and efficiency properties. Despite the fact that many practical and theoretical algorithms have successfully attempted to provide Pareto optimal solutions, they have focused on attempting to reach Pareto Optimality using horizontal approaches, where optimality is calculated taking into account every participant at the same time. Sometimes, this may prove to be a difficult task (e.g., conflict, mistrust, no information sharing, etc.). In this paper, we explore the possibility of achieving Pareto Optimal outcomes in a group by using a bottom-up approach: discovering Pareto optimal outcomes by interacting in subgroups. We analytically show that the set of Pareto optimal outcomes in a group covers the Pareto optimal outcomes within its subgroups. This theoretical finding can be applied in a variety of scenarios such as negotiation teams, multi-party negotiation, and team formation to social recommendation. Additionally, we empirically test the validity and practicality of this proof in a variety of decision making domains and analyze the usability of this proof in practical situations.

Keywords: Pareto optimality · Agreement technologies · Group decision making · Multi-agent systems · Artificial intelligence

1 Introduction

Group decision making, in which a group of agents with conflicting preferences aim to reach mutually acceptable decisions, has been studied within different disciplines. In social choice theory, voting methods have been applied to choose the most desired alternatives, while negotiation mechanisms have been proposed to find unanimous agreements in order to resolve the conflict of interests among groups of agents. Multi-objective optimization methods, distributed or not, have

© Springer International Publishing AG 2017
R. Aydoğan et al. (Eds.): COREDEMA 2016, LNAI 10238, pp. 19–35, 2017.
DOI: 10.1007/978-3-319-57285-7_2

also been developed to find optimal solutions for group decision making settings. One of the desired properties of such a solution is Pareto optimality, proposed by the Italian economist Vilfredo Pareto. Its desirability comes from the fact that, concerning non-Pareto optimal solutions, at least one of the objectives can be improved without worsening the performance of the rest of objectives. Hence, rational decision makers should see no objection in moving from a non-Pareto optimal solution to a Pareto optimal solution.

Reaching Pareto optimal agreements is not straightforward in practice. In open and dynamic environments, decision makers may not know each other's preferences completely. In such cases, the participants may try to reach an approximation of those solutions. Even it becomes more complicated to find Pareto optimal solutions when the number of participants increases, as the number of interactions required to achieve an optimal deal for the group may increase due to internal conflicts or lack of trust.

A number of works in the field focus on finding a global Pareto optimal solution by involving all agents at the same time [13, 14, 20, 37], which may lead to complicated interactions and lengthy decision making processes. However, we believe that, in many situations, agents can benefit from taking a bottom-up approach: calculating Pareto optimal outcomes in subgroups. In other words, we pursue the question of whether or not it is possible to estimate some Pareto optimal outcomes without knowing or predicting the preferences of all agents. In essence, solving the Pareto optimal set problem in a smaller group may be less complicated than in larger groups (e.g., less privacy concerns, less interactions needed, more willingness to cooperate, etc.) and it may provide a relatively important ratio of the final Pareto Optimal outcomes. Such kind of property can be used in some complex group decision making scenarios. Imagine that a group of agents is negotiating in unison with an unknown opponent [29, 31, 33]. If the agents can find the Pareto optimal outcomes within the team, they may use these outcomes in their bidding strategy to reach a Pareto optimal agreement with their opponent.

In this paper we explore bottom-up strategies. For that, first we prove that any Pareto optimal outcome in a subgroup is also Pareto optimal in a larger group that contains the subgroup, as long as agents' preferences are strict linear order. Second, we empirically simulate how bottom-up approaches may perform in realistic scenarios. More specifically, we show that we can obtain a reasonable ratio of the Pareto optimal outcomes within a group of agents by only finding the Pareto optimal outcomes within the subgroup of these agents.

The remainder of this paper is organized as follows: first we present a proof of how Pareto optimal solutions in subgroups are also Pareto optimal in larger groups when agents have strict, transitive, and complete preferences. Section 3 discusses some of the implications of the proof, and how it can be applied to solve a wide variety of problems in multi-agent systems. In Sect. 4, we empirically validate the theory in practice and analyze empirically compare the ratio of Pareto optimal outcomes within subgroups to the Pareto optimal outcomes within the entire group in a wide variety of real domains. After discussing the related work, we finally conclude the paper with future lines of work.

2   Pareto Optimality in Subgroups

In this section we prove that any Pareto optimal outcome in a subgroup of agents is also Pareto optimal in any group of agents containing the subgroup. First, we provide some of the necessary definitions and introduce some notation.

Let $\mathcal{A} = \{a_1, ..., a_n\}$ be a set of agents where k is the index of agent a_k and $\mathcal{A}' = \{a_1, ..., a_m\}$ be a superset of $\mathcal{A}$, $\mathcal{A} \subset \mathcal{A}'$ where $m > n$. $\mathcal{O}$ is the set of all possible solutions in a given domain, and $o \in \mathcal{O}$ represents a possible solution in the domain. We assume that $\succeq_i$ represents agent's a_i preference relation over outcomes in $\mathcal{O}$. If $o \succeq_i o'$ then agent a_i likes o at least as well as o', we write $o \succ_i o'$ to denote a strict preference for o and $o = o'$ to denote indifference. We assume that the agents' preference relations are strict, transitive and complete.

An outcome o^* is Pareto optimal with respect to $\mathcal{A}$ and $\mathcal{O}$, denoted by $po(o^*, \mathcal{A}, \mathcal{O})$ iff

$$\nexists o \in \mathcal{O} \ \exists j \leq n \bigwedge_{i=1}^{n} o \succeq_i o^* \wedge o \succ_j o^*.$$

We denote the set of all Pareto optimal outcomes over $\mathcal{A}$ by $\mathcal{O}_{\mathcal{A}}^* = \{o^* \in \mathcal{O} \mid po(o^*, \mathcal{A}, \mathcal{O})\}$.

Theorem 1. *Given a set of outcomes $\mathcal{O}$. For all two sets of agents $\mathcal{A}$ and $\mathcal{A}'$, if $\mathcal{A} \subset \mathcal{A}'$, then $\mathcal{O}_{\mathcal{A}}^* \subset \mathcal{O}_{\mathcal{A}'}^*$.*

Proof. Let us assume by reductio ad absurdum that $\mathcal{A} \subset \mathcal{A}'$, but $\mathcal{O}_{\mathcal{A}}^* \not\subset \mathcal{O}_{\mathcal{A}'}^*$. This means there exists an $o^* \in \mathcal{O}_{\mathcal{A}}^*$ such that $o^* \notin \mathcal{O}_{\mathcal{A}'}^*$. Expanding the definition of Pareto optimal outcomes, we have

$$o^* \notin \{o \in \mathcal{O} \mid \nexists o' \in \mathcal{O} . \exists k \leq m, \bigwedge_{i=1}^{m} o' \succeq_i o \wedge o' \succ_k o\}.$$

This means there must exist an $o \in \mathcal{O}$ and a $k \leq m$ such that $\bigwedge_{i=1}^{m} o \succeq_i o^* \wedge o \succ_k o^*$. We consider two scenarios: either $a_k \in \mathcal{A}$ or $a_k \notin \mathcal{A}$.

- If $a_k \in \mathcal{A}$ then o is an outcome that dominates o^* over $\mathcal{A}$, which is not possible as o^* is Pareto optimal over $\mathcal{A}$.
- Otherwise, $k > n$, so we have $\bigwedge_{i=1}^{n} o \succeq_i o^*$. In that case, as o^* is Pareto optimal over $\mathcal{A}$, the condition is only true if all of the agents in $\mathcal{A}$ are indifferent between o and o^*. As preferences are strict, that cannot be true either.

Since both sides lead to a contradiction, we have proven the theorem.

At this point the reader may be wondering how the theorem above behaves in a scenario where agents' preferences are not strict. As we will discuss later, the likeliness of such as scenario is small, but the conclusion of the theorem above may in fact not hold in that case. Basically, an outcome that is Pareto optimal in a subgroup $\mathcal{A}$ may not be Pareto optimal in the group $\mathcal{A}'$ when all of the agents in $\mathcal{A}$ are indifferent between such outcome and another Pareto optimal outcome. Then, one of the two outcomes may not be Pareto optimal with $\mathcal{A}'$ when one of the agents in the group is not indifferent between those outcomes. Nevertheless, as we shall outline in Sect. 4.2, such situations are rare in practice, as all of the agents need to be indifferent between outcomes. This becomes increasingly unlikely as the group size grows and thus, for large enough groups, we can consider that the theorem is true for practically any scenario.

There are several practical implications to the set/superset Pareto relationship. The first one is that a negotiation team [31] can discover a prospective set of Pareto optimal outcomes by just considering the preferences of the team. With high probabilities, these deals will also be Pareto optimal when engaging in a negotiation with and additional agent. However, the consequences of this theorem can be also applied to other domains like multilateral negotiations or group decision making. In the next section, we discuss some of the prospective applications of this finding.

3 Prospective Applications

In Sect. 2 we have demonstrated that, the vast majority of the times, an outcome that is Pareto optimal in a subgroup of agents will also remain Pareto optimal in a larger group. However, the reader may still be wondering about the usability of such proof in practice. In this section, we will discuss the usability of the proof in a wide variety of practical domains. It should be highlighted that we are not depicting achieving Pareto optimality as a simple task, not even calculating a small portion of it. In fact, it is usually one of the most difficult goals for optimization algorithms. However, there is value in computing Pareto optimality in smaller/less complex problems as long as we are able to use those solutions in a most difficult problem, which is exactly the situation that arises while making practical use of our proof. Now, imagine the following situations:

- **Negotiation teams:** In this scenario, a group of individuals negotiate as a party with opponent(s) to achieve a deal [28–31,33]. In that case, finding the outcomes that are Pareto optimal within the team may play in favor of the team as (i) if the team sticks to these outcomes while negotiating with opponents, it can ensure efficiency in the final outcome, (ii) the set of calculated deals may be reused in multiple negotiations with different opponents as they remain Pareto optimal, and (iii) finding Pareto optimal outcomes once may reduce the time spent in negotiation threads as the team exactly knows which outcomes are more beneficial for team members. On top of that, one can also assume that team members may be more willing to share information with teammates, which may make easier the search for Pareto optimal outcomes inside the team.
- **Multi-party negotiations:** Some participants in a multi-party negotiation [4,8,11,13,14,37] may decide to collude and bias the agreement with their

preferences. For that, the subgroup of agents may calculate Pareto optimal outcomes within the subgroup, and decide on the Pareto optimal outcomes that they plan to use in the upcoming multi-party negotiation. This way, there may be higher probabilities for the negotiation to finish with an outcome that satisfies the subgroups' interests and that is efficient. Another possible application for this proof in multi-party settings is precisely the idea of looking for Pareto optimal agreements within subgroups of agents. For instance, agents with high degrees of trust may decide to share some information that facilitates the search of Pareto optimal outcomes within the subgroup. Then, once outcomes are found in subgroups, these may be shared among all of the agents, and the whole group may need to decide on the most appropriate Pareto optimal outcome.

- **Decision making in open environments**: Open multi-agent systems [3, 15,32] have the particularity of being systems where agents enter and leave the system dynamically. In such environments, decision making tasks may suffer from the same characteristic and agents may enter and leave decision making tasks as needed, resulting in a real time problem. For those situations, agents in a decision making task may benefit from a continuous search for Pareto optimal outcomes. As new agents join the task, those Pareto optimal outcomes calculated should be kept as they will remain Pareto optimal in the new group. When agents leave, remaining group members can get rid of some outcomes that have become dominated in the new setting.

- **Team/coalition formation**: Teams of agents [2] can be iteratively built considering the number of Pareto optimal outcomes within the current team and the new Pareto optimal outcomes that may arise when adding a new members. In general, when the agent added to the team is more dissimilar to current team members, the more Pareto optimal outcomes will be added when the agent joins the team. Hence, it can be used a measure of team similarity/dissimilarity.

- **Multi-objective optimization**: A more general application for this proof is multi-objective optimization [9]. Initially, an agent may need to optimize a problem with n objective functions. If the agent computes a set of Pareto optimal outcomes for such a problem, it can keep those outcomes for future optimizations considering additional goals or objectives.

As the reader may have noticed, the range of applications where this approach could be applied is varied. We are not claiming that those are the sole applications for this approach, and there may be others in domains like social choice [6], group recommendations [24], and so forth.

4   Experimental Study

Section 2 shows theoretically that Pareto optimal outcomes within a group of agents having complete, transitive and strict preferences are still Pareto optimal when the group size increases with incoming agents. Even when preferences are non strict, we expect for the theorem to hold in most of the cases. In this section, we empirically analyze the prospective performance and applicability of bottom-up approaches. For that purpose, we selected a variety of domains:

- **Sushi domain:** The sushi domain [18] is a widely used dataset in decision making tasks. The dataset contains 5000 preference profiles over 10 types of sushi. Each preference profile has strictly ranked all the types of sushi.
- **AGH course selection:** This dataset contains information about 153 students that stated their preferences on 6 courses offered by AGU University of Science and Technology in 2004 [36].
- **Book crossing domain:** This is a well-known dataset in recommender systems [38]. The original dataset contains information about 278,858 users that have produced 1,149,780 ratings on 271,379 books. As we require preferences to be complete on at least a subset of items, we kept 7 users that had rated 23 books in common. The users that we kept were calculated so that the number of items rated in common was maximized.
- **Movielens domain:** This is a popular domain in recommender systems [25], being one of the *de facto* benchmarks when testing recommender algorithms. The original dataset contains 138,000 users that have emitted ratings on 27,000 movies. As we require preferences to be complete, for this study, we picked the 10 users that had provided more recommendations in the dataset and chose the movies that had been rated by all these 10 users. After reducing the dataset, we obtained 10 preference profiles that had rated a total of 298 movies.
- **Holiday domain:** This is a multi-party negotiation domain available in Genius [22]. In this scenario, decision makers need to decide on the details of a holiday trip that they are going to take together. More specifically, the participants can decide on their destination, the duration for the trip, the budget, the activities to be done in the holiday, and the transportation method. In total, 9 preference profiles over 1024 possible outcomes are available. These preferences have been elicited from TU Delft computer science students, but not with serious plans for a joint holiday in mind.
- **Symposium domain:** This is another multi-party negotiation domain that is available in Genius [22]. The scenario is on the organization of conferences where the decision makers need to decide on where a conference will be held and schedules for the talks. There are 9 preference profiles over 2305 possible outcomes. These preferences have been elicited from faculty members in computer science of TU Delft experienced in organizing conferences, but not having a specific conference in mind.
- **Party domain:** This is a multi-party negotiation domain where agents decide on the details of a party that they are going to host together [22]. Even though the original domain does not provide real user preferences, we carried out an experiment where we elicited preferences from students in a Master level AI course. Students were asked to input their real preferences via Genius based on their tastes for hosting parties. More specifically, the issues in the negotiation scenario are the type of food, the type of drinks, the location for the party,

the type of invitations to be sent, the type of music, and how to cleanup after the party. In total, we elicited 24 real preference profiles over 3072 outcomes.

From a global perspective, the sushi, agh, and book domain are *small* attending to the number of outcomes. These domains correspond to decision making domains where outcomes are non customizable objects (e.g., a movie, a book, a course, etc.). The data in the Movielens domain is less sparse and we were able to find 10 users that had rated 298 outcomes in common. This is again a domain where outcomes are non customizable, but the size of the domain is one order of magnitude larger than that of the small domains. The three remaining multi-party negotiation domains (i.e., holiday, symposium, and party domain) represent scenarios where the final outcome can be customized via the negotiable issues. As a result, the number of possible outcomes is larger. We consider these domains and the Movielens domain as the *large domains* in our study.

4.1   Validation and Performance Analysis

Our performance metric is the ratio of the Pareto optimal outcomes within a subgroup with a size of $\{2, ..., n-1\}$ to the Pareto optimal outcomes within the n-sized group. If the ratio remains low even for large subgroups, then this means that the performance of our theoretical finding may be of little value in practice, as only a small ratio of the final Pareto outcomes may be achievable. However, if the ratio is large, then it may indicate that bottom-up approaches may be valuable. Additionally, common sense indicates that, the larger the subgroup, the higher the ratio of final Pareto optimal outcomes that may be obtained in the subgroup. However, one question that arises is the actual speed by which the ratio of final Pareto outcomes increases, and whether or not subgroups may be able to calculate a respectable ratio of the final Pareto optimal outcomes.

For testing the practical performance of our bottom-up approaches, we randomly generated groups of size n based on the preference profiles available for each domain. For each randomly generated group, we built all possible subgroups with varying sizes $\{2, .., n-1\}$ and estimated the Pareto optimal set in each (sub)group. More specifically, for each domain we tested a maximum of 1000 groups[1] of size $n = \{5, 7, 9\}$[2].

The results of this experiment can be observed in Fig. 1. As expected, the results show that the larger the subgroup is, the larger the average ratio of the final Pareto Optimal set that we get. The increase is clearly continuous for all of the domains and group sizes. When we look at the results for groups of 7 and 9 members we observe a non-linear increase with the size of the subgroup. This non-linear increase is not as evident in the case of 5 members' groups, as in that case we only have 3 data points[3].

---

[1] The total number is $min(1000, \binom{m}{n})$, where m is the total number of available preference profiles and n is the size of the group.

[2] Except for the Book domain, where we only have 7 preference profiles.

[3] Even non-linear functions may look like linear when the number of points is reduced.

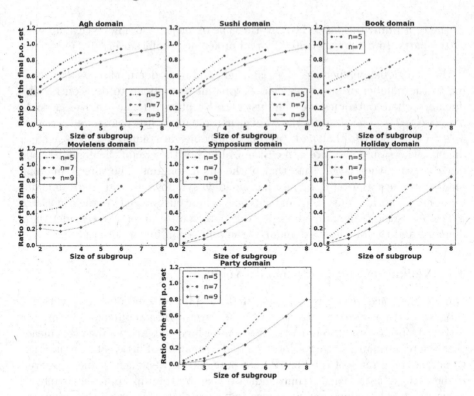

Fig. 1. Average ratio of the final Pareto optimal obtained in subgroups of different size

One should highlight that for $n - 1$ agents in the subgroup, n being the total number of agents in the group, the average ratio of the Pareto optimal set obtained in the subgroup is always over 50% of the final set, being close to 80% in some cases (e.g., smaller domains, larger groups). This is a good result, especially for negotiation team scenarios [29,31,33], where the team could calculate the Pareto set inside the team and use those outcomes in the negotiation with an opponent. This is a clear case where a subgroup of size $n - 1$ can be formed (i.e., all of the team members) and, according to the experimental results, obtain a notably high ratio of final Pareto optimal outcomes. Consequently, they can propose Pareto optimal bids without knowing their opponent's preferences.

The result is also notable for smaller subgroups. For instance, in groups of size 5, we are able to obtain between an average of 68% of the final Pareto set for small domains and 32% for the larger domains with just about half of the group members (i.e., 3). In the case of groups of size 7, we get 68% of the final Pareto set for small domains and 28% for larger domains with just about half of the group members (i.e., 4). Similarly, for groups of size 9 we are able to obtain an average of 76% of the final Pareto set in small domains, and 30% in large domains with just about half of group members (i.e., 5).

The trends in the graphics and the results mentioned above also may suggest that larger domains may result in lower ratios of the final Pareto optimal frontier achievable by subgroups. Nevertheless, the results can still be considered as positive for the studied domain sizes as we have been able to observe above. Despite the data trend, it is still premature to draw any conclusion as it would be necessary to experiment with a wider range of domain sizes and more domains from each size. Studying the changes in the behavior of the proof for larger domains is part of our future work. However, it is not very feasible to elicit the preferences of humans for very large domains (e.g., 10,000, 100,000, etc.)

4.2 Applicability Analysis

There are still other aspects that we need to analyze to determine the applicability of bottom-up approaches in real situations. Even though considerable ratios of the final Pareto optimal set are obtainable within subgroups, this may be useless in practice if the total number of Pareto optimal outcomes is very close to all possible outcomes. In those cases, there would be no point in calculating Pareto optimal outcomes in subgroups, as almost any outcome would be Pareto optimal. Therefore, we are interested in checking that the set of final Pareto optimal outcomes does not dramatically approach the total number of outcomes. In [26], O'Neill studied how Pareto optimality was affected by the number of agents participating in a decision making process. To put it simply, the author proved that the number of Pareto optimal outcomes grows exponentially with the number of agents, with the assumption that all preference profiles are equally probable. Additionally, he proposed a formula to estimate the number of outcomes that are expected to be Pareto optimal based on the size of the domain m, and the number of agents in the group n: $E(K_{m,n}) = -\sum_{i=1}^{m}(-1)^i \binom{m}{i}\frac{1}{i^{n-1}}$.

He also stated that the size of the domain had an effect on the number of outcomes that were Pareto optimal: larger outcome spaces tend to slow down the exponential growth of the Pareto optimal set, although the growth is still exponential. Of course, for drawing such a conclusion, the author had to assume that all preference profiles were equally probable. We argue that, in practice, all preference profiles are not equally probable as in some domains not all of the outcomes may be equally feasible (e.g., high prices in a team of buyers, popular choices in movies, popular choices in travel destinations, etc.). Hence, we argue that the exponential growth may not be as fast as in the theoretical case, and bottom-up approaches may be applicable to more scenarios.

In order to examine this theoretical finding in practice, we calculated the ratio of the Pareto optimal outcomes to the total number of outcomes for each domain and group size. Figure 2 shows the average ratio of outcomes that are Pareto optimal for different groups sizes and domains. In these graphs, blue dots represent the average ratios calculated in real scenarios while green dots denote the theoretical estimation provided by [26] for domains of the same size. In addition to this, for each data point we provide the total number of cases[4]

---

[4] Again, the total number is $min(1000, \binom{m}{n})$.

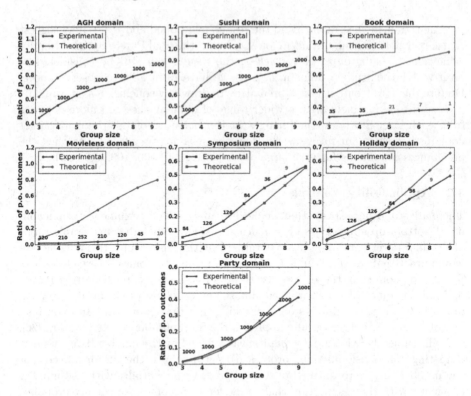

Fig. 2. Average ratio of the final Pareto optimal set obtained with subgroups of different size (Color figure online)

that were considered for calculating the average. Numbers in red represent less than 30 samples and such averages should be ignored.

As it can be observed in Fig. 2, the growth in the number of outcomes that are Pareto optimal is usually slower in real domains than in the theoretical estimation. Being more specific, we observe that only the symposium domain shows a similar behavior to that of the theoretical case. The rest of the domains deviate from the theoretical behavior sooner or later, showing a slower saturation. We can observe that this difference is specially acute in the Movielens, Book, Sushi, and Agh domain, which are the ones whose preferences have been rigorously elicited from real users (except for the party domain). This may reinforce our initial intuition, that, in real domains, the exponential growth on the number of Pareto optimal outcomes may not be as drastic as in the theoretical case. In other domains like the party and the holiday domain, the difference is less acute but still existent.

In fact, if one analyzes the proposed domains one by one, it is possible to realize that there are general preferential trends. This is clear in domains like Movielens or the Book domain, where we know that some movies and some books tend to be more popular than others. For instance, *The Shawshank Redemption* is one of the most popular movies of all times, and it has been able to obtain average ratings of 9.3 over 10 stars in sites like *IMDB*[5], where it has been voted by more than 1 million users. Similarly, we can find books like *Harry Potter and the Deathly Hallows* that have received an average rating of 4.59 over 5 stars with more than 1 million ratings on sites like *GoodReads*[6]. Finding users that did not like these items has low odds, and as a consequence we can state that not all preference profiles are equally probable. Not only there are general trends in users preferences, but many times we find that there are clusters of users with similar preferences [35]. For instance, in the book domain, we can expect that users that have liked *The Lord of the Rings* will also like other fantasy themed books like *Song of Ice and Fire*. This is the type of patterns exploited by recommender systems, and suggests that the number of likely preference profiles is even smaller.

With respect to the other small domains (e.g., AGH, Sushi), we analyzed the preferences of users. In fact, for analyzing the preferences of users on items we performed a Borda count with all of the preference profiles. We could observe that, in the Sushi domain, there are also some popular choices the *toro* (a total score of 39445) and some choices that are usually the least liked by users like the *kappa-maki* (a total score of 14928). In the case of the AGH domain, we could also observe that one of the courses (e.g., course 3) was the most preferred one with a score of 731, whereas the least preferred score had almost half the score. This means that in these domains, preferences are not equally distributed and one should not expect such an exponential growth as in the theoretical case.

With respect to negotiation domains, we elicited real preferences from the Party domain, whereas we used the preference profiles provided by Genius in the Holiday and Symposium domain. Interestingly, we could observe that real users in the Party domain tend to consider the type of food, the type of drinks, and the music as the most important attributes. Even in some specific attributes, we could find that there were popular choices like for instance *Beer only* for drinks, and *Finger-food* and *Chips and Nuts* for food choices. With respect to the rest of negotiation domains, it has to be considered that they were not strictly and rigorously elicited like in the case of the party domain. Users were not contextualized in a specific scenario and their preferences were just elicited from their previous experiences in similar scenarios. In the case of the Holiday domain, we were able to observe some patterns like users considering the duration and the activities as the most important attributes. The users usually preferred longer durations to shorter durations, and we observed a slight positive inclination towards *Historical Places* and *Restaurants*. Even in the rest of less important attributes we were able to find some patterns like the fact that most users preferred *Miami* and *Amsterdam* as destinations. These patterns again show that not all preference profiles are equally likely, and that is reflected in the fact that the experimental growth depicted for Fig. 2 is slower than the theoretical growth. On the other hand, the Symposium domain is closer to the theoretical expectation. This may

---

[5] http://www.imdb.com. Visited on 16th November 2015.
[6] http://www.goodreads.com/. Visited on 16th November 2015.

Table 1. Average % of false positives calculated in a subgroup

Group size	Subgroup size						
	2	3	4	5	6	7	8
5	7%	4%	1%	–	–	–	–
7	5%	2%	1%	0.7%	0.3%	–	–
9	4%	2%	1%	0.7%	0.4%	0.2%	0.07%

be explainable due to the fact that the Symposium domain preferences were not elicited thinking on an specific symposium. In contrast to the Holiday domain, which did not follow a rigorous preference elicitation process either, in the Symposium domain it is harder to relate to the scenario, as it includes totally fictional speakers (e.g. *Mr. Talkolot*), whereas in the holiday domain one always can think about his/her own preferences on a trip. This may explain why the increase in the ratio of Pareto optimal outcomes is similar to the theoretical case where preference profiles are equally probable. It should be highlighted that in many negotiation domains, preferences are made different to test the performance of negotiation algorithms in conflicting scenarios.

The fact that, as we have shown, not all preference profiles are equally likely makes bottom-up approaches more applicable to real life scenarios than the results depicted in theory [26]. However, it should be noted that, even though the growth is slower, the graphics still suggest an increase with the size of the group and eventually the proof may not be applicable for domains involving a large number of agents. These results raise an interesting trade-off that should be analyzed in the future: the relation between the performance of bottom-up approaches, which increases with the subgroup size, and its applicability, which decreases with the group size, as nearly all outcomes may be Pareto optimal.

There is another additional issue to be studied concerning the applicability of bottom-up approaches. As the reader may have guessed, the aforementioned domains do not guarantee strict preferences. Therefore, some Pareto optimal outcomes calculated in subgroups may not be Pareto optimal in the whole group (we call these false positives). In order to study this, we measured the ratio of false positives in the previous experimental setting. The results are summarized in Table 1. As it can be observed, the percentage of false positives remains low for every possible scenario, and it tends to decrease with the size of the subgroup. This matches our initial intuition, and shows that the proof presented in this paper practically holds in every situation. Hence, this result supports the applicability of bottom-up approaches in practice.

5 Related Work

Since its introduction by the Italian mathematician Vilfred Pareto, Pareto optimality has been an efficiency and stability concept that has had an impact on many disciplines and areas of knowledge. Not only it has been studied in mathematics, but Pareto optimality has been considered a cornerstone in some computer science areas like artificial intelligence, specially in those fields concerned with making decisions by means of automated software (e.g., multi-agent systems, multi-objective optimization, etc.).

Despite its increasing popularity in computer science areas, most of the studies have dedicated their efforts on reaching Pareto optimal solutions. For instance, many researchers in automated negotiation have successfully focused on achieving Pareto or near Pareto optimal agreements. Fatima *et al.* studied the case of two agents negotiating issues based on an endogenous agenda, and analyzed conditions and strategies that led to Pareto optimal agreements. In [20], the authors propose a general framework for bilateral negotiations where agents are able to reach near Pareto optimal outcomes by decomposing the negotiation process into iso-utility curves, from where outcomes are proposed based on the similarity to the last offer proposed by the opponent. Later, authors in [34] refine the models to make it capable of working with non-linear utility functions and addressing the issue of devices with limited computational capabilities by applying genetic algorithms. Ehtamo *et al.* [14] propose a centralized mechanism for achieving Pareto optimal outcomes based on real valued linear additive utility functions and information sharing. Recently, Hara *et al.* [13] proposed a mediated mechanism based on genetic algorithms that is capable of achieving near Pareto optimal outcomes for multi-party negotiations where agents preferences present non-linear relationships and change over time. In addition to using Pareto optimality to measure the effectiveness of negotiation outcome, Marsa-Maestre *et al.* use the structure of the Pareto Frointer to decide the degree of competitiveness of a given negotiation scenario [23].

The concept of Pareto optimally is not only widely used in automated negotiation but also used in other application areas in multiagent systems. For example, Kash *et al.* study the problem of fair division of resources in scenarios where agents enter and leave the system dynamically [19]. In this work, they define the concept of dynamic Pareto optimality for such scenarios and under which conditions and mechanisms the efficiency property can be accomplished. The main difference with this work resides in the fact that our approach, although it can be applied to dynamic environments, it focuses on scenarios where agents have to decide on a non-divisible and discrete outcome space. Amador *et al.* [1] propose a task allocation method for agents with temporal constraints that is capable of providing envy free and Pareto optimal solutions under specific conditions. Other works like [27] have extended the concept of Pareto optimality to argumentation frameworks. The authors study different agent attitudes, how they relate to the problem of efficiency in abstract argumentation dialogues, and define several situations and scenarios that lead to Pareto optimal arguments. They focus on characterizing Pareto optimal solutions in argumentation dialogues while our proposal is much more general as it relates to one of the underlying properties of theoretical Pareto optimality, which can be applicable to a wide variety of domains.

Another field related to our study is that of multi-objective optimization. Pareto optimality is a well-known efficiency measure in multi-objective optimization [16,17,21]. Similarly to our multiagent decision setting, researchers in centralized multi-objective optimization have noticed the exponential increase on the number of Pareto optimal outcomes with the number of objective functions [7,10]. Due to this unfortunate property of Pareto optimality, some researchers have offered practical alternatives to the selection of Pareto optimal outcomes. Di Pierro *et al.* define the concept of k optimality for deciding over Pareto optimal outcomes. Basically, a non-dominated outcome is defined as k-optimal when that outcome is non-dominated over every possible combination of k objectives. Thus, it results in a stronger concept of optimality that may help to choose a solution over a set of Pareto optimal outcomes. We want to highlight the practical usability of k-optimality on future decision making mechanisms for agents and how it complements our current findings. First, based on our proof, a subgroups of agents may calculate Pareto optimal outcomes on subgroups and communicate them to the rest of subgroups. Then, a mechanism may be devised to allow agents to select a k-optimal outcome over calculated Pareto optimal outcomes.

Finally, economic and theoretical studies are also a source of related work. As introduced in the text, [26] analyzed how the number of Pareto optimal outcomes exponentially increases with the number of agents by assuming that all preference profiles are equally probable. In our present study, we have, among other contributions, shown how real domains in practice behave with regards to Pareto optimality. More specifically, we have shown that, despite the increase in the number of Pareto optimal outcomes with the number of agents, the growth speed is not as quick as portrayed by [26]. This is, as far as we know, our closest work in the study of the underlying properties of Pareto optimality. Of course, there have been other successful studies on Pareto optimality for specific domains and problems like characterizing fairness, or studying the relationship between monotonic solutions and Pareto optimality [5,12], but their focus of study has not been on the exploration of bottom-up approaches for reaching Pareto optimality.

6   Conclusion

In this paper, we have explored the applicability and performance of bottom-up approaches for reaching Pareto optimal outcomes in groups. Our analysis shows that Pareto optimal outcomes in a group remain optimal when increasing the number of agents in the group in many practical scenarios. This has implications for bottom-up approaches, as Pareto optimal outcomes may be calculated in subgroups first, and then be used in scenarios involving the whole group.

We performed experimental analysis on preferences elicited from users in real-life scenarios and validated that this principle can be applied to a wide range of domains. Our results on performance and applicability indicate that we are able to calculate a significant ratio of the final Pareto optimal frontier within subgroups. Conversely, we analyzed the applicability of our approach by considering how the ratio of Pareto outcomes increases with the size of the group. Our findings highlight that this increase is not as abrupt as expected in theoretical studies, as not all preference profiles are equally likely in many real-life domains. Still, the increase of the ratio of final Pareto optimal outcomes points to a necessary trade off in practice, which we plan to analyze in the future.

Another interesting aspect that requires more study is deciding on the right Pareto optimal outcomes for the group. The concept of a Pareto optimal outcome does not automatically ensure it is going to be acceptable for the group; for instance, an outcome with the maximum utility for a group member and the minimum utility for another group member may be Pareto optimal, but should definitely not be deemed acceptable for the group. Therefore, a mechanism should be devised to ensure that either those Pareto optimal outcomes calculated in subgroups are beneficial for the group, or a posterior negotiation or social choice procedure should help group members to select the most appropriate outcome for the group afterwards.

Additionally, as a future work, we plan to design novel negotiation approaches for intra-team negotiations that benefit from our findings. In particular, we plan to design a negotiation strategy for negotiation teams, which first calculate the Pareto optimal solutions within the team using our approach, and then target that set of Pareto optimal proposals when negotiating with the opponent.

References

1. Amador, S., Okamoto, S., Zivan, R.: Dynamic multi-agent task allocation with spatial and temporal constraints. In: Proceedings of the International Conference on Autonomous Agents and Multi-agent Systems, pp. 1495–1496. International Foundation for Autonomous Agents and Multiagent Systems (2014)
2. Anagnostopoulos, A., Becchetti, L., Castillo, C., Gionis, A., Leonardi, S.: Online team formation in social networks. In: Proceedings of the 21st International Conference on World Wide Web, pp. 839–848. ACM (2012)
3. Argente, E., Botti, V., Carrascosa, C., Giret, A., Julian, V., Rebollo, M.: An abstract architecture for virtual organizations: the thomas approach. Knowl. Inf. Syst. **29**(2), 379–403 (2011)
4. Aydoğan, R., Hindriks, K.V., Jonker, C.M.: Multilateral mediated negotiation protocols with feedback. In: Marsa-Maestre, I., Lopez-Carmona, M.A., Ito, T., Zhang, M., Bai, Q., Fujita, K. (eds.) Novel Insights in Agent-based Complex Automated Negotiation. SCI, vol. 535, pp. 43–59. Springer, Tokyo (2014). doi:10.1007/978-4-431-54758-7_3
5. Bogomolnaia, A., Moulin, H.: Size versus fairness in the assignment problem. Games Econ. Behav. **90**, 119–127 (2015)
6. Brandt, F., Conitzer, V., Endriss, U.: Computational social choice. In: Multiagent system, pp. 213–283 (2012)
7. Corne, D.W., Knowles, J.D.: Techniques for highly multiobjective optimisation: some nondominated points are better than others. In: Proceedings of the 9th Annual Conference on Genetic and Evolutionary Computation, GECCO 2007, pp. 773–780. ACM, New York (2007)

8. Jonge, D., Sierra, C.: NB^3: a multilateral negotiation algorithm for large, non-linear agreement spaces with limited time. Auton. Agents Multi-agent Syst. **29**(5), 896–942 (2015)

9. Deb, K., Agrawal, S., Pratap, A., Meyarivan, T.: A fast elitist non-dominated sorting genetic algorithm for multi-objective optimization: NSGA-II. In: Schoenauer, M., Deb, K., Rudolph, G., Yao, X., Lutton, E., Merelo, J.J., Schwefel, H.-P. (eds.) PPSN 2000. LNCS, vol. 1917, pp. 849–858. Springer, Heidelberg (2000). doi:10.1007/3-540-45356-3_83

10. di Pierro, F.: Many-objective evolutionary algorithms and applications to water resources engineering. Ph.D. thesis, University of Exeter (2006)

11. Esparcia, S., Sanchez-Anguix, V., Aydoğan, R.: A negotiation approach for energy-aware room allocation systems. In: Corchado, J.M., et al. (eds.) Highlights on Practical Applications of Agents and Multi-Agent Systems, vol. 365, pp. 280–291. Springer, Heidelberg (2013)

12. García-Segarra, J., Ginés-Vilar, M.: The impossibility of paretian monotonic solutions: a strengthening of Roths result. Oper. Res. Lett. **43**(5), 476–478 (2015)

13. Hara, K., Ito, T.: A mediation mechanism for automated negotiating agents whose utility changes over time. In: Twenty-Seventh AAAI Conference on Artificial Intelligence (2013)

14. Heiskanen, P., Ehtamo, H., Hämäläinen, R.P.: Constraint proposal method for computing pareto solutions in multi-party negotiations. Eur. J. Oper. Res. **133**(1), 44–61 (2001)

15. Hewitt, C.: Open information systems semantics for distributed artificial intelligence. Artif. Intell. **47**(1–3), 79–106 (1991)

16. Horn, J., Nafpliotis, N., Goldberg, D.E.: A niched pareto genetic algorithm for multiobjective optimization. In: Proceedings of the First IEEE Conference on Evolutionary Computation, IEEE World Congress on Computational Intelligence, pp. 82–87. IEEE (1994)

17. Xiao-Bing, H., Wang, M., Di Paolo, E.: Calculating complete and exact pareto front for multiobjective optimization: a new deterministic approach for discrete problems. IEEE Trans. Cybern. **43**(3), 1088–1101 (2013)

18. Kamishima, T.: Nantonac collaborative filtering: recommendation based on order responses. In: Proceedings of the Ninth ACM SIGKDD International Conference on Knowledge Discovery and Data Mining, pp. 583–588. ACM (2003)

19. Kash, I., Procaccia, A.D., Shah, N.: No agent left behind: dynamic fair division of multiple resources. J. Artif. Intell. Res. **51**, 579–603 (2014)

20. Lai, G., Li, C., Sycara, K.: Efficient multi-attribute negotiation with incomplete information. Group Decis. Negot. **15**(5), 511–528 (2006)

21. Li, H., Zhang, Q.: Multiobjective optimization problems with complicated pareto sets, MOEA/D and NSGA-II. IEEE Trans. Evol. Comput. **13**(2), 284–302 (2009)

22. Lin, R., Kraus, S., Baarslag, T., Tykhonov, D., Hindriks, K., Jonker, C.M.: Genius: an integrated environment for supporting the design of generic automated negotiators. Comput. Intell. **30**(1), 48–70 (2014)

23. Marsa-Maestre, I., Klein, M., Jonker, C.M., Aydoğan, R.: From problems to protocols: towards a negotiation handbook. Decis. Support Syst. **60**, 39–54 (2014)

24. Masthoff, J.: Group recommender systems: combining individual models. In: Ricci, F., Rokach, L., Shapira, B., Kantor, P.B. (eds.) Recommender Systems Handbook, pp. 677–702. Springer, USA (2011)

25. Miller, B.N., Albert, I., Lam, S.K., Konstan, J.A., Riedl, J.: Movielens unplugged: experiences with an occasionally connected recommender system. In: Proceedings of the 8th International Conference on Intelligent User Interfaces, pp. 263–266. ACM (2003)
26. O'Neill, B.: The number of outcomes in the pareto-optimal set of discrete bargaining games. Math. Oper. Res. **6**(4), 571–578 (1981)
27. Rahwan, I., Larson, K.: Pareto optimality in abstract argumentation. In: AAAI, pp. 150–155 (2008)
28. Sanchez-Anguix, V., Dai, T., Semnani-Azad, Z., Sycara, K., Botti, V.: Modeling power distance and individualism/collectivism in negotiation team dynamics. In: 45 Hawaii International Conference on System Sciences (HICSS-45), pp. 628–637 (2012)
29. Sanchez-Anguix, V., Julian, V., Botti, V., Garcia-Fornes, A.: Reaching unanimous agreements within agent-based negotiation teams with linear and monotonic utility functions. IEEE Trans. Syst. Man Cybern. Part B **42**(3), 778–792 (2012)
30. Sanchez-Anguix, V., Julian, V., Botti, V., Garcia-Fornes, A.: Studying the impact of negotiation environments on negotiation teams' performance. Inf. Sci. **219**, 17–40 (2013)
31. Sanchez-Anguix, V., Aydoğan, R., Julian, V., Jonker, C.: Unanimously acceptable agreements for negotiation teams in unpredictable domains. Electr. Commer. Res. Appl. **13**(4), 243–265 (2014)
32. Sanchez-Anguix, V., Espinosa, A., Hernandez, L., Garcia-Fornes, A.: MAMSY: a management tool for multi-agent systems. In: Demazeau, Y., Pavón, J., Corchado, J.M., Bajo, J. (eds.) 7th International Conference on Practical Applications of Agents and Multi-agent Systems (PAAMS), vol. 55, pp. 130–139. Springer, Heidelberg (2009)
33. Sanchez-Anguix, V., Julian, V., Botti, V., García-Fornes, A.: Tasks for agent-based negotiation teams: analysis, review, and challenges. Eng. Appl. Artif. Intell. **26**(10), 2480–2494 (2013)
34. Sánchez-Anguix, V., Valero, S., Julián, V., Botti, V., García-Fornes, A.: Evolutionary-aided negotiation model for bilateral bargaining in ambient intelligence domains with complex utility functions. Inf. Sci. **222**, 25–46 (2013)
35. Sarwar, B.M., Karypis, G., Konstan, J., Riedl, J.: Recommender systems for large-scale e-commerce: scalable neighborhood formation using clustering. In: Proceedings of the fifth International Conference on Computer and Information Technology, vol. 1. Citeseer (2002)
36. Skowron, P., Faliszewski, P., Slinko, A.: Achieving fully proportional representation is easy in practice. In: Proceedings of the International Conference on Autonomous Agents and Multi-agent Systems, pp. 399–406. International Foundation for Autonomous Agents and Multiagent Systems (2013)
37. Zhenh, R., Chakraborty, N., Dai, T., Sycara, K.: Automated multilateral negotiation on multiple issues with private information. INFORMS J. Comput. **28**(4), 612–628 (2015)
38. Ziegler, C.-N., McNee, S.M., Konstan, J.A., Lausen, G.: Improving recommendation lists through topic diversification. In: Proceedings of the 14th International Conference on World Wide Web, pp. 22–32. ACM (2005)

The Role of Execution Errors in Populations of Ultimatum Bargaining Agents

Fernando P. Santos[1,2(✉)], Jorge M. Pacheco[2,3], Ana Paiva[1],
and Francisco C. Santos[1,2]

[1] INESC-ID and Instituto Superior Técnico, Universidade de Lisboa,
Taguspark, Av. Prof. Cavaco Silva, 2780-990 Porto Salvo, Portugal
fernando.pedro@tecnico.ulisboa.pt
[2] ATP-Group, 2780-990 Porto Salvo, Portugal
[3] CBMA and Departamento de Matemática e Aplicações, Universidade do Minho,
Campus de Gualtar, 4710-057 Braga, Portugal

Abstract. The design of artificial intelligent agents is frequently accomplished by equipping individuals with mechanisms to choose actions that maximise a subjective utility function. This way, the implementation of behavioural errors, that systematically prevent agents from using optimal strategies, often seems baseless. In this paper, we employ an analytical framework to study a population of Proposers and Responders, with conflicting interests, that co-evolve by playing the prototypical Ultimatum Game. This framework allows to consider an arbitrary discretisation of the strategy space, and allows us to describe the dynamical impact of individual mistakes by Responders, on the collective success of this population. Conveniently, this method can be used to analyse other continuous strategy interactions. In the case of Ultimatum Game, we show analytically how seemingly disadvantageous errors empower Responders and become the source of individual and collective long-term success, leading to a fairer distribution of gains. This conclusion remains valid for a wide range of selection pressures, population sizes and mutation rates.

1 Introduction

The attempt to model artificial intelligent agents, revealing human-like behaviour, is often implemented through utility-maximisation heuristics, as *rationality* fits the role of stylised model of human behaviour. When empirical evidence shows that humans systematically deviate from the rational model, explanations suggest the lack of information or computational power. Consequently, the concept of bounded rationality relaxes the strongest assumptions of the pure rational model [15,27]. Either way, the existence of seemingly irrational decisions is often disadvantageous, if one considers agents in isolation.

Agents are not only intended to act alone in environments, however. Often, they interact in multiagent systems, whose decentralised nature of decision making, huge number of opponents and evolving behaviour stems a complex adaptive system [19]. When agents interact with a static environment, the provided reward functions are well-defined and the implementation of traditional

© Springer International Publishing AG 2017
R. Aydoğan et al. (Eds.): COREDEMA 2016, LNAI 10238, pp. 36–50, 2017.
DOI: 10.1007/978-3-319-57285-7_3

learning algorithms turns to be feasible. Yet, in the context of the mentioned large-scale multiagent systems, the success of agents strongly depends on the actions employed by the opponents, very much in the same way as we observe in the evolutionary dynamics of social and biological ecosystems [21,29]. The adaptation of agents, and the learning procedures devised, face important challenges that must be considered [37]. Likewise, the strong considerations about what means to be a rational agent in Artificial Intelligence should be relaxed, or extended. This endeavour can be conveniently achieved through the employment of new tools from, e.g., population dynamics [21] and complex systems research [20], in order to grasp the effects of implementing agents whose strategies, even rational in the context of static environments, may turn to be disadvantageous when successively applied by members of a dynamic population.

In this paper, we present a paradigmatic scenario in which behavioural errors are the source of long-term success. We assume that the goals and strategies of agents are formalised through the famous Ultimatum Game (**UG**) [11], where the conflicting interests of Proposers and Responders likely result in an unfair outcome favouring the former individuals. Additionally, we simulate a finite population of adaptive agents that co-evolve by imitating the best observed actions. We focus on the changes regarding the frequency of agents adopting each strategy, over time. This process of social learning, essentially analogous to the evolution of animal traits in a population, enables us to use the tools of Evolutionary Game Theory (EGT), originally applied in the context of theoretical biology [18]. We start by describing analytically the behavioural outcome in a discretised strategy space of the UG, and in the limit of rare mutations. Additionally, we test the robustness of the results obtained, showing that this analytical approximation remains valid for an arbitrary (i) strategy space, (ii) selection pressure and (iii) mutation rates, via comparison with results from agent-based computer simulations. We shall highlight that this framework, together with a small part of the derived results, were briefly introduced in a short paper [35].

The structure of this paper will continue as follows: Sect. 2 presents the related work in the scope of the game we experiment with, in the field of EGT and, specifically, in its connections with multiagent learning (MAL). Section 3 will present the methods employed, namely, the analytical model that we employ to study evolution as a stochastic process and the analogous agent-based Monte Carlo simulations. In Sect. 4, we present the results derived from both methods. Finally, Sect. 5 is used to provide concluding remarks about the role of execution errors, the nature of its long-term benefits and its relation with the own irrational action.

2   Background

In the present work, we assume that the success of agents is directly derived from the UG [11]. The rules of this game are simple: two players interact in two distinct roles. One is called the *Proposer* and the other is denominated *Responder*. The game is composed by two subgames, one played by each role.

First, some amount of a given resource, e.g. money, is conditionally endowed to the Proposer, and this agent must then suggest a division with the Responder. Secondly, the Responder will accept or reject the offer. The agents divide the money as it was proposed, if the Responder accepts. By rejecting, none of them will get anything. The actions available to the Proposers compose a very large set, constituted by any desired division of the resource. The strategies of the Responders are typically acceptance or rejection, depending on the offer made. We can transform this sequential game in a simultaneous one, if one notes that the strategy of the Responders may be codified *a priori* in a minimum threshold of acceptance [22,38]. This game condenses a myriad of situations in daily life encounters and in economic interactions. Its use is threefold ideal for the situation we want to analyse; for one way, it allows a simple and objective qualification of utility, as we assume that the success of each agent is uniquely defined by the payoffs earned in the context of this game; for other, this game metaphor is the source of multiple studies that account for an irrational behaviour by human beings [4,11], considerably hard to justify mathematically; lastly, by being the last round of a bargaining process, the pertinence of this game and its predicted outcome is specially important in artificial intelligence, namely in the design of artificial bargaining agents [14,16,17].

The rational behaviour in UG can be defined using a game-theoretical equilibrium analysis, through a simple backward induction. Facing the decision of rejecting (earn 0) or accepting (earn some money), the responder would always prefer to accept any arbitrarily small offer. Secure about this certain acceptance, the Proposer will offer the minimum possible, maximising his own share. Denoting by p the fraction of the resource offered by the Proposer, $p \in [0, 1]$, and by q the acceptance threshold of the Responder, $q \in [0, 1]$, acceptance will occur whenever $p \geq q$ and the *subgame perfect equilibrium* [16] of this game is defined by values of p and q slightly above 0. This outcome is said to be unfair, as it presents a profound inequality between the gains of Proposer and Responder. The strategies of agents that value fairness are characterised by prescribing a more equalitarian outcome: a fair Proposer suggests an offer close to 0.5 and a fair Responder rejects unfair offers, much lower than 0.5 (i.e. $p = 0.5$ and $q = 0.5$).

The rational predictions regarding this game were repeatedly refuted by experimental results. The methods employed to make sense of human decision making and adopted behaviour in UG have, necessarily, to be extended beyond pure rational choice models. The need to disuse optimal methods to model human behaviour, and the relevance of including culturally dependent features, were pointed out in previous works [1,27]. To overcome the limitation of an optimal rational model, methods related with psychological features and machine learning techniques were proposed [28]. We follow a different path, adopting methods from population ecology, as EGT. EGT was, in the past, successfully used to predict how individual choices may influence the collective dynamics of self-regarding agents, from cells to climate negotiations — see, e.g., [21,29,33,38,45]. We employ the UG as a game metaphor, without assuming individual or collective rationality. In a social context, EGT describes individuals who revise their strategies through social learning, being influenced by the behaviours and achievements of others [12,25,38].

These dynamics of peer-influence allows one to evaluate the extent of the errors and the impact of the own irrational action.

One of the most traditional tools to describe the dynamics of an evolutionary game model is the replicator equation [40]. This equation, justified in a context of trait evolution in biology or cultural evolution across human societies, poses that populations are infinite and evolution will proceed favouring strategies that offer a fitness higher than the average fitness of the population. The fact that replicator equation describes a process of social learning does not prevent it from being convenient in understanding individual learning. A lot of effort has been placed in bridging the gap between replicator dynamics and multiagent learning [2]. Borgers and Sarin showed that there is indeed an equivalence between replicator dynamics and a simple reinforcement learning model (*Cross learning*) [3]. Also, the relationship between Q-learning and replicator dynamics was positively evidenced [43]. It is also important to highlight that EGT is not confined to infinite populations as the replicator equation. The finite nature of real multiagent systems poses the need to consider stochastic effects related with the probabilistic sampling of peers to interact and imitate, a feature that may significantly impact the resulting description of the evolutionary dynamics and the obtained results [13,33]. This is particularly relevant within multiagent systems research. Thus, in both analytical and numerical computations, we consider evolution as a stochastic process occurring in finite populations [42].

The role of erroneous behaviour during UG encounters was modelled in the past, however in different flavours. Rand et al. studied, both analytically and resorting to experiments, the role of mistakes and stochastic noise in the imitation process of strategies [26]. While that work focus on the role of mutations (or exploration rate) and selection strength (see next section for more details), here of focus on strategic noise, affecting directly the adopted strategies by agents and not the own strategy update process. Notwithstanding, we verify the same general principle: increasing stochasticity, either through high execution errors, low selection strength or small population sizes, has a positive effect on Responders' fitness and overall population fairness. Also in [10] the authors studied errors in executing actions, considering a two-strategy version of UG (the so-called Minigame). The role of errors (in the strategic update process, however) was also studied in the context of multiplayer Ultimatum Games (MUG), both in EGT models [34] and populations with reinforcement learning agents [31]. Next, we present the steps to model the role of execution errors considering large populations of agents, and an arbitrary strategy-space discretisation of UG.

3   Model and Methods

To study the impact of errors in the long-term fitness of agents, we employ two distinct methods. In the first, we describe the prevailing (emergent) behaviours analytically, while resorting to two approximations: we discretise the strategy space of the Ultimatum Game and assume a small mutation (or exploration) probability.

These simplifications allow a convenient analytical computation of the most prevailing states, without the need of massive simulations. Notwithstanding, we complement our study with a second method, achieved through simulations that consider the full Ultimatum Game. The simulations are repeated for 100 times (runs) and during 5000 generations. We conclude that the analytical framework proposed provides equivalent results, and may constitute a convenient way of accessing the role of errors in the natural selection of behaviours.

In both methods we consider the existence of two populations (Proposers and Responders) each one composed by Z agents. The adoption of strategies will evolve following an imitation process. The successful individuals will be imitated, thereby, their strategies will prevail in the population. This process of imitation, akin to social learning, fits well with studies that argue for the importance of observing others in the acquisition of behavioural traits [12, 25]. We assume that at each step two agents are chosen, one that will imitate (agent A) and one whose fitness and strategy will serve as model (agent B). The imitation probability will be calculated using a function — $(1+e^{-\beta(f_B-f_A)})^{-1}$ — that grows monotonously with the fitness difference $f_B - f_A$ [42]. The variable β in the equation above is well-suited to control the selection pressure, allowing to manipulate the extent to which imitation depends on the fitness difference. Whenever $\beta \to 0$, a regime of random drift is attained, in which the imitation occurs irrespectively of the game played, whereas for $\beta \to +\infty$ the imitation will occur deterministically, as even an infinitesimal fitness difference will persuade the imitation of the fitter individual. It is worth to note that, when deciding about imitation, an agent will only observe the fitness of the other agent and the respective strategy; the agents do not have full-information about all interactions of all agents, neither observe the outcome of all individual interactions.

It is also worth to point out that our model copes with fitness, rather than utility. A utility function could vary from agent to agent and could be defined, for instance, to incorporate equality preferences [8], or even a risk-aversion component in the Proposers decision making. Differently, here fitness is uniquely defined by the payoffs of the game, and defines which strategies prevail. The differences between coping with behavioural deviations from rationality through the inclusion of parameters in the utility functions or the study of learning models, is well discussed in [6].

3.1   Analytical Framework

Let us assume that a Proposer and a Responder may choose one of S strategies, corresponding to increasing divisions of 1. A Proposer choosing strategy $m \in \{1, 2, ..., S\}$ will offer the corresponding to $p_m = \frac{1}{S}m$ and a Responder choosing strategy $n \in \{1, 2, ..., S\}$ will accept any offer equal or above $q_n = \frac{1}{S}n$. The two-person encounter between a Proposer and a Responder thus yield $1 - p_m$ to the Proposers and p_m to the Responder if the proposal is accepted $(n : q_n \leq p_m)$ and 0 to both agents otherwise.

We are concerned with the role of systematic errors in the execution of the desired strategy, namely, by the Responders. The class of these errors should not be mixed with errors implemented in learning procedures, which favour exploration over exploitation, and may naturally provide advantages in deriving optimal policies (as ϵ-greedy methods or *softmax* action selection [39]). Indeed, the errors considered in this paper do not provide a direct feedback to their practitioners and they do not interfere in the social learning procedure. We assume that each Responder with strategy n (and threshold of acceptance q_n) will actually use a threshold of q'_n, calculated as $q'_n = q_n + U(-\epsilon, \epsilon)$, where $U(-\epsilon, \epsilon)$ corresponds to an error sampled from a uniform distribution between $-\epsilon$ and ϵ. Thereby, a Responder (using strategy n) accepts an offer $p_m \in [q_n - \epsilon, q_n + \epsilon]$ with a probability given by $P(q'_n \leq p_m) = P(q_n + U(-\epsilon, \epsilon) \leq p_m) = P(U(-\epsilon, \epsilon) \leq p_m - q_n) = \int_{-\epsilon}^{p_m - q_n} \frac{1}{2\epsilon} d(p_m - q_n) = \frac{p_m - q_n + \epsilon}{2\epsilon}$. The probability of acceptance is 0 if $p_m < q_n - \epsilon$ and is 1 if $p_m \geq q_n + \epsilon$. The resulting payoff of a pair (proposal, acceptance threshold) is, thereby, linearly weighted by the probability of acceptance, considering the execution error (ϵ).

This allows us to compute the average payoffs of each strategy in each inter-action, its average fitness and respective transition probabilities (see below). As we assume a well-mixed population, the fitness is given by the average payoff earned when playing with all the agents in the opposite population. Considering the two populations (Proposers and Responders), we say that the population of Proposers is opposite to the population of Responders, and *vice-versa*. Pay-off will be defined by encounters between agents from opposite populations and imitation will happen within a population. Thereby, considering the existence of S different strategies in the opposite population of the one from which agent A belongs; denoting k_i as the number of agents using strategy i, in the opposite population of A; and regarding $R_{j,i}$ as the payoff (reward) earned by an agent A using strategy j, against an agent with strategy i (calculated following the rules of UG with execution errors as detailed above), the fitness of agent A is given by

$$f_{A_j} = \sum_{i=1}^{S} \frac{k_i}{Z} R_{j,i} \tag{1}$$

To model the dynamical behaviour of agents when two strategies are present in the population, we adopt the pairwise comparison rule (see [42]), where the imitation probability increases with the fitness difference (see above). Assuming that two agents are randomly sampled from the population in which k_i agents are using strategy i (the remaining are using strategy j), the probability of having ± 1 individual using strategy i is given by

$$T^{\pm}(k_i) = \frac{Z - k_i}{Z} \frac{k_i}{Z - 1} (1 + e^{\mp \beta(f_i(\overline{k}_s) - f_j(\overline{k}_s))})^{-1} \tag{2}$$

assuming that in the opposite population the number of agents using another strategy s is $\overline{k}_s$ and that the population size is Z. Note that $\frac{Z - k_i}{Z}$ (and $\frac{k_i}{Z-1}$) represent the sampling probabilities of choosing one agent with strategy $j(i)$ and $(1 + e^{\mp \beta(f_i(\overline{k}_s) - f_j(\overline{k}_s))})^{-1}$ translates the imitation probability.

Additionally, with probability μ, a mutation occurs and individuals change their strategy to a random one, exploring a new behaviour regardless the observation of others. The imitation process described above will occur with probability $(1-\mu)$. As said, if we assume that $\mu \to 0$ [5,9,30,33,44], we are able to derive analytical conclusions through a simpler apparatus. This simplified limit turns out to be valid over a much wider interval of mutation regimes [33,44]. Also, while this assumption reduces the random exploration of behaviours, it does not prevent us from considering other stochastic effects, as ϵ, the execution error of Responders. Under this regime in which mutations are extremely rare, a *mutant* strategy will either fixate in the population or will completely vanish [9]. The time between two mutation events is usually so large that the population will always evolve to a monomorphic state (i.e., all agents using the same strategy) before the next mutation occurs. Thus, the dynamics can be approximated by means of a Markov chain whose states correspond to the different monomorphic states of the populations. This fact allows us to conveniently use Eq. (2) in the calculation of transition probabilities, as will be detailed below. Moreover, the time that the populations spend in polymorphic populations is merely transient, thereby disregarded [9,13].

The transitions between states are described through the fixation probability of every single mutant of strategy i in every resident population of strategy j, that translate how easy is for a strategy originated by a rare mutation, to fixate in a population. A strategy i will fixate in a population composed by $Z - 1$ individuals using strategy j with a probability given by [23]

$$\rho_{i \to j}(\overline{k}_s) = \left(\sum_{l=0}^{Z-1} \prod_{k=1}^{l} \frac{T^-(\overline{k}_s)}{T^+(\overline{k}_s)} \right)^{-1} \tag{3}$$

where $\overline{k}_s$ is the number of individuals using strategy s, in the opposite population. Also, while we are calculating the fixation probability in a specific population, the opposite one will remain in the same monomorphic state. This fact allow us to even simplify the calculations [42]. Writing $f_i(\overline{k}_s) - f_j(\overline{k}_s)$ as $\Delta f(\overline{k}_s)$ and noting that $T^-(\overline{k}_s)/T^+(\overline{k}_s) = e^{-\beta \Delta f(\overline{k}_s)}$, Eq. (3) reduces to,

$$\rho_{i \to j}(\overline{k}_s) = \frac{1 - e^{-\beta \Delta f(\overline{k}_s)}}{1 - e^{-Z \beta \Delta f(\overline{k}_s)}} \tag{4}$$

These probabilities define an embedded Markov Chain, governed by the stochastic matrix T, in which $T_{i,j} = \rho_{i \to j}$ defines the fixation probability of a mutant with strategy i in a population with $Z - 1$ individuals using strategy j. To calculate π, the stationary distribution of this Markov Process, we compute the normalised eigenvector associated with the eigenvalue 1 of the transposed of T. $\pi_{a,b}$ represents the fraction of time, on average, that is spent when the population of Proposers is using strategy a and the population of Responders is using strategy b. The number of possible states depends on the discretisation chosen, regarding the strategy space considered in Ultimatum Game. If the Proposer and Responder have, each, S available strategies, there are S^2 different monomorphic states. The resulting average fitness is provided by the average fitness of a population in each monomorphic state, weighted by the time spent in that state. Thereby, the average fitness of the population of Proposers is given by $\overline{f} = \sum_{a=1,b=1}^{S} \pi_{a,b} R_{a,b}$ and the average fitness of the population of Responders is given by $\overline{f} = \sum_{a=1,b=1}^{S} \pi_{a,b} R_{b,a}$. Our results refer to $S = 20$. We tested for $S = 10, 20, 30, 40$ and the conclusions remain the same.

3.2   Agent Based Simulations

The simplifications considered in the previous subsection enable the description of the system as a convenient stochastic process, whose dynamics can be studied without effort. Yet, to know whether the results achieved are sound, we proceeded through agent based simulations, in which agents may choose a continuity of strategies (i.e. $S \to \infty$) and mutations are arbitrary.

We employ a general procedure to simulate evolving agents in the context of EGT. At each time step, a population is picked with probability 0.5. From that population, two agents are chosen (agent A and agent B). The fitness of each agent is calculated by using their strategy against all agents from the opposite population, each with their own strategy. Agent A will then imitate agent B with a probability provided by the sigmoid function — $(1 + e^{-\beta(f_B - f_A)})^{-1}$ — presented in the beginning of this section. With a small probability of μ, imitation will not take place and agent A updates the own strategy to a randomly picked one, between 0 and 1. In biology, this corresponds to a genetic mutation while, in social learning and cultural evolution (and also in typical reinforcement learning algorithms [39]), this mimics the random exploration of behaviours.

The same procedure takes place in the opposite population. When $2Z$ steps of imitation occur, Z in each population, we say that one generation has elapsed. We evolve our system for 5000 generations, and we save the average fitness and average strategy used, for each population. In the beginning, agents start with random strategies, sampled from a uniform distribution between 0 and 1. We repeat the simulation for 50 times, each time starting with random conditions. The results presented (average fitness and average strategy) correspond to a time average over all generations and an ensemble average over all repetitions. In all plays done by the Responders, a noise factor will be added to their base strategy. Thus, the real strategy employed by Responders will correspond to q', their base strategy (q), plus $U(-\epsilon, \epsilon)$, a random value between $-\epsilon$ and ϵ sampled from a uniform distribution in each interaction. Additionally, we followed the same procedure yet assuming a normal distribution with ϵ defining the variance and q defining the mean of the distribution. The same conclusions were obtained, however, the optimal value of ϵ that maximises the Responders' fitness is lower than the one observed with a uniform distribution (but still higher than 0).

4   Results

In this section we report the analytical and numerical results. Anticipating the detailed presentation, we show that the fitness of the Responders will be maximised if they commit a significant execution error, sampled from an interval close to $[-0.3, 0.3]$. Both methodologies are in consonance with this conclusion.

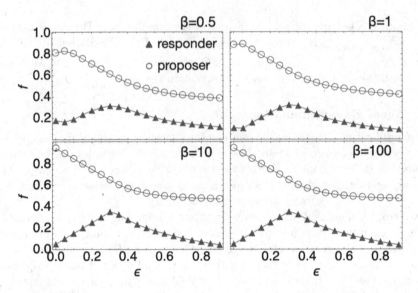

Fig. 1. Analytical results, reporting the average fitness (f) of Proposers (empty circles), average fitness of Responders (filled triangles) for different spans of error committed by the Responders while choosing a strategy, ϵ. It is notorious that it is beneficial for the Responder to behave erroneously, to some extent. If Responders reject irrationally some proposals, the Proposers have to adapt and start to offer more, beneficing, in the long run, the Responders; If Responders reject too much, they will harm themselves and the population of Proposers, as they will waste too much proposals. $Z = 100$, $S = 20$.

In Fig. 1 we show how the average fitness of Proposers and Responders is affected by changing the range of possible execution errors (ϵ) committed by Responders. For different β the conclusion remains equivalent: if the error increases, Responders are endowed with increased fitness. The Proposers are always harmed by the erroneous behaviour of Responders. The *subgame perfect equilibrium* prediction poses that Proposers will earn all the pot, by offering almost nothing to the Responder and assuming an unconditional acceptance by this agent. Yet, if it is assumed that Responders will commit execution errors, which, in the case of heighten the threshold of acceptance may be seen as an irrational behaviour, the Proposers necessarily have to adapt to have their proposals accepted and earn some payoff. This adaptation leads to increased offers (see Fig. 3), favouring the average fitness of the Responders. Additionally, we note that if the Responders error unreasonably, both Proposers and Responders will be impaired.

One may argue that the results presented in Fig. 1 strongly depend on the simplifying assumptions made: the discretisation of strategy space; the assumption of having an equivalence between an average error committed by all agents and the different errors committed individually, within a range; the assumption that most of the time, populations are in a steady monomorphic state,

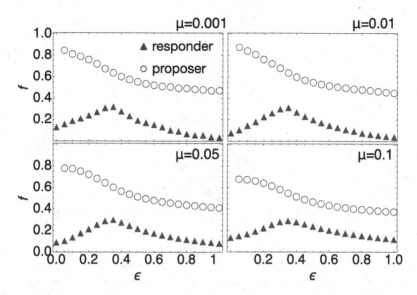

Fig. 2. Results from agent-based computer simulations, reporting the average fitness (f) of Proposers (empty circles), average fitness of Responders (filled triangles) for different spans of error committed by the Responders while choosing a strategy. It is notorious that it is beneficial for the Responder to behave erroneously, to some extent. The results confirm that for a wide range of mutation values (μ), the conclusions regarding the role of execution error (ϵ) in the emergence of fairness remain valid. $Z = 100$, $\beta = 10$

only perturbed by rare mutations. Yet, Fig. 2 shows that our conclusions, and the applicability of the analytical model, are more general than one may initially expect. Figure 2 reports the almost exact same results as Fig. 1 whereas in this case, they refer to agent based simulations. In these simulations, the assumptions made are disregarded: agents may use any strategy between 0 and 1, each Responder commits a different error within the same range, every time an interaction occurs and no impositions are posed, regarding the time spent in monomorphic states.

The results arguing for an optimal value of error that maximises the fitness achieved by Responders, are also robust for different values of Z (population size), μ (mutation rate) and β (selection pressure). We tested with μ ranging from 0.001 to 0.1 (Fig. 2), and the conclusions remain valid. Further analytical results regarding β and Z can be accessed in Figs. 4 and 5.

In Fig. 3 we present the emerging strategies of Proposers (p), regarding the execution error by the Responders (ϵ). The fairer offers made by the Proposers coincide with the highest fitness achieved by the Responders (when $\epsilon = 0.3$).

Using both methods (analytical and simulations) it is also possible to assess the impact of β (intensity of selection) and Z (population size) in the emerging average fitness (Figs. 4 and 5). Again, the analytical and numerical results

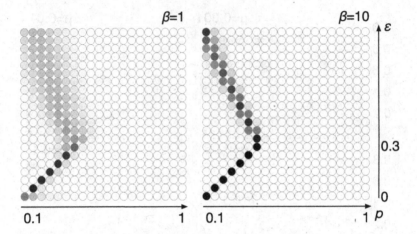

Fig. 3. Prevailing behaviour of Proposers (p) for different execution errors (ϵ) and selection pressure (β), calculated using the proposed analytical framework. Circles coloured using a grayscale represent the stationary distribution over possible *base strategies*, calculated analytically. Darker colours mean that the system spends more time in the corresponding state. It is possible to observe that the Proposers maximise their offers (towards fairer proposals) when $\epsilon = 0.3$. That increased offer coincides with the increase in the average fitness earned by the Responders. $Z = 100$, $S = 20$

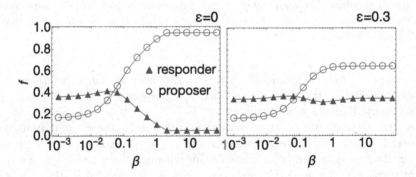

Fig. 4. Analytical results showing the role of selection pressure (β) in the overall fitness (f) of Proposers (empty circles) and Responders (filled triangles), considering two different execution errors by Responders $\epsilon = 0$ and $\epsilon = 0.3$. An increase in β undermines the fitness of Responders. For high intensities of selection, the advantages for Responders of behaving erratically is evident. $Z = 100$, $S = 20$

coincide. Increasing β and Z promotes determinism in the imitation process (see Sect. 3). Thereby, if the strategy update depends on the fitness difference between agents and no execution errors are considered, the system evolves into a state in which Proposers offer less and Responders accept everything. As an outcome, Proposers keep almost all the payoffs. Even employing a different methodology, these results (regarding the connection between stochasticity and fairness) are in line with the discussion performed in [26,34].

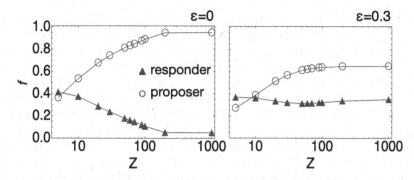

Fig. 5. Analytical results showing the role of different population sizes (Z) in the overall fitness (f) of Proposers (empty circles) and Responders (filled triangles), considering two different execution errors by Responders $\epsilon = 0$ and $\epsilon = 0.3$. An increase in Z undermines the fitness of Responders, similarly to what happened with an increase in β. In fact, high values of Z translate into a population more deterministic, as the fixation of disadvantageous traits by stochastic perturbations turns to be harder. Again, for high population sizes, it is clear the advantage for Responders of behaving erratically. $\beta = 10$, $S = 20$

5   Discussion

In this paper, we apply a novel analytical framework to study UG in a finite population, with an arbitrary state space discretisation. This framework enables the evaluation of stochastic parameters (i.e. selection pressure and different population sizes) in the dynamics of strategy usage in UG. We are able to show, both analytically and through agent-based simulations, how execution errors (ϵ) may promote increased fitness and fairer offers in UG. If the Responders are induced to commit execution errors (which should not be confused with a mixed strategy, mutation or exploration rate), the seemingly disadvantageous nature of errors turns to be, indeed, an illusion. As Responders error, the Proposers need to adapt and necessarily have to propose generous offers to cover possible errors. Yet, it is also important to understand the extent to which should Responders error. Clearly, being overly erroneous is not beneficial. Other than avoiding the proper adaptation of Responders through the adoption and use of strategies that conduce to fair payoffs, an exaggeration in error span would waste too much proposals, harming both Proposers and Responders. This said, we find an optimal error value in the range $[-0.3, 0.3]$ (i.e., $\epsilon = 0.3$), meaning that, if Responders evolve their base strategy to be close to 0, they would still reject low offers, up to a 0.3 of the total amount help by the Proposer. Despite the plethora of experimental studies in the context of UG, where humans are asked to play this game, a common result is that proposals giving the responder shares below 0.25 are rejected with a very high probability [7], which is interestingly close to the results we obtain.

Finally, we shall highlight that the model we propose avoids the rationality supposition of classical game theory, by assuming that strategies are adopted as the outcome of an evolutionary process of social learning. The relation between our conclusions and eventual results derived from an equilibrium analysis that incorporates noise, as *trembling hand perfect equilibrium* or *quantal response equilibrium*, are naturally interesting. However, by using those game theoretical tools, one would ease the fact that games are often played by agents within adaptive populations, and overall, what seems rational as an individual behaviour may not constitute a good option regarding the collective results [24, 36]. Indeed, in our model, we may identify actions that, even if not rational at an individual scale, turn to be justifiable from an evolutionary point of view. Execution errors may be seen as a pernicious individual feature that provides collective benefits. Resorting to a multi-level selection mechanism [41], our results may indicate how little pressure evolution may exert to diminish those errors, leading to a plausible argumentation for the natural selection of "erroneous" behaviours, fostered by psychological and emotional factors [4]. Moreover, the fixation of these execution errors is the source of a fairer distribution of payoffs in the UG, as the gains of Responders approximate the gains of the Proposers. As future work, we intend to adapt the proposed framework to analyse the role of errors in group decision making (specifically in multiplayer ultimatum games), where fairness and conflicting interests are paramount [32, 34].

References

1. Azaria, A., Richardson, A., Rosenfeld, A.: Autonomous agents and human cultures in the trust-revenge game. Auton. Agents Multi Agent Syst. **30**(3), 1–20 (2015)
2. Bloembergen, D., Tuyls, K., Hennes, D., Kaisers, M.: Evolutionary dynamics of multiagent learning: a survey. J. Artif. Intell. Res. **53**, 659–697 (2015)
3. Börgers, T., Sarin, R.: Learning through reinforcement and replicator dynamics. J. Econ. Theor. **77**(1), 1–14 (1997)
4. Camerer, C.: Behavioral Game Theory: Experiments in Strategic Interaction. Princeton University Press, Princeton (2003)
5. Encarnao, S., Santos, F.P., Santos, F.C., Blass, V., Pacheco, J.M., Portugali, J.: Paradigm shifts and the interplay between state, business and civil sectors. R. Soc. Open Sci. **3**, 160753 (2016)
6. Erev, I., Roth, A.E.: Maximization, learning, and economic behavior. Proc. Natl. Acad. Sci. USA **111**, 10818–10825 (2014)
7. Fehr, E., Fischbacher, U.: The nature of human altruism. Nature **425**(6960), 785–791 (2003)
8. Fehr, E., Schmidt, K.M.: A theory of fairness, competition, and cooperation. Q. J. Econ. **114**(3), 817–868 (1999)
9. Fudenberg, D., Imhof, L.A.: Imitation processes with small mutations. J. Econ. Theor. **131**(1), 251–262 (2006)
10. Gale, J., Binmore, K.G., Samuelson, L.: Learning to be imperfect: the ultimatum game. Game Econ. Behav. **8**(1), 56–90 (1995)
11. Güth, W., Schmittberger, R., Schwarze, B.: An experimental analysis of ultimatum bargaining. J. Econ. Behav. Organ. **3**(4), 367–388 (1982)

12. Heyes, C.M.: Social learning in animals: categories and mechanisms. Biol. Rev. **69**(2), 207–231 (1994)
13. Imhof, L.A., Fudenberg, D., Nowak, M.A.: Evolutionary cycles of cooperation and defection. Proc. Natl. Acad. Sci. USA **102**(31), 10797–10800 (2005)
14. Jennings, N.R., Faratin, P., Lomuscio, A.R., Parsons, S., Wooldridge, M.J., Sierra, C.: Automated negotiation: prospects, methods and challenges. Group Decis. Negot. **10**(2), 199–215 (2001)
15. Kahneman, D.: Maps of bounded rationality: psychology for behavioral economics. Am. Econ. Rev. **93**(5), 1449–1475 (2003)
16. Kraus, S.: Strategic Negotiation in Multiagent Environments. MIT press, Cambridge (2001)
17. Lin, R., Kraus, S.: Can automated agents proficiently negotiate with humans? Commun. ACM **53**(1), 78–88 (2010)
18. Maynard-Smith, J., Price, G.: The logic of animal conflict. Nature **246**, 15 (1973)
19. Miller, J.H., Page, S.E.: Complex Adaptive Systems: An Introduction to Computational Models of Social Life. Princeton University Press, Princeton (2009)
20. Mitchell, M.: Complexity: A Guided Tour. Oxford University Press, Oxford (2009)
21. Nowak, M.A.: Evolutionary Dynamics: Exploring the Equations of Life. Harvard University Press, Cambridge (2006)
22. Nowak, M.A., Page, K.M., Sigmund, K.: Fairness versus reason in the ultimatum game. Science **289**(5485), 1773–1775 (2000)
23. Nowak, M.A., Sasaki, A., Taylor, C., Fudenberg, D.: Emergence of cooperation and evolutionary stability in finite populations. Nature **428**(6983), 646–650 (2004)
24. Pinheiro, F.L., Pacheco, J.M., Santos, F.C.: From local to global dilemmas in social networks. PLoS ONE **7**(2), e32114 (2012)
25. Pinheiro, F.L., Santos, M.D., Santos, F.C., Pacheco, J.M.: Origin of peer influence in social networks. Phys. Rev. Lett. **112**(9), 098702 (2014)
26. Rand, D.G., Tarnita, C.E., Ohtsuki, H., Nowak, M.A.: Evolution of fairness in the one-shot anonymous ultimatum game. Proc. Natl. Acad. Sci. USA **110**(7), 2581–2586 (2013)
27. Rosenfeld, A., Kraus, S.: Modeling agents through bounded rationality theories. In: IJCAI 2009 Proceedings of the 21st International Joint Conference on Artificial Intelligence, vol. 9, pp. 264–271 (2009)
28. Rosenfeld, A., Zuckerman, I., Azaria, A., Kraus, S.: Combining psychological models with machine learning to better predict people's decisions. Synthese **189**(1), 81–93 (2012)
29. Santos, F.C., Pacheco, J.M.: Risk of collective failure provides an escape from the tragedy of the commons. Proc. Natl. Acad. Sci. USA **108**(26), 10421–10425 (2011)
30. Santos, F.C., Pacheco, J.M., Skyrms, B.: Co-evolution of pre-play signaling and cooperation. J. Theor. Biol. **274**(1), 30–35 (2011)
31. Santos, F.P., Santos, F.C., Melo, F.S., Paiva, A., Pacheco, J.M.: Dynamics of fairness in groups of autonomous learning agents. In: Osman, N., Sierra, C. (eds.) AAMAS 2016. LNCS (LNAI), vol. 10002, pp. 107–126. Springer, Cham (2016). doi:10.1007/978-3-319-46882-2_7
32. Santos, F.P., Santos, F.C., Melo, F.S. Paiva, A., Pacheco, J.M.: Learning to be fair in multiplayer ultimatum games. In: Proceedings of the 2016 International Conference on Autonomous Agents and Multiagent Systems, International Foundation for Autonomous Agents and Multiagent Systems, pp. 1381–1382 (2016)
33. Santos, F.P., Santos, F.C., Pacheco, J.M.: Social norms of cooperation in small-scale societies. PLoS Comput. Biol. **12**(1), e1004709 (2016)

34. Santos, F.P., Santos, F.C., Paiva, A., Pacheco, J.M.: Evolutionary dynamics of group fairness. J. Theor. Biol. **378**, 96–102 (2015)
35. Santos, F.P., Santos, F.C., Paiva, A., Pacheco, J.M.: Execution errors enable the evolution of fairness in the ultimatum game. In: Proceedings of the 22nd European Conference on Artificial Intelligence (ECAI 2016), vol. 285, p. 1592. IOS Press (2016)
36. Schelling, T.C.: Micromotives and Macrobehavior. WW Norton & Company, New York City (2006)
37. Shoham, Y., Powers, R., Grenager, T.: If multi-agent learning is the answer, what is the question? Artif. Intell. **171**(7), 365–377 (2007)
38. Sigmund, K.: The Calculus of Selfishness. Princeton University Press, Princeton (2010)
39. Sutton, R.S., Barto, A.G.: Introduction to Reinforcement Learning. MIT Press, Cambridge (1998)
40. Taylor, P.D., Jonker, L.B.: Evolutionary stable strategies and game dynamics. Math. Biosci. **40**(1), 145–156 (1978)
41. Traulsen, A., Nowak, M.A.: Evolution of cooperation by multilevel selection. Proc. Natl. Acad. Sci. USA **103**(29), 10952–10955 (2006)
42. Traulsen, A., Nowak, M.A., Pacheco, J.M.: Stochastic dynamics of invasion and fixation. Phys. Rev. E **74**(1), 011909 (2006)
43. Tuyls, K., Verbeeck, K., Lenaerts, T.: A selection-mutation model for q-learning in multiagent systems. In: AAMAS 2003 Proceedings of the Second International Joint Conference on Autonomous Agents and Multiagent Systems, pp. 693–700 (2003)
44. Van Segbroeck, S., Pacheco, J.M., Lenaerts, T., Santos, F.C.: Emergence of fairness in repeated group interactions. Phys. Rev. Lett. **108**(15), 158104 (2012)
45. Vasconcelos, V.V., Santos, F.C., Pacheco, J.M., Levin, S.A.: Climate policies under wealth inequality. Proc. Natl. Acad. Sci. USA **111**(6), 2212–2216 (2014)

Nonlinear Negotiation Approaches for Complex-Network Optimization: A Study Inspired by Wi-Fi Channel Assignment

Ivan Marsa-Maestre[1]([⊠]), Enrique de la Hoz[1], Jose Manuel Gimenez-Guzman[1], David Orden[2], and Mark Klein[3]

[1] Computer Engineering Department,
University of Alcala, Alcalá de Henares, Spain
{ivan.marsa,enrique.delahoz,josem.gimenez}@uah.es
[2] Department of Physics and Mathematics,
University of Alcala, Alcalá de Henares, Spain
david.orden@uah.es
[3] Center for Collective Intelligence, MIT, Cambridge, USA
m_klein@mit.edu

Abstract. In this paper, we study a problem family inspired by a prominent network optimization problem (graph coloring), enriched and extended towards a real-world application (Wi-Fi channel assignment). We propose a utility model based on this scenario, and we generate an extensive set of test cases, against which we run both a complete information optimizer and two nonlinear negotiation approaches –a hill-climber and an approach based on simulated annealing (SA). We show that, for the larger-scale scenarios, the SA negotiation approach significantly outperforms the optimizer while running in roughly one tenth of the computation time. Also, we point out interesting patterns regarding the relative performance of the two approaches depending on the properties of the underlying graphs.

1 Introduction

In the last years, complex networks have attracted a lot of interest within the AI community, both due to the inherent challenge of some network-structured optimization problems (e.g. to be NP-hard) and due to the enormous potential for real-world applications (many important real-world problems have network structures). An important sub-class involves autonomous, self-interested entities (e.g. drivers in a transportation network). The self-interested nature of these entities cause the network to deviate from socially-optimal behaviour.

Taking this into account, it is not surprising that problems which combine a networked structure and self-interested parties have been drawing attention from the AI community. Different fields of research are working on the challenges these problems raise, but, so far, with only mixed success. Optimization techniques are especially suited to address large-scale systems with an underlying network

© Springer International Publishing AG 2017
R. Aydoğan et al. (Eds.): COREDEMA 2016, LNAI 10238, pp. 51–65, 2017.
DOI: 10.1007/978-3-319-57285-7_4

structure, usually with a "divide and conquer" approach. However, their performance severely decreases as the complexity of the system increases [30], and with the presence of autonomous entities which deviate from the globally optimal solution, thus harming the social goal. Automated negotiation has proven to be valuable to support decision-making process in scenarios where it is necessary to find an agreement quickly and with conflicting interests involved [31]. Potential applications of automated negotiation range from e-commerce [26] to task distribution problem solving, resource sharing or cooperative design [34]. One of the most important advantages of automated negotiation is that it takes into account the conflict of interests from the beginning. This enables finding more stable solutions (agreements) which make participating agents less prone to deviating from the socially optimal solution to favour their privately optimal solution. Although there is significant work on game theory and bargaining in complex networks, the nonlinear negotiation community has made only few, very specific incursions in complex networked problems [6].

We want to explore the possibilities of using non-linear negotiation techniques [22] to solve complex network problems involving self interested parties. To this end, we are working on the problem of frequency assignment in Wi-Fi infrastructure networks. In this problem, different Wi-Fi providers have to collectively decide how to distribute the channels used by their APs in order to minimize interference between nodes and thus maximize the utility (i.e. network throughput) for their clients. This is a particularly interesting problem, since it is strongly related to the Frequency Assignment Problem (which has been extensively studied from the perspective of discrete optimization), to the prominent mathematical graph coloring problem [35], and to distributed constraint optimization models [13].

Graph coloring have attracted researchers due to its theoretical challenges and real-world applications [21]. One of the most prominent problems of coloring vertices of a graph is frequency assignment [2], with models ranging from the most basic, forbidding monochromatic edges, to the most general, like including interference restrictions and an objective function. Some works like [4,12,33] consider graph coloring considering the distance between colors and vertices, i.e., with hard restrictions. On the other hand, in [2] we can find a survey of optimization techniques for graph coloring considering soft restrictions. In our case, and differently from the above-mentioned works, we focus in coloring the network with a set of predefined spectrum of colors and with a matrix of interferences between them, with the objective of minimizing some function that depends on the resulting interferences.

In relation to previous works involving optimal frequency assignment in Wi-Fi networks, it is important to note that there is an scarcity of works in this topic, probably due to its high complexity, being NP-hard [5]. In fact, in [5] we can find an overview frequency assignment techniques in Wi-Fi environments. Probably, the most remarkable proposals are [24,25]. These works are specially interesting to this work as they use graph coloring as their main tool. Other works that also use graphs for frequency assignment are [23,27], although they do not consider Wi-Fi peculiarities. A proposal that coordinates Wi-Fi access points to assign frequency channels without the use of graphs can be found in [3].

However, the focus of our work is different from all these works as we are interested in demonstrating that nonlinear negotiation techniques are powerful tools to solve the complex problem of frequency assignment in Wi-Fi networks. More specifically, we want to test the hypotheses that our nonlinear negotiation approaches can be used as an efficient alternative to centralized, generic optimization tools, and that network properties have an impact on the relative performance of the different techniques. This work contributes to achieve this objective in the following ways:

- We model the problem of Wi-Fi channel assignment, using an abstract model based on a multilayer graph and a nonlinear utility model (Sect. 2).
- We propose to solve this problem using nonlinear automated negotiation techniques, and define the corresponding negotiation scenario (Sect. 3).
- We generate a large set of scenario instances for this problem, we select a set of metrics based on graph theory to analyze them, and we perform extensive experimentation on this set of instances, comparing our negotiation approaches to two reference techniques: a random channel assignment and a complete-information nonlinear optimizer based on particle swarms (Sect. 4).

The experimental results (Sect. 5) show that one of the benchmarked negotiation approaches (single text mediation with simulated annealing) significantly outperforms the optimizer for the larger-scale scenarios, both in computation time and social welfare. Also, interesting patterns regarding the influence of network properties on the relative performance of the approaches are identified. The last section summarizes our contributions and sheds light on future lines of research.

2   Problem Modelling

2.1   Wi-Fi Architecture

IEEE 802.11 technology, commercially known as Wi-Fi, is a very popular and widespread technology, whose most used standard operates commonly in the 2.4 GHz frequency band. Due to the high number of Wi-Fi devices that coexist in these frequencies, this band is usually congested, a situation often worsened by other devices like Bluetooth, ZigBee, microwave ovens, baby monitors or cordless phones. For those reasons, it is of paramount importance that Wi-Fi devices smartly manage the use of the radio spectrum. The 2.4 GHz band is divided into 11 partially overlapped channels [29], so it is important to choose the most advantageous one to minimize interferences.

The most widely deployed Wi-Fi architecture is infrastructure mode, where there are two types of devices in the network: access points (APs) and wireless devices (WDs) such as laptops, smartphones... In infrastructure mode, wireless devices are wirelessly connected to a single AP, which is generally a wireless

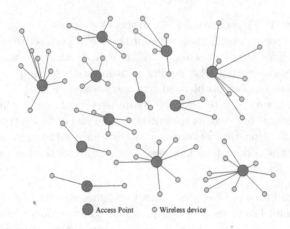

Fig. 1. Wi-Fi architecture.

router, and are able to communicate to other devices only through that AP. For that reason, WDs are also called clients. In Fig. 1 we show a graphical representation of a scenario with 12 APs and 60 WDs.

2.2   Modelling Based on a Multilayer Graph

Graphs are one of the most commonly used tools for modelling the frequency assignment problems, because of the relation of this problem to the graph coloring problem, which has been widely studied by the mathematical community [35]. In graph coloring, an abstract graph is considered, defined by a set of vertices along with some edges connecting them, and the objective is to assign one color to each vertex, in such a manner that the minimum possible number of colors should be used, while avoiding monochromatic edges. In the commonly used model, graph nodes represent elements that should be assigned a frequency while edges represent element pairs that should not be assigned the same frequency. This way, colors act as frequencies and hetero-chromatic edges guarantee element pairs with different frequencies. Although widely used, Tragos et al. [7] conclude that the model is not accurate enough, because it does not reflect all the information. For instance, the authors suggest that the information regarding adjacent channel interferences should be incorporated into the graph.

To model the Wi-Fi channel assignment problem we propose a multilayer network graph [17], where each layer represents a different relationship between network elements, as shown in Fig. 2. In this graph we can distinguish two types of vertices: APs and WDs. *Layer a* captures the infrastructure links between Wi-Fi APs and WDs, i.e. the links shown in Fig. 1. Note that every WD is associated to its closest AP, and that, since APs are the ones who set the channel to be used by their associated clients, all nodes connected in *layer a* will use the same channel (color) to communicate. On the other hand, *layer b* captures the potential interferences between nearby vertices. To be more specific, *layer b* links node pairs where

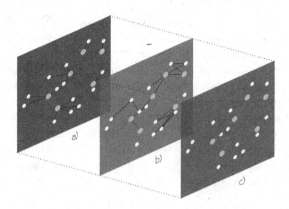

Fig. 2. Multilayer graph model.

the distance between them is below the corresponding interference radius R (that depends on the sensitivity of the receiver): AP–AP pairs will be linked provided that the distance condition is met, AP–WD pairs only when the device is not associated to that AP, and WD–WD pairs only if both devices are associated to different APs, since the communications among the elements connected to the same AP are coordinated and do not interfere. In Sect. 2.3 we describe the interference model in more detail. Finally, *layer c* captures the idea that usually there is a small number of communication providers to which the APs belongs to. This last layer is the key to model the automated negotiation, since the fact that a provider may choose to sacrifice the throughput of a given access point in favor of others is what will enable the existence of utility trade-offs during negotiations. It is important to note that this layers are not associated to communication infrastructure layers or in any way represent communication restrictions between APs. It is usual to have APs connected to wired networks so that they can communicate with each other.

2.3 Interferences and Utility of the Solutions

To model interference power between two elements, we weigh each edge of the interference graph (*layer b* in the multilayer model) based on three factors:

1. We consider a weight for each color pair ij that we have called the co-channel index, which can be understood as the interference between color i and color j. It is worth noting that the usual coloring problem only takes into account the particular case of interferences between vertices of the same color, while our extension of the problem allows considering also interferences between adjacent colors or colors in a certain distance range, to take into account the partial overlapping between frequency channels in Wi-Fi. To model this effect, we have used the values obtained for this index in [29], where authors provide a matrix where each value (i, j) represents the interference, as seen in channel i, motivated by a transmission on channel j.

2. We consider the distance between edge endpoints. This way, the weight assigned to a colored edge ij will be different depending on how far apart its endpoints are, following the propagation model described in [11]. This represents another extension to the usual coloring problem, because now vertices have also certain positions and this means that our graph is no longer abstract but geometrical.
3. We include the effect of the amount of data into the weights, including a factor (called activity index) that accounts for the fact that a higher bandwidth data flow will occupy the wireless channel a higher fraction of the time. In other words, higher bandwidth flows will generate more harmful interference signals, as they will occupy the spectrum for a higher ratio of time.

Once there is a model for interfering signals, the signal to noise ratio for terminal i $(SINR_i)$ can be computed as the ratio between the received desired signal and the sum of the received undesired interferences. Note that each AP will have a $SINR$ value for every terminal that is associated to it. In that case, we will assume that its $SINR$ will be the minimum of all of them, which is in fact the worst case.

To quantify the goodness of the different network colorings, we have used the concept of utility, which is closely related to the perceived throughput and $SINR$. According to [1], in a wireless network the throughput equals a maximum value when the $SINR$ is over a certain value $SINR_{max}$ and monotonically decreases with the reduction of $SINR$ until an insufficient value of $SINR$, called $SINR_{min}$, is reached, when the throughput falls to zero. We can consider the utility seen by node i (U_i) as a normalized throughput, so it can be defined as a value ranging from 0 to 1, with 0 corresponding to the situations when there is a very low-quality reception and the devices cannot keep connected (throughput equals to zero), and 1 corresponding to the case when the signal quality is excellent (throughput equals to its maximum value). Threshold values for $SINR$ have been defined from the values presented in [10]. Finally, the utility value for a specific provider P_i (U_{P_i}) is computed as the sum of the utility values for all its APs and the clients associated to these APs.

3   Automated Negotiation Techniques for Channel Selection

In this work, we propose to tackle the network-structured channel assignment problem in Wi-Fi using automated negotiation techniques. Automated negotiation is a quite wide field [9] but most authors agree that a negotiation problem can be characterized by a negotiation domain (who negotiates and what to negotiate about), an interaction protocol (which rules govern the negotiation process), and a set of decision mechanisms or *strategies* that guide the negotiating agents through every phase of the interaction protocol [8]. In the following we define our particular negotiation problem along these three dimensions.

3.1   Negotiation Domain

For the scope of this work, we assume a multiattribute negotiation domain, where a deal or solution to the problem is defined as the set of attributes (*issues*), and each one of them can be in a certain range. In our case, for a channel assignment problem with n_{AP} access points, a solution or deal S can be expressed as $S = \{s_i | i \in 1, ..., n_{AP}\}$, where $s_i \in \{1, ..., 11\}$ represents the assignation of a Wi-Fi channel to the i-th access point.

In this work, we assume that there are two network providers (commonly Internet Service Providers, ISPs), thus APs belong to one of the providers. Each provider only has control over the channel assignment for its own access points. According to this situation, $P = \{p_1, p_2\}$ will be the set of agents that will negotiate the channel assignment. We find adequate to focus in the two-provider case because there are more works in complex bilateral negotiations than for the multilateral case (three or more agents).

Finally, each one of these agents will compute its utility for a certain solution according to the model described in the previous section. The problem settings (high cardinality of the solution space and attribute interdependence) will make the utility functions highly complex, with multiple local optima.

3.2   Interaction Protocol

There are many interaction protocols for negotiations, from the classical alternating offers model [32] to auction-based protocols [14]. From the assumption that the negotiation scenarios coming from Wi-Fi channel assignment will be highly nonlinear, and according to the discussion in [22], we have chosen a simple text mediation protocol [18]. In its simplest version, the negotiation protocol will be as follows:

1. It starts with a randomly-generated candidate contract (S_0^c). This means to assign each AP a random channel.
2. In each iteration t, the mediator proposes a contract S_t^c to the rest of agents (i.e. the providers).
3. Each agent either accepts or rejects the contract S_t^c .
4. The mediator generates a new contract S_{t+1}^c from the previous contracts and from the votes received from the agents and the process moves to step 2.

This process goes on until a maximum number of iterations is reached. The protocol, as defined, is rather generic and must be completed with the definition of the decision mechanism to be used by the negotiating agents and the mediator.

3.3   Decision Mechanisms

For the mediator, we have implemented a single-text mediation mechanism [18] for the generation of new contracts, which works as follows:

- If at time t all agents have accepted the presented contract S_t^c, this contract will be used as the base contract S^b to generate the next contract S_{t+1}^c. Otherwise, the last mutually accepted contract will be used.
- To generate the next candidate contract S_{t+1}^c, the mediator takes the base contract S_b and mutates one of its issues randomly. In our case of study, this would correspond to choosing a random access point and selecting a new random channel for it.
- After a fixed number of iterations, the mediator advertises the last mutually accepted contract as final.

For the agents, we have considered two different mechanisms to vote about the candidate contracts S^c:

- _Hill-climber (HC):_ In this case, the agent behaves as a greedy utility maximizer. The agent will only accept a contract when it has at least the same utility for her than the previous mutually accepted contract.
- _Annealer (SA):_ In this case, we use a widespread nonlinear optimization technique called _simulated annealing_ [18]. When a contract yields a utility loss against the previous mutually accepted contract, there will be a probability for the agent to accept it nonetheless. This probability P_a depends on the utility loss associated to the new contract Δu, and also depends on a parameter known as _annealing temperature_ τ, so that $P_a = e^{\frac{-\Delta u}{\tau}}$. Annealing temperature begins at an initial value, and linearly decreases to zero throughout the successive iterations of the protocol.

The choice of these two mechanisms is not arbitrary. _Simulated annealing_ techniques have yielded very satisfactory results in negotiation for nonlinear utility spaces [20], and are the basis for several of other works [22]. Furthermore, as discussed in [18], the comparison between _hill-climbers_ and _annealers_ allows to assess whether the scenario under consideration is a highly complex one, since in such scenarios greedy optimizers tend to get stuck in local optima, while the _simulated annealing_ optimizer tends to escape from them.

4 Scenarios, Benchmarks and Metrics

4.1 Considered Scenarios

In this paper, we make the common assumption that Wi-Fi nodes (APs and clients) are static elements. As in our problem there is not any element that evolves with time, we deal with the problem of evaluating the performance of a particular channel assignment strategy by means of the computation described in Sect. 2.

Moreover, the choice of the configuration parameters for the studied scenarios has been driven by considering typical or reasonable power transmission and sensitivity parameters from a realistic point of view [15]. We have also made the assumption that both APs and clients are randomly distributed throughout the environment, and that clients associate to the AP which is closer to them. With these assumptions, we have generated scenarios varying the number of APs (15, 50 and 100) and the number of clients per AP (1 and 5). For each of these combinations of parameters we generated 50 different graphs, for a total of 300 scenarios. This allowed us to have a wide range of problem sizes (from tens of nodes to roughly one thousand nodes), and also a wide diversity (due to the randomization of node placement). Keep in mind that there is more variability on the number of APs and clients than the one suggested by the parameter set, since we removed from the scenario any AP which had no nearby clients, and vice versa. Finally, for each scenario, we randomly assigned half of the APs to each provider.

4.2 Analysed Techniques

In addition to the negotiation techniques under study, presented in Sect. 3.3, we have included a comparison with two reference techniques:

- *Random Reference*: as a first base line, in this technique each AP chooses a channel randomly.
- *Particle Swarm Optimization (ALPSO)*: additionally to our negotiators based on *simulated annealing*, we wanted to have, as a reference, a nonlinear optimizer using complete information. We have chosen a parallel augmented Lagrange multiplier particle swarm optimizer, which solves nonlinear non-smooth constrained problems using an augmented Lagrange multiplier approach to handle constraints [16].

4.3 Graph Metrics for Performance Evaluation

One of the long-term purposes of our work is to study how the network structural properties of a problem influence the performance of optimization and negotiation approaches used to address it. To this end, we have selected a number of graph metrics from the literature to analyze our experimental results. The selected metrics are the following:

- *Graph order:* the number of nodes in the graph.
- *Graph diameter:* the longest distance between any pair of nodes in the graph [28].
- *Wiener index:* gives a measure of graph complexity from the distances in the graph. It is computed as $W(G) = \frac{1}{2} \sum_{i=0}^{|N|} \sum_{j=0}^{|N|} d(n_i, n_j)$, where $d(n_i, n_j)$ is the shortest distance between nodes [36].
- *Graph density:* the ratio between the number of edges in the graph and the maximum possible number of edges (that is, for a fully-connected graph).

- *Clustering coefficient:* a measure of the degree to which nodes in a graph tend to cluster together. The cluster coefficient of a graph is computed as the average of the local clustering coefficient of its nodes, which is the ratio between the number of links between a node's neighbors and the maximum possible number of links between them (that is, if they were fully connected).
- *Average betweenness centrality.* Centrality metrics measure the importance of a node within a graph. In particular, betweenness centrality of a node is the ratio of shortest paths in the graph which traverse the node [19].

One of our long-term hypothesis is that these metrics may be used as a basis for mechanism selection in networked problems involving self-interested parties. As a first step in this track, in this paper we have used these metrics to compare the relative performance of the benchmarked approaches.

5   Experimental Results and Discussion

In this section, we describe and discuss the results of our experiments. For each of the aforementioned 300 scenarios, we did 20 repetitions with each of the benchmarked techniques, recording the achieved social welfare (sum of utilities for both providers) and the computation time.

Firstly, we study the performance of the evaluated techniques in the different scenario categories according to the scenario generation parameters (number of APs and number of clients per AP). Table 1 shows the average utility obtained by each approach for all the graphs in each category. We can see that, for the less complex scenarios, all approaches but *random* perform reasonably well, with a non-significant little advantage for the hill climber (*HC*). As the scenarios grow more complex, we can see the performance of the *random* approach turns worse, which is reasonable since the size of the solution space becomes larger. We can also note significant increasing distance between the performances of the hill climber and the annealer (*SA*) negotiators. This confirms our hypothesis that these scenarios are highly nonlinear [18]. We can also see that, for the

Table 1. Utility for different techniques.

(APs,WDs)	Random		HC		SA		ALPSO	
	avg	std	avg	std	avg	std	avg	std
(15, 15)	12.45	1.90	15.88	0.02	15.86	0.04	15.86	0.03
(15, 75)	30.57	5.18	52.53	1.35	53.85	0.50	52.95	0.93
(50, 50)	29.17	4.15	50.40	0.89	51.08	0.52	50.06	0.98
(50, 250)	60.28	9.44	125.24	4.71	134.96	2.34	125.51	3.80
(100, 100)	45.37	5.48	84.90	2.39	88.33	1.52	83.53	2.25
(100, 500)	86.21	11.68	188.13	7.93	208.23	4.33	191.43	6.25

Table 2. Run time (in seconds) for different techniques.

(APs,WDs)	HC		SA		ALPSO	
	avg	std	avg	std	avg	std
(15, 15)	0.53	0.21	0.64	0.22	0.25	0.19
(15, 75)	5.79	1.22	5.96	1.23	5.86	2.00
(50, 50)	5.22	1.16	5.40	1.17	11.91	5.02
(50, 250)	69.39	6.44	69.32	6.36	285.89	74.37
(100, 100)	22.01	2.96	22.15	2.99	108.14	31.39
(100, 500)	330.38	17.23	326.90	16.61	3225.63	817.93

more complex scenarios, the SA negotiator significantly outperforms the particle swarm optimizer ($ALPSO$). This is a remarkable result, specially taking into account that SA reaches the optimum faster than the $ALPSO$ optimizer. Table 2 shows the average computation times for both approaches. We can see that, in the largest scenarios, the SA negotiator is roughly 10 times faster than the complete information optimizer.

To account for the diversity of scenarios within each category, we have analyzed the results of the best performing approach (SA) against the complete-information reference (ALPSO) with respect to the different metrics discussed in Sect. 4.3. Figure 3 shows, for each metric, the ratio between the average utility achieved by SA in the 20 runs for a given graph, and the average utility obtained by ALPSO for the same graph (hence the dashed line in the figures corresponds to the ALPSO 1.0 baseline). We can see there is an approximately linear increasing gain for SA with graph order, with ALPSO doing better for low-order graphs and SA getting to gains up to 10% for the larger graphs (Fig. 3a). This is coherent with the results in Table 1. We can see an inversely proportional trend with the average betweenness centrality (Fig. 3b). The SA negotiator performs better for low centrality values, which seems reasonable because in these graphs there will be more peripheral nodes (i.e. with less interfering nodes) than central nodes (i.e. with more interfering nodes), which should make negotiations easier. The same reasoning explains the results with respect to density (Fig. 3c). The negotiator fares better in the less dense graphs (i.e. where there are less interference links).

There are other interesting patterns arising from the metrics analysis. For instance, Figs. 3d and 3e suggest that there may be optimal values of graph diameter and graph cluster coefficient, respectively, regarding the performance of the SA negotiator. However, further analysis would be needed to rule out other possible explanations. For instance, it is reasonable to expect very little room for improvement of the negotiator in the extremely high clustering coefficient cases (almost complete graph, all nodes interfere with each other).

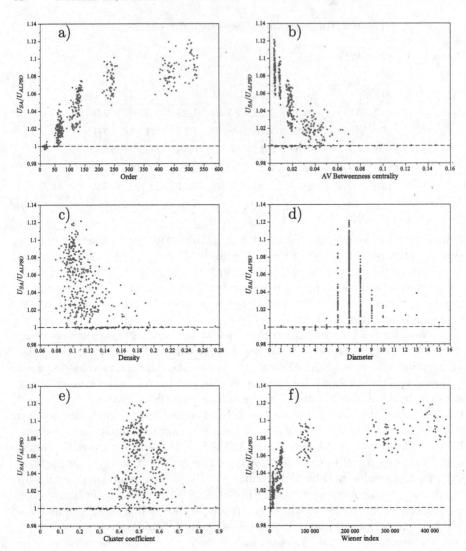

Fig. 3. Utility of SA relative to ALPSO for different graph metrics.

6   Conclusions and Future Work

This paper presents a problem inspired by an extension of the prominent graph coloring problem, enriched towards a real application domain (Wi-Fi channel assignment), which has been extensively studied from the discrete optimization perspective, but has not received attention from the negotiation community. We study a negotiated approach to address this problem, which is, to our knowledge, the first attempt to apply nonlinear negotiation techniques to real complex network scenarios. Experiments show that our approach based on simulated annealing significantly outperforms the optimizer used as a reference in both social welfare and computation time. This is a relevant result, since scalability is the main drawback to apply negotiation approaches to complex systems.

Although our experiments yield satisfactory results, there are still a variety of avenues for further research. As discussed in the previous sections, a range of bilateral and multilateral negotiation protocols and agent decision mechanisms can be studied. A more in-depth metric analysis is needed, specially to determine if the observed correlations among metrics are inherent or caused by a scenario generation bias. Finally, we are interested in fully-distributed negotiations, where the need for mediation can be substituted by a form of distributed social choice.

Acknowledgements. This work has been supported by the Spanish Ministry of Economy and Competitiveness grants TIN2016-80622-P, TIN2014-61627-EXP, MTM2014-54207, and TEC2013-45183-R and by the University of Alcalá through CCG2015/EXP-053.

References

1. Bazzi, A.: On uncoordinated multi user multi RAT combining. In: Vehicular Technology Conference (VTC Fall), pp. 1–6. IEEE, 5–8 September 2011
2. Aardal, K.I., Van Hoesel, S.P., Koster, A.M., Mannino, C., Sassano, A.: Models and solution techniques for frequency assignment problems. Ann. Oper. Res. **153**(1), 79–129 (2007)
3. Abusubaih, M., Gross, J., Wolisz, A.: An inter-access point coordination protocol for dynamic channel selection in IEEE 802.11 wireless LANs. In: 2007 1st IEEE Workshop on Autonomic Communications and Network Management (ACNM 2007) (2007)
4. Bodlaender, H.L., Kloks, T., Tan, R.B., van Leeuwen, J.: λ-coloring of graphs. In: Reichel, H., Tison, S. (eds.) STACS 2000. LNCS, vol. 1770, pp. 395–406. Springer, Heidelberg (2000). doi:10.1007/3-540-46541-3_33
5. Chieochan, S., Hossain, E., Diamond, J.: Channel assignment schemes for infrastructure-based 802.11 WLANs: A survey. IEEE Commun. Surv. Tutorials **12**(1), 124–136 (2010)
6. De Jonge, D., Sierra, C.: NB^3: A multilateral negotiation algorithm for large, non-linear agreement spaces with limited time. Auton. Agent. Multi-Agent Syst. **29**(5), 896–942 (2015)
7. Tragos, E.Z., Zeadally, S., Fragkiadakis, A.G., Siris, V.A.: Spectrum assignment in cognitive radio networks: A comprehensive survey. IEEE Commun. Surv. Tutorials **15**(3), 1108–1135 (2013). Third Quarter
8. Fatima, S.S., Wooldridge, M., Jennings, N.R.: Optimal negotiation strategies for agents with incomplete information. In: Meyer, J.-J.C., Tambe, M. (eds.) ATAL 2001. LNCS (LNAI), vol. 2333, pp. 377–392. Springer, Heidelberg (2002). doi:10.1007/3-540-45448-9_28
9. Fatima, S., Kraus, S., Wooldridge, M.: Principles of Automated Negotiation. Cambridge University Press, Cambridge (2014)
10. Geier, J.: How to: Define Minimum SNR Values for Signal Coverage. http://www.wireless-nets.com/resources/tutorials/define_SNR_values.html

11. Green, D.B., Obaidat, A.S.: An accurate line of sight propagation performance model for ad-hoc 802.11 wireless LAN (WLAN) devices. In: 2002 IEEE International Conference on Communications, ICC 2002, vol. 5, pp. 3424–3428 (2002)

12. Griggs, J.R., et al.: Graph labellings with variable weights, a survey. Discrete Appl. Math. **157**(12), 2646–2658 (2009)

13. Grubshtein, A., Meisels, A.: A distributed cooperative approach for optimizing a family of network games. In: Brazier, F.M.T., Nieuwenhuis, K., Pavlin, G., Warnier, M., Badica, C. (eds.) Proceedings of the 5th International Symposium on Intelligent Distributed Computing-IDC 2011. Intelligent Distributed Computing V, vol. 382, pp. 49–62. Springer, Heidelberg (2012)

14. Hattori, H., Klein, M., Ito, T.: Using iterative narrowing to enable multi-party negotiations with multiple interdependent issues. In: Proceedings of the 6th International Joint Conference on Autonomous Agents and Multiagent Systems, AAMAS 2007, pp. 247:1–247:3. ACM, New York (2007)

15. de la Hoz, E., Gimenez-Guzman, J.M., Marsa-Maestre, I., Orden, D.: Automated negotiation for resource assignment in wireless surveillance sensor networks. Sensors **15**(11), 29547–29568 (2015)

16. Jansen, P., Perez, R.: Constrained structural design optimization via a parallel augmented lagrangian particle swarm optimization approach. Comput. Struct. **89**(13–14), 1352–1366 (2011)

17. Kivelä, M., Arenas, A., Barthelemy, M., Gleeson, J.P., Moreno, Y., Porter, M.A.: Multilayer networks. J. Complex Netw. **2**(3), 203–271 (2014)

18. Klein, M., Faratin, P., Sayama, H., Bar-Yam, Y.: Negotiating complex contracts. Group Decis. Negot. **12**(2), 111–125 (2003)

19. Koschützki, D., Lehmann, K.A., Peeters, L., Richter, S., Tenfelde-Podehl, D., Zlotowski, O.: Centrality indices. In: Brandes, U., Erlebach, T. (eds.) Network Analysis. LNCS, vol. 3418, pp. 16–61. Springer, Heidelberg (2005). doi:10.1007/978-3-540-31955-9_3

20. Lang, F., Fink, A.: Learning from the metaheuristics: Protocols for automated negotiations. Group Decis. Negot. **24**(2), 299–332 (2015)

21. Malaguti, E., Toth, P.: A survey on vertex coloring problems. Int. Trans. Oper. Res. **17**(1), 1–34 (2010)

22. Marsa-Maestre, I., Lopez-Carmona, M.A., Velasco, J.R., Ito, T., Klein, M., Fujita, K.: Balancing utility and deal probability for auction-based negotiations in highly nonlinear utility spaces. In: Proceedings of the 21st International Joint Conference on Artifical Intelligence, pp. 214–219. Morgan Kaufmann Publishers Inc., San Francisco (2009)

23. McDiarmid, C., Reed, B.: Channel assignment and weighted coloring. Networks **36**(2), 114–117 (2000)

24. Mishra, A., Banerjee, S., Arbaugh, W.: Weighted coloring based channel assignment for WLANs. ACM SIGMOBILE Mob. Comput. Commun. Rev. **9**(3), 19–31 (2005)

25. Mishra, A., Brik, V., Banerjee, S., Srinivasan, A., Arbaugh, W.A.: A client-driven approach for channel management in wireless LANs. In: INFOCOM (2006)

26. Myerson, R.B., Satterthwaite, M.A.: Efficient mechanisms for bilateral trading. J. Econ. Theory **29**(2), 265–281 (1983)

27. Narayanan, L.: Channel assignment and graph multicoloring. In: Handbook of Wireless Networks and Mobile Computing, vol. 8, pp. 71–94 (2002)

28. Newman, M.: Networks: An Introduction. Oxford University Press, Oxford (2010)

29. Ng, S.W.K., Szymanski, T.H.: Interference measurements in an 802.11n wireless mesh network testbed. In: 25th IEEE Canadian Conference on Electrical Computer Engineering (CCECE), pp. 1–6, April 2012
30. Pelikan, M., Sastry, K., Goldberg, D.E.: Multiobjective estimation of distribution algorithms. In: Pelikan, M., Pelikan, K., CantúPaz, E. (eds.) Scalable Optimization via Probabilistic Modeling, vol. 33, pp. 223–248. Springer, Heidelberg (2006)
31. Ren, F., Zhang, M., Sim, K.M.: Adaptive conceding strategies for automated trading agents in dynamic, open markets. Wirel. Healthc. **46**(3), 704–716 (2009)
32. Rubinstein, A.: Perfect equilibrium in a bargaining model. Econometrica **50**(1), 97–109 (1982)
33. Sharp, A.: Distance coloring. In: Arge, L., Hoffmann, M., Welzl, E. (eds.) ESA 2007. LNCS, vol. 4698, pp. 510–521. Springer, Heidelberg (2007). doi:10.1007/978-3-540-75520-3_46
34. Sim, K.M., Shi, B.: Concurrent negotiation and coordination for grid resource coallocation. Trans. Syst. Man Cber. Part B **40**(3), 753–766 (2010)
35. Tuza, Z., Gutin, G., Plurnmer, M., Tucker, A., Burke, E., Werra, D., Kingston, J.: Colorings and related topics. In: Handbook of Graph Theory. Discrete Mathematics and its Applications, pp. 340–483. CRC Press, December 2003
36. Wiener, H.: Structural determination of paraffin boiling points. J. Am. Chem. Soc. **69**(1), 17–20 (1947)

Incremental Computation of Grounded Semantics for Dynamic Abstract Argumentation Frameworks

Sergio Greco and Francesco Parisi[✉]

Department of Informatics Modeling, Electronics and System Engineering,
University of Calabria, Rende, Italy
{greco,fparisi}@dimes.unical.it

Abstract. Abstract argumentation has emerged as a central field in Artificial Intelligence. Although the underlying idea is very simple and intuitive, most of the semantics proposed so far suffer from a high computational complexity. For this reason, in recent years, an increasing amount of work has been done to define efficient algorithms. However, so far, the research has concentrated on the definition of algorithms for static frameworks, whereas argumentation frameworks (AFs) are highly dynamic in practice. Surprisingly, the definition of evaluation algorithms taking into account such dynamic aspects has been mostly neglected. In this paper, we address the problem of efficiently recomputing the extensions of AFs which are updated by adding/deleting arguments or attacks. In particular, after identifying some properties that hold for updates of AFs under several well-known semantics, we focus on the most popular unique-status semantics (namely, the *grounded* semantics) and present an algorithm for its incremental computation, well-suited to dynamic applications where updates to an initial AF are frequently performed to take into account new available knowledge.

1 Introduction

Abstract argumentation has emerged as a central field in Artificial Intelligence [3,10,26,42,44,45]. Although the underlying idea is very simple and intuitive, most of the semantics proposed so far suffer from a high computational complexity [22–25,28–32]. Complexity bounds and evaluation algorithms for argumentation frameworks (AFs) have been deeply studied in the literature, but this research focused on 'static' frameworks, whereas, in practice, AFs are not static systems [4,5,19,27,39]. Typically an AF represents a temporary situation as new arguments and attacks continuously can be added/removed to take into account new available knowledge. This may change significantly the conclusions that can be derived. For instance, when a new attack is added to an AF, existing attacks may cease to apply and new attacks become applicable.

Surprisingly, the definition of evaluation algorithms and the analysis of the computational complexity taking into account such dynamic aspects have been mostly neglected, whereas in these situations incremental computation techniques can greatly improve performance. Sometimes changes to the AF can

© Springer International Publishing AG 2017
R. Aydoğan et al. (Eds.): COREDEMA 2016, LNAI 10238, pp. 66–81, 2017.
DOI: 10.1007/978-3-319-57285-7_5

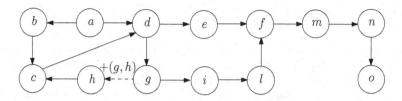

Fig. 1. AFs $\mathcal{A}_0$ and $\mathcal{A} = +(g, h)(\mathcal{A}_0)$

make small changes to the set of conclusions, and recomputing the whole semantics from scratch can be avoided. For instance, consider the situation shown in Fig. 1: the initial AF $\mathcal{A}_0$, where h is not attacked by any other argument, is updated to AF $\mathcal{A}$ by adding attack (g, h). According to the most popular argumentation semantics, i.e. *grounded, complete, ideal, preferred, stable,* and *semi-stable* [15,20,21], the initial AF $\mathcal{A}_0$ admits the extension $E_0 = \{a, h, g, e, l, m, o\}$, whereas the extension for the updated framework $\mathcal{A}$ becomes $E = \{a, c, g, e, l, m, o\}$. As it will be shown later, for the grounded semantics the extension E can be efficiently computed incrementally by looking only at a small part of the AF, which is "influenced by" the update operation. This part is just $\{h, c\}$ in our example, and we will show that the membership of the other arguments to E does not depend on the update operation, and thus we do not need to compute them again after performing update $+(g, h)$.

Contributions. The main contributions are as follows:

- We introduce the concept of *influenced set* consisting of the arguments whose status could change after an update. The influenced set refines the previously proposed set of *affected arguments* [4,39] and makes the computation more efficient.
- We present an incremental algorithm for recomputing the grounded extension. It is very efficient as it (iteratively) computes the status of influenced arguments only and when it finds that the status of arguments derived at some step cannot be changed by subsequent steps then it stops.
- We present experimental results showing the effectiveness of our approach.

Plan of the paper. We start by discussing related works in Sect. 2, and reviewing Dung's abstract argumentation framework in Sect. 3, where updates are introduced. Next, we identify some sufficient conditions on the updates that guarantee that the semantics of an AF does not change, and introduce the concept of influenced set in Sect. 4. Then we provide our algorithm for incrementally computing the grounded semantics in Sect. 5. In Sect. 6 we present experimental results on two datasets showing that our incremental approach outperforms the computation from scratch of the grounded semantics. Finally, we draw conclusions and discuss future work in Sect. 7, where we also discuss how the results presented in the paper carry over to the case of sets of updates to be performed simultaneously.

2 Related Work

There have been several efforts coping with dynamics aspects of abstract argumentation. In [12,13] the principles according to which the extension does not change when the set of arguments/attacks are changed have been studied. However, this work does not consider how the extensions of an AF evolve when new arguments are added or some of the old ones are removed. [17,18] addressed the problem of revising the set of extensions of an AF, and studied how the extensions can evolve when a new argument is considered. However, they focus on adding only one argument interacting with one initial argument (i.e. an argument which is not attacked by any other argument). The work in [17,18] has been extended in [11], where the evolution of the set of extensions after performing a change operation (addition/removal of arguments/interaction) is studied. Dynamic argumentation has been applied to decision-making of an autonomous agent in [1], where it is studied how the acceptability of arguments evolves when a new argument is added to the decision system. However, they do not compute the whole extensions and also focused on the case where only one argument is added to the system.

The division-based method, proposed in [39] and refined in [4], divides the updated framework into two parts: *affected* and *unaffected*, where only the status of affected arguments is recomputed after updates. However, the set of affected arguments consists of those that are reachable from the updated arguments, which is often larger than the set that actually needs to be considered when recomputing the extension. For the AF of Fig. 1, all the arguments in the chains originated by h turn out to be 'affected'. But we only need to recompute the status of h and c after the update. Recently, [48] introduced a matrix representation of AFs and proposed a matrix reduction that, when applied to dynamic AFs, resembles the division-based method in [39]. In [5,9] an approach exploiting the concept of splitting of logic programs [40] was adopted to deal with dynamic argumentation. However, the technique considers weak expansions of the initial AF, where added arguments never attack previous ones. Recently, [16] studied the relationship between argumentation and logic programming [14,35,36].

[8] investigated whether and how it is possible to modify a given AF in such a way that a desired set of arguments becomes an extension, whereas [43] studied equivalence between two AFs when further information (another AF) is added to both simultaneously. [6] focused on specific expansions where new arguments and attacks may be added but the attacks among the old arguments remain unchanged, while [7] characterized update and deletion equivalence, where adding as well as deleting arguments and attacks is allowed (deletions were not considered in [6,43]).

To the best of our knowledge, this is the first paper that exploits the initial extension E_0 of an AF $\mathcal{A}_0$ not only for computing the set $\mathcal{I}(u, \mathcal{A}_0, E_0)$ of arguments influenced by an update u but also for recomputing the status of the arguments in $\mathcal{I}(u, \mathcal{A}_0, E_0)$ by applying early termination conditions. A short version of this paper appeared in [37].

3   Preliminaries

We assume the existence of a set Arg whose elements are called *arguments*. An *(abstract) argumentation framework* [20] *(AF)* is a pair $\langle A, \Sigma \rangle$, where $A \subseteq Arg$ is a finite set whose elements are referred to as *arguments*, and $\Sigma \subseteq A \times A$ is a binary relation over A whose elements are referred to as *attacks*. Essentially, an AF is a directed graph in which the arguments are represented by the nodes and the attack relation is represented by the set of directed edges. An argument is an abstract entity whose role is entirely determined by its relationships with other arguments.

Given arguments $a, b \in A$, we say that a *attacks* b iff $(a, b) \in \Sigma$. An argument a *attacks* a set $S \subseteq A$ iff $\exists b \in S$ such that a *attacks* b.

We use $S^+ = \{b \mid \exists a \in S : (a, b) \in \Sigma\}$ and $S^- = \{b \mid \exists a \in S : (b, a) \in \Sigma\}$ to denote the sets of all arguments that are attacked by S and attack S, respectively.

A set $S \subseteq A$ *defends* a iff $\forall b \in A$ such that b *attacks* a, there is $c \in S$ such that c *attacks* b.

A set $S \subseteq A$ of arguments, is said to be

(i) *conflict-free*, if there are no $a, b \in S$ such that a *attacks* b;
(ii) *admissible*, if it is conflict-free and it defends all its arguments.

An argumentation semantics specifies the criteria for identifying a set of arguments considered to be "reasonable" together, called *extension*. A *complete extension* (co) is an admissible set that contains all the arguments that it defends. A complete extension S is said to be:

- *preferred (pr)* iff it is maximal (w.r.t. $\subseteq$);
- *semi-stable (ss)* iff $S \cup S^+$ is maximal (w.r.t. $\subseteq$);
- *stable (st)* iff it attacks each argument in $A \setminus S$;
- *grounded (gr)* iff it is minimal (w.r.t. $\subseteq$);
- *ideal (id)* iff it is contained in every preferred extension and it is maximal (w.r.t. $\subseteq$).

Given an AF $\mathcal{A}$ and a semantics $\mathcal{S} \in \{\text{co}, \text{pr}, \text{ss}, \text{st}, \text{gr}, \text{id}\}$, we use $\mathcal{E}_\mathcal{S}(\mathcal{A})$ to denote the set of $\mathcal{S}$-extensions of $\mathcal{A}$.

All the above-mentioned semantics except the stable admit at least one extension, and the grounded and ideal admit exactly one extension [15,20,21]. That is, for $\mathcal{S} \in \{\text{co}, \text{pr}, \text{ss}, \text{gr}, \text{id}\}$ it is the case that $\mathcal{E}_\mathcal{S}(\mathcal{A}) \neq \emptyset$, while $\mathcal{E}_{\text{st}}(\mathcal{A})$ may be empty. Semantics gr and id are called *unique status* semantics as $|\mathcal{E}_{\text{gr}}(\mathcal{A})| = |\mathcal{E}_{\text{id}}(\mathcal{A})| = 1$, whereas the others are called *multiple status* semantics. It is well-known that, for any AF $\mathcal{A}$, $\mathcal{E}_{\text{gr}}(\mathcal{A}) \subseteq \mathcal{E}_{\text{co}}(\mathcal{A})$ and $\mathcal{E}_{\text{id}}(\mathcal{A}) \subseteq \mathcal{E}_{\text{co}}(\mathcal{A})$, and $\mathcal{E}_{\text{st}}(\mathcal{A}) \subseteq \mathcal{E}_{\text{ss}}(\mathcal{A}) \subseteq \mathcal{E}_{\text{pr}}(\mathcal{A}) \subseteq \mathcal{E}_{\text{co}}(\mathcal{A})$.

Example 1. Consider the AF $\mathcal{A}_0$ shown in Fig. 2. Then, the set of admissible sets is $\{ \emptyset, \{a\}, \{d\}, \{a, d\}, \{b, d\} \}$, and $\mathcal{E}_\mathcal{S}(\mathcal{A}_0)$ with $\mathcal{S} \in \{\text{co}, \text{pr}, \text{ss}, \text{st}, \text{gr}, \text{id}\}$ is as reported in the second column of Fig. 3.   □

S	$\mathcal{E}_S(\mathcal{A}_0)$	$\mathcal{E}_S(\mathcal{A}_1)$	$\mathcal{E}_S(\mathcal{A}_2)$
co	$\{\{d\},\{a,d\},\{b,d\}\}$	$\{\emptyset,\{a,d\}\}$	$\{\emptyset,\{a,d\},\{b,c\}\}$
pr	$\{\{a,d\},\{b,d\}\}$	$\{\{a,d\}\}$	$\{\{a,d\},\{b,c\}\}$
ss	$\{\{a,d\},\{b,d\}\}$	$\{\{a,d\}\}$	$\{\{a,d\},\{b,c\}\}$
st	$\{\{a,d\},\{b,d\}\}$	$\{\{a,d\}\}$	$\{\{a,d\},\{b,c\}\}$
gr	$\{\{d\}\}$	$\{\emptyset\}$	$\{\emptyset\}$
id	$\{\{d\}\}$	$\{\{a,d\}\}$	$\{\emptyset\}$

Fig. 2. AF $\mathcal{A}_0$ Example 1.   **Fig. 3.** Sets of extensions for the AF of Example 1, and changes in the sets after performing updates $+(b,d)$ and $-(c,b)$.

The argumentation semantics can be also defined in terms of *labelling*. A labelling for an AF $\mathcal{A} = \langle A, \Sigma \rangle$ is a total function $L : A \rightarrow \{\text{IN}, \text{OUT}, \text{UN}\}$ assigning to each argument a label. $L(a) = \text{IN}$ means that argument a is accepted, $L(a) = \text{OUT}$ means that a is rejected, while $L(a) = \text{UN}$ means that a is undecided.

Let $in(L) = \{a \mid a \in A \wedge L(a) = \text{IN}\}$, $out(L) = \{a \mid a \in A \wedge L(a) = \text{OUT}\}$, and $un(L) = \{a \mid a \in A \wedge L(a) = \text{UN}\}$. In the following, we also use the triple $\langle in(L), out(L), un(L) \rangle$ to represent L.

A labelling L is said to be *admissible (or legal)* if $\forall a \in in(L) \cup out(L)$ (i) if $L(a) = \text{OUT}$ then $\exists b \in A$ such that $(b,a) \in \Sigma$ and $L(b) = \text{IN}$; and (ii) if $L(a) = \text{IN}$ then $L(b) = \text{OUT}$ for all $b \in A$ such that $(b,a) \in \Sigma$. L is a complete labelling iff conditions (i) and (ii) hold for all $a \in A$.

Between complete extensions and complete labellings there is a bijective mapping defined as follows: for each extension E there is a unique labelling $L = \langle E, E^+, A \setminus (E \cup E^+) \rangle$ and for each labelling L there is a unique extension $in(L)$. We say that L is the labelling *corresponding* to E.

In the following, we say that the *status of an argument* a w.r.t. a labelling L (or its corresponding extension $in(L)$) is IN (resp., OUT, UN) iff $L(a) = \text{IN}$ (resp., $L(a) = \text{OUT}$, $L(a) = \text{UN}$). We will avoid to mention explicitly the labelling (or the extension) whenever it is understood.

Updates. An *update* u for an AF $\mathcal{A}_0$ consists in modifying $\mathcal{A}_0$ into an AF $\mathcal{A}$ by adding or removing arguments or attacks.

In the following, we focus on updates consisting of adding/deleting one attack between arguments belonging to $\mathcal{A}_0$. As we discuss in Sect. 7, focusing on single attack updates is not a limitation as *multiple (attack) updates* to be performed simultaneously can be simulated by means of a single attack update.

Concerning the addition (resp. deletion) of a set of isolated arguments, it is easy to see that if $\mathcal{A}$ is obtained from $\mathcal{A}_0$ through the addition (resp. deletion) of a set S of isolated arguments, then, let E_0 be an extension for $\mathcal{A}_0$, $E = E_0 \cup S$ (resp. $E = E_0 \setminus S$) is an extension for $\mathcal{A}$ that can be trivially computed. Of course, if arguments in S are not isolated, we can first delete all attacks involving arguments in S; adding an attack between an argument in $\mathcal{A}_0$ and a new argument can be simulated as well.

We use $+(a,b)$ (resp. $-(a,b)$) to denote the addition (resp. deletion) of an attack (a,b), and $u(\mathcal{A}_0)$ to denote the application of update $u = \pm(a,b)$ to $\mathcal{A}_0$.

Updating an AF implies that its semantics (sets of extensions or labellings) changes, as shown in the following example.

Example 2. Consider the AF $\mathcal{A}_0$ of Example 1. For each semantics S, the set $\mathcal{E}_S(\mathcal{A}_1)$ of extensions for $\mathcal{A}_1 = +(b,d)(\mathcal{A}_0)$ is reported in the third column of Fig. 3. If update $-(c,b)$ is performed on $\mathcal{A}_1$, then $\mathcal{E}_S(\mathcal{A}_2)$ with $\mathcal{A}_2 = -(c,b)(\mathcal{A}_1)$ is as shown on the last column of Fig. 3. □

4 Influenced Arguments

In this section, we first identify conditions ensuring that a given S-extension continues to be an S-extension after an update, and then introduce the *influenced set* that will be used to limit the set of arguments that needs to be recomputed after an update. In addition, arguments not in the influenced set can be used to derive extensions for the updated AF.

The following two propositions introduce sufficient conditions guaranteeing that a given S-extension is still an S-extension after performing an update.

Proposition 1. *Let $\mathcal{A}_0$ be an AF, $u = +(a,b)$ an update, S a semantics, $E_0 \in \mathcal{E}_S(\mathcal{A}_0)$ an extension of $\mathcal{A}_0$ under semantics S, and L_0 the labelling corresponding to E_0. Then $E_0 \in \mathcal{E}_S(u(\mathcal{A}_0))$ if*

- $S \in \{co, st, gr\}$ *and one of the following conditions holds:*
  - $L_0(a) \neq$ IN *and* $L_0(b) \neq$ IN,
  - $L_0(a) =$ IN *and* $L_0(b) =$ OUT;
- $S \in \{pr, ss, id\}$ *and* $L_0(b) =$ OUT.

Proposition 2. *Let $\mathcal{A}_0$ be an AF, $u = -(a,b)$, $S \in \{co, pr, ss, st, gr\}$, and $E_0 \in \mathcal{E}_S(\mathcal{A}_0)$ an extension of $\mathcal{A}_0$ under S. Then $E_0 \in \mathcal{E}_S(u(\mathcal{A}_0))$ if one of the following conditions holds:*

(1) $L_0(a) =$ OUT;
(2) $L_0(a) =$ UN *and* $L_0(b) =$ OUT.

Example 3. Consider the AFs $\mathcal{A}_1 = +(b,d)(\mathcal{A}_0)$ and $\mathcal{A}_2 = -(c,b)(\mathcal{A}_1)$, where $\mathcal{A}_0$ is the AF of Example 2. For $S \in \{co, pr, ss, st\}$, extension $\{a,d\}$ of $\mathcal{A}_1$ is still an extension of $\mathcal{A}_2$ as $L_0(c) =$ OUT (see Fig. 3). The grounded extension $\emptyset$ of $\mathcal{A}_1$ is still a grounded extension of $\mathcal{A}_2$, whereas the ideal extension $\{a,d\}$ of $\mathcal{A}_1$ is not the ideal extension of $\mathcal{A}_2$. □

Given an AF $\mathcal{A} = \langle A, \Sigma \rangle$ and an argument $b \in A$, we denote as $Reach_\mathcal{A}(b)$ the set of arguments that are reachable from b in $\mathcal{A}$. We now introduce the *influenced set*.

Definition 1 (Influenced set). Let $\mathcal{A} = \langle A, \Sigma \rangle$ be an AF, $u = \pm(a,b)$ an update, E an extension of $\mathcal{A}$ under a given semantics $\mathcal{S}$, and let

$$
\mathcal{I}_0(u, \mathcal{A}, E) = \begin{cases} \emptyset & \text{if } E \in \mathcal{E}_{\mathcal{S}}(u(\mathcal{A})) \text{ [i.e., the conditions of Prop. 1/2 hold] } or \\ & \exists (z,b) \in \Sigma \text{ s.t. } z \in E \wedge z \notin Reach_{\mathcal{A}}(b); \\[2mm] \{b\} & otherwise; \end{cases}
$$

- $\mathcal{I}_{i+1}(u, \mathcal{A}, E) = \mathcal{I}_i(u, \mathcal{A}, E) \cup \{y \mid \exists (x,y) \in \Sigma \text{ s.t. } x \in \mathcal{I}_i(u, \mathcal{A}, E) \wedge \not\exists (z,y) \in \Sigma \text{ s.t. } z \in E \wedge z \notin Reach_{\mathcal{A}}(b)\}$.

The *influenced set* of update u w.r.t. AF $\mathcal{A}$ and the extension E is $\mathcal{I}(u, \mathcal{A}, E) = \mathcal{I}_n(u, \mathcal{A}, E)$ such that $\mathcal{I}_n(u, \mathcal{A}, E) = \mathcal{I}_{n+1}(u, \mathcal{A}, E)$. ☐

Thus, the set of arguments that are influenced by an update of the status of b are those that can be reached from b without using any intermediate argument y whose status is known to be OUT because it is determined by an argument $z \in E$ which is not reachable from (and thus not influenced by) b.

Example 4. For the AF $\mathcal{A}_0 = \langle A_0, \Sigma_0 \rangle$ of Fig. 1, whose grounded extension is $E_0 = \{a, h, g, e, l, m, o\}$, we have that $Reach_{\mathcal{A}_0}(h) = A_0 \setminus \{a, b\}$, and the influenced set of $u = +(g, h)$ is $\mathcal{I}(u, \mathcal{A}_0, E_0) = \{h, c\}$. Note that $d \notin \mathcal{I}(u, \mathcal{A}_0, E_0)$ since it is attacked by $a \in E_0$. Thus the arguments that can be reached only using d cannot belong to $\mathcal{I}(u, \mathcal{A}_0, E_0)$ either.

For $\mathcal{A} = u(\mathcal{A}_0)$, whose the grounded extension is $E = \{a, c, g, e, l, m, o\}$, we have that $S = \mathcal{I}(u, \mathcal{A}, E)$ is still $\{h, c\}$. Therefore, only the status of arguments in S could change and their status can be determined by considering a restricted AF containing only arguments in $S \cup S^-$. ☐

Proposition 3. *Given an AF $\mathcal{A} = \langle A, \Sigma \rangle$, an update $u = \pm(a, b)$, and an extension E, the complexity of computing the influenced set of u w.r.t. $\mathcal{A}$ and E is $O(|\Sigma|)$.*

All the arguments not belonging to the influenced set of an update will still belong to an extension of the updated AF.

Theorem 1. *Let $\mathcal{A}_0$ be an AF, and $\mathcal{A} = u(\mathcal{A}_0)$ be the AF resulting from performing update $u = \pm(a, b)$ on $\mathcal{A}_0$. Let $E_0 \in \mathcal{E}_{\mathcal{S}}(\mathcal{A}_0)$ be an extension for $\mathcal{A}_0$ under any semantics $\mathcal{S} \in \{co, pr, ss, st, gr, id\}$. Let $\overline{\mathcal{I}} = Arg \setminus \mathcal{I}(u, \mathcal{A}_0, E_0)$ be the set of the arguments that are not influenced by u in $\mathcal{A}_0$ w.r.t. E_0. Then, either $\mathcal{E}_{\mathcal{S}}(\mathcal{A}) = \emptyset$ or there is an extension $E \in \mathcal{E}_{\mathcal{S}}(\mathcal{A})$ for $\mathcal{A}$ such that $(E \cap \overline{\mathcal{I}}) = (E_0 \cap \overline{\mathcal{I}})$.*

Observe that the set of extensions may be empty only for the stable semantics. For all of the other semantics, the theorem suggests the following strategy for computing an extension of the updated AF: derive it by first projecting out the set of arguments not influenced by the update and then extend the so-obtained set by using the information provided by it.

We conclude this section by introducing a refinement of Proposition 1 that makes use of the influenced set. This result will be used in the next section to restrict the input AF.

Proposition 4. *Let $\mathcal{A}_0$ be an AF, $u = +(a,b)$, $S \in \{co, pr, ss, st, gr\}$, and $E_0 \in \mathcal{E}_S(\mathcal{A}_0)$ an extension of $\mathcal{A}_0$ under S. Then $E_0 \in \mathcal{E}_S(u(\mathcal{A}_0))$ if*

- *one of the conditions of Proposition 1 holds or*
- *the next three conditions hold:*
  - *(1) $L_0(a) = $ OUT,*
  - *(2) $L_0(b) = $ IN, and*
  - *(3) either (i) $S \in \{co, st, ss, pr\}$ or (ii) $a \notin \mathcal{I}(u, \mathcal{A}_0, E_0)$ and $S = gr$.*

Example 5. Consider AFs $\mathcal{A}_0$ and $\mathcal{A}_1 = +(b,d)(\mathcal{A}_0)$ of Examples 1 and 3. For $S \in \{co, pr, ss, st\}$, extension $E_0 = \{a,d\}$ for $\mathcal{A}_0$ is still an extension of the AF $\mathcal{A}_1$ as $L_0(b) = $ OUT and $L_0(d) = $ IN (see Fig. 3). However, the grounded extension $E_0' = \{d\}$ for $\mathcal{A}_0$ is not guarantee to be a grounded extension for $\mathcal{A}_1$ as neither Proposition 1 nor conditions 1) and 3.*ii*) of Proposition 4 hold (b is UN and $b \in \mathcal{I}(+(b,d), \mathcal{A}_0, E_0')$). □

5 Recomputing the Grounded Semantics

Given an AF $\mathcal{A}_0$, the grounded extension E_0 for $\mathcal{A}_0$, an update u for $\mathcal{A}_0$ yielding $\mathcal{A} = u(\mathcal{A}_0)$, we address the problem of efficiently computing the grounded extension E of the updated AF $\mathcal{A}$ starting from E_0.

For any AF $\mathcal{A} = \langle A, \Sigma \rangle$ and set $S \subseteq A$ of arguments, we denote with $\Pi(S, \mathcal{A}) = \langle S, \Sigma \cap S \times S \rangle$ the subgraph of $\mathcal{A}$ induced by the nodes in S. Moreover, given two AFs $\mathcal{A}_1 = \langle A_1, \Sigma_1 \rangle$ and $\mathcal{A}_2 = \langle A_2, \Sigma_2 \rangle$, we denote as $\mathcal{A}_1 \sqcup \mathcal{A}_2 = \langle A_1 \cup A_1, \Sigma_1 \cup \Sigma_2 \rangle$ the union of the two AFs.

Our algorithm first identifies the restricted subgraph of the given AF containing the arguments influenced by the update.

Definition 2. (Restricted AF for grounded semantics). Given an AF $\mathcal{A} = \langle A, \Sigma \rangle$, a grounded extension E for $\mathcal{A}$, and an update $u = \pm(a,b)$, the restricted AF of $\mathcal{A}$ w.r.t. E and u (denoted as $\mathcal{R}_{gr}(u, \mathcal{A}, E)$) is as follows.

- $\mathcal{R}_{gr}(u, \mathcal{A}, E)$ is empty if $\mathcal{I}(u, \mathcal{A}, E)$ is empty or one of the conditions of Proposition 4 holds.
- $\mathcal{R}_{gr}(u, \mathcal{A}, E) = \Pi(\mathcal{I}(u, \mathcal{A}, E), u(\mathcal{A})) \sqcup T_1 \sqcup T_2$ where:
  - T_1 is the union of the AFs $\langle \{a,b\}, \{(a,b)\} \rangle$ s.t. (a,b) is an attack of $u(\mathcal{A})$ and $a \notin \mathcal{I}(u, \mathcal{A}, E)$, $a \in E$, and $b \in \mathcal{I}(u, \mathcal{A}, E)$;
  - $T_2 = \langle \{c \,|\, Check(c)\}, \{(c,c) \,|\, Check(c)\} \rangle$, where $Check(c)$ is true if $\exists (e,c) \in \Sigma$ such that $c \in \mathcal{I}(u, \mathcal{A}, E)$ and $e \notin \mathcal{I}(u, \mathcal{A}, E)$ and $e \notin E \cup E^+$. □

Hence, AF $\mathcal{R}_{gr}(u, \mathcal{A}, E)$ contains, in addition to the subgraph of $u(\mathcal{A})$ induced by $\mathcal{I}(u, \mathcal{A}, E)$, additional nodes and edges containing needed information on the "external context", i.e. information about the status of arguments which are attacking some argument in $\mathcal{I}(u, \mathcal{A}, E)$. Specifically, if there is in $u(\mathcal{A})$ an edge from node $a \notin \mathcal{I}(u, \mathcal{A}, E)$ whose status is IN to node $b \in \mathcal{I}(u, \mathcal{A}, E)$, then we add the edge (a,b) so that, as a does not have incoming edges in $\mathcal{R}_{gr}(u, \mathcal{A}, E)$, its status is confirmed to be IN. Moreover, if there is in $u(\mathcal{A})$ an edge from a node

$e \notin \mathcal{I}(u, \mathcal{A}, E)$ to a node $c \in \mathcal{I}(u, \mathcal{A}, E)$ such that e is UN, we add edge (c, c) to $\mathcal{R}_{gr}(u, \mathcal{A}, E)$ so that the status of c cannot be IN. Using fake arguments/attacks to represent external contexts has been exploited in a similar way in [2], where decomposability properties of argumentation semantics are studied.

Example 6. Continuing Example 4, $\mathcal{R}_{gr}(+(g, h), \mathcal{A}_0, E_0)$ consists of the subgraph induced by $\mathcal{I}(u, \mathcal{A}_0, E_0) = \{h, c\}$ as well as the edge (g, h) which is an attack towards argument $h \in \mathcal{I}(u, \mathcal{A}_0, E_0)$ coming from argument g outside $\mathcal{I}(u, \mathcal{A}_0, E_0)$ labelled as IN. Hence, $\mathcal{R}_{gr}(+(g, h), \mathcal{A}_0, E_0) = \langle A_d, \Sigma_d \rangle$ with $A_d = \{g, h, c\}$ and $\Sigma_d = \{(g, h), (h, c)\}$. □

Example 7. Consider the AF $\mathcal{A}_0 = \langle \{a, b, c, d, e, f, g\}, \{(a, b), (b, a), (c, d), (d, c), (a, c), (b, c), (f, c), (g, f)\}\rangle$ and the update $u = +(e, d)$. We have that

(i) the grounded extension of $\mathcal{A}_0$ is $E_0 = \{g, e\}$ (i.e. arguments a, b, c, d are all labeled as UN);

(ii) the influenced set is $\mathcal{I}(u, \mathcal{A}_0, E_0) = \{c, d\}$; and

(iii) the restricted AF is $\mathcal{R}_{gr}(u, \mathcal{A}_0, E_0) = \langle \{c, d\}, \{(c, d), (d, c)\}\rangle \sqcup T_1 \sqcup T_2$ where $T_1 = \langle \{e, d\}, \{(e, d)\}\rangle$ and $T_2 = \langle \{c\}, \{(c, c)\}\rangle$.

That is, $\mathcal{R}_{gr}(u, \mathcal{A}_0, E_0) = \langle \{c, d, e\}, \{(c, d), (d, c), (e, d), (c, c)\}\rangle$. □

Algorithm 1 first checks if the restricted AF (computed w.r.t. update $u = \pm(a, b)$) is empty (Line 3). If this is the case, then $E = E_0$. Otherwise, the status of arguments in $S = \mathcal{I}(u, \mathcal{A}_0, E_0)$ needs to be recomputed and the extension E of $u(\mathcal{A}_0)$ is constructed at Line 6 by combining the arguments in E_0 not belonging to the influenced part and the arguments returned by Function *IFP* (incremental fixpoint), which is invoked with AF $\mathcal{A}_d = \langle A_d, \Sigma_d \rangle$ (the restricted graph of $\mathcal{A}$) and starting extension $E_0 \cap A_d$ (the restriction of E_0 to A_d).

Function *IFP* first computes the set of nodes which are labelled IN and an initial set of nodes which are labelled OUT. If no argument can be labelled IN, it returns the empty set. Otherwise, it iteratively applies function G that takes as input the set of arguments S_{OUT} which have been labeled OUT so far and the subset $\Delta_{OUT} \subseteq S_{OUT}$ of arguments which have been labelled OUT in the last step, and returns the arguments $b \in \Delta_{OUT}^+$ such that for every attack $(a, b) \in$

Algorithm 1. Incr-Grounded-Sem($\mathcal{A}_0, u, E_0$)

Input: AF $\mathcal{A}_0 = \langle A_0, \Sigma_0 \rangle$, $u = \pm(a, b)$, grounded extension E_0;
Output: Revised grounded extension E
1: Let $S = \mathcal{I}(u, \mathcal{A}_0, E_0)$;
2: Let $\mathcal{A}_d = \langle A_d, \Sigma_d \rangle = \mathcal{R}_{gr}(u, \mathcal{A}_0, E_0)$;
3: **if** $(A_d = \emptyset)$ **then**
4:     $E = E_0$;
5: **else**
6:     $E = (E_0 \setminus S) \cup IFP(\mathcal{A}_d, E_0 \cap A_d)$;

Function 1. $IFP(\mathcal{A}, E_0)$

Input: AF $\mathcal{A} = \langle A, \Sigma \rangle$, Extension E_0;
Output: Extension E
1: $S_{\text{IN}} = \Delta_{\text{IN}} = \{\, a \mid \not\exists(c, a) \in \Sigma \,\}$;
2: **if** $(S_{\text{IN}} = \emptyset)$ **then**
3:      **return** S_{IN}
4: $S_{\text{OUT}} = \Delta_{\text{OUT}} = \Delta_{\text{IN}}^{+}$;
5: **repeat**
6:      $\Delta_{\text{IN}} = G(S_{\text{OUT}}, \Delta_{\text{OUT}}) \setminus S_{\text{IN}}$;
7:      $\Delta_{\text{OUT}} = \Delta_{\text{IN}}^{+} \setminus S_{\text{OUT}}$;
8:      $S_{\text{IN}} = S_{\text{IN}} \cup \Delta_{\text{IN}}$;
9:      $S_{\text{OUT}} = S_{\text{OUT}} \cup \Delta_{\text{OUT}}$;
10: **until** $\Delta_{\text{IN}} \subseteq E_0$
11: **if** $(\Delta_{\text{IN}} = \emptyset)$ **then**
12:      **return** S_{IN};
13: **else**
14:      **return** $S_{\text{IN}} \cup (E_0 \setminus (S_{\text{IN}} \cup S_{\text{OUT}}))$;

Σ, argument $a \in S_{\text{OUT}}$ (i.e. a is labelled OUT).[1] Function G returns the set Δ_{IN} of arguments which are labeled IN at Line 6. Arguments labeled OUT are immediately derived by taking Δ_{IN}^{+}, that is the arguments which are attacked by some argument which has been labelled as IN (Line 7). Function G is iteratively applied until, in the last step of the **repeat** loop, all arguments derived are confirmed to be in the extension E_0 of the AF $\mathcal{A}_0$ being updated (i.e., $\Delta_{\text{IN}} \subseteq E_0$). Finally, if Δ_{IN} is empty, then it just returns the set of arguments labeled as IN (in this case, the status of all the arguments in the restricted AF has been recomputed by function G), otherwise it returns S_{IN} union the arguments in E_0 whose status has not been recomputed by function G.

Example 8. Consider the AF $\mathcal{A}_0$ of Fig. 1 where $E_0 = \{a, h, g, e, l, m, o\}$ and $\mathcal{I}(u, \mathcal{A}_0, E_0) = \{h, c\}$. Algorithm 1 computes the grounded extension E of the AF $\mathcal{A} = +(g, h)(\mathcal{A}_0)$ as follows. The restricted AF $\mathcal{A}_d = \langle A_d, \Sigma_d \rangle = \mathcal{R}_{\text{gr}}(u, \mathcal{A}_0, E_0)$ is computed (at Line 2) obtaining $A_d = \{g, h, c\}$ and $\Sigma_d = \{(g, h), (h, c)\}$. As A_d is not empty, Function IFP with actual parameters $\mathcal{A}_d$ and $E_0 \cap A_d = \{g, h\}$ is called at Line 6. Function IFP first computes $S_{\text{IN}} = \Delta_{\text{IN}} = \{g\}$ and $S_{\text{OUT}} = \Delta_{\text{OUT}} = \{h\}$. Next, at the first iteration of the **repeat** loop, it is computed $\Delta_{\text{IN}} = G(\{h\}, \{h\}) = \{c\}$ (Line 6) and $\Delta_{\text{OUT}} = \emptyset$ (Line 7) as there is no argument attacked by c in $\mathcal{A}_d$. Then the function terminates returning the set $\{g, c\}$ and E turns out to be the set $\{a, g, e, l, m, o\} \cup \{g, c\}$.   □

Theorem 2. *For any AF $\mathcal{A} = \langle A, \Sigma \rangle$, the complexity of computing $IFP(\mathcal{A}, E_0)$, with $E_0 \subset A$, is $O(|A| \times \bar{d}^2)$, where $\bar{d}$ is the maximum input degree of a node (i.e., the maximum number of attacks towards an argument in A).*

---

[1] Similarly to the characteristic function F of an AF [20], function G infers new arguments that can be labelled IN. But it is more efficient as it only uses arguments labelled in the last step.

Theorem 3. *For any AF $\mathcal{A}_0 = \langle A_0, \Sigma_0 \rangle$ with grounded extension E_0, and $u = \pm(a, b)$, the complexity of Algorithm* Incr-Grounded-Sem$(\mathcal{A}_0, u, E_0)$ *is $O(|\Sigma_0| + |\mathcal{I}(u, \mathcal{A}_0, E_0)| \times \bar{d}^2)$, where $\bar{d}$ is the maximum input degree of a node.*

Theorem 4. *Given an AF $\mathcal{A}_0$, an update $u = \pm(a, b)$ for $\mathcal{A}_0$ yielding $\mathcal{A} = u(\mathcal{A}_0)$, and the grounded extension E_0 of $\mathcal{A}_0$, Algorithm 1 computes the grounded extension E of $\mathcal{A}$.*

6   Experimental Results

We implemented a prototype for incremental computation of argumentation semantics using the Java argumentation libraries provided by the *Tweety* project [47].

Datasets. We used two datasets taken from the International Competition on Computational Models of Argumentation (ICCMA)[2]:

(i) REAL consists of 19 AFs $\langle A_0, \Sigma_0 \rangle$ with $|A_0| \in [5K, 100K]$ and $|\Sigma_0| \in [7K, 143K]$;
(ii) SYN consists of 24 AFs $\langle A_0, \Sigma_0 \rangle$ with $|A_0| \in [1K, 4K]$ and $|\Sigma_0| \in [14K, 172K]$.

The AFs in the two datasets have a different structure: on average, $|Reach_{\mathcal{A}_0}(a)|$ is around 2200 for arguments a in SYN, while it is about 10 for REAL; moreover, the average number of attacks per argument for REAL is 1.5 while it is 26 for SYN.

Algorithms. For each AF $\mathcal{A}_0 = \langle A_0, \Sigma_0 \rangle$ in each dataset, we first computed the grounded extension E_0. Then, we randomly selected an update u of the form $+(a, b)$ (with $a, b \in A_0$ and $(a, b) \notin \Sigma_0$) or $-(a, b)$ (with $(a, b) \in \Sigma_0$). Next, we executed the following algorithms:

(i) *BaseG* which computes the grounded semantics E of the updated AF $u(\mathcal{A}_0)$ from scratch. It finds the fixpoint of the characteristic function of an AF as implemented in the libraries of *Tweety* [47]. This algorithm was also used to compute the initial extension E_0 which is taken as input by the incremental algorithms;
(ii) *Incr-Grounded-Sem* (*IncrG* for short) which incrementally computes the grounded extension E by implementing Algorithm 1 (note that it also includes the computation of the influenced set and the restricted AF).

All experiments have been carried out on an Intel Core i7-4790 CPU 3.60 GHz with 16 GB RAM running Ubuntu 14.04 64bit. All data points reported on the figures are averages over 20 trials (except those for *BaseG* which are averages of 5 trials, as it can take hours in some cases due to the huge size of the datasets considered).

---

[2] http://argumentationcompetition.org.

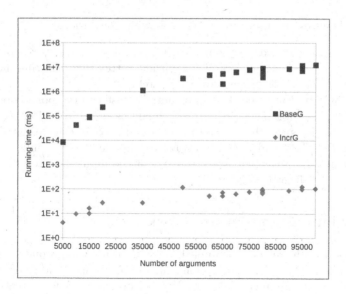

Fig. 4. Run times (ms) of *BaseG* and *IncrG* over **REAL**.

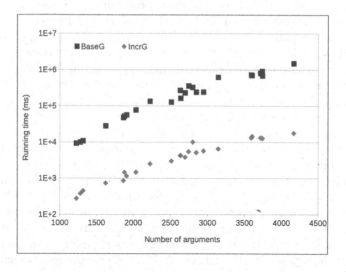

Fig. 5. Run times (ms) of *BaseG* and *IncrG* over **SYN**.

Results. Figures 4 and 5 report the run times (log scale) of *BaseG* and *IncrG* for computing the grounded extensions of the updated AFs versus the number of arguments over **REAL** and **SYN**, respectively.[3] The experiments also showed that, on average, the size of the influenced set w.r.t. that of the input AF for **REAL** (resp. **SYN**) is about 0.01% (resp. 1%).

---

[3] Data points with the same x-axis value are due to AFs in the datasets having the same number of arguments.

From these results, we can draw the following conclusions:

- The overall time needed by our algorithm for incrementally computing the grounded extension is orders of magnitude better than the time needed to recompute the whole extension from scratch.
- The definition of influenced set substantially restricts the portion of the AF to be analysed for recomputing the semantics of an AF after performing an update. It is worth noting that this means that even using *any non-incremental* algorithm taking as input the restricted AF would result in a performance improvement, since the size of the input data to be processed would be significantly smaller.

7   Conclusions and Future Work

We presented an incremental approach for computing the grounded extension of updated AFs. Our algorithm exploits the initial extension of an AF for computing the set of arguments influenced by an update, and for detecting early termination conditions during the recomputation of the status of the arguments. The experiments showed that the incremental computation outperforms the base (non-incremental) computation. In fact, the time needed by our algorithm for incrementally computing the grounded extension is orders of magnitude better than the time needed to recompute the whole extension from scratch.

Although in this paper we focused on updates consisting of adding/removing only one attack, our technique can be extended to deal with the case of multiple updates. Indeed, in [38] a construction is provided for reducing the application of a set of updates $\{+(a_1, b_1), \ldots, +(a_n, b_n), -(a'_1, b'_1), \ldots, -(a'_m, b'_m)\}$ on AF $\mathcal{A}_0$ to the application of a single attack update $+(v, w)$ on an AF obtained from $\mathcal{A}_0$ by adding some new arguments/attacks and replacing some existing ones. Thus, this construction can be used to simulate the simultaneous application of a set of updates by a single attack update of the type considered in this paper.

Moreover, our approach can be extended to work in the case of the incremental computation of the ideal extension of an AF. In fact, the definition of influenced set can be used as it is to compute the part of the AF consisting of the arguments whose status can change after performing an update, and an appropriate definition of restricted AF $\mathcal{R}_{id}(u, \mathcal{A}, E)$ for the ideal semantics can be provided [38]. Once the restricted AF is identified, even a non-incremental algorithm taking as input the restricted AF could be used to recompute the status of influenced arguments.

We plan to continue our work along two directions. First, we will investigate the application of the techniques developed in this paper to other (multiple status) semantics. Indeed, the influenced set is defined already for non-deterministic semantics, and the identification of restricted AFs for these semantics would enable the use of existing (non-incremental) algorithms taking as input a smaller AF for computing extensions. We envisage the definition of incremental algorithms that make use of initial extensions for computing extensions after updates for multiple status semantics where we need to deal with the additional issue that extensions can be split/merged after an update.

Our second direction of research for future work is related to the recent investigations of the integration of argumentation and database repairing techniques [46]. In fact, database reparation is often modelled as interactive reasoning process [41], and the user can profitably exploit argumentation techniques to identify and resolve the conflicts between tuples, possibly specifying preferences among repairs suggested by the system [33,34]. Given the interactive nature of this process, we believe it would benefit from the use of incremental algorithms for the computation of the arguments justifying repairs, and thus plan to explore this issue in the future.

References

1. Amgoud, L., Vesic, S.: Revising option status in argument-based decision systems. J. Log. Comput. **22**(5), 1019–1058 (2012)
2. Baroni, P., Boella, G., Cerutti, F., Giacomin, M., van der Torre, L.W.N., Villata, S.: On the input/output behavior of argumentation frameworks. Artif. Intell. **217**, 144–197 (2014)
3. Baroni, P., Caminada, M., Giacomin, M.: An introduction to argumentation semantics. Knowl. Eng. Rev. **26**(4), 365–410 (2011)
4. Baroni, P., Giacomin, M., Liao, B.: On topology-related properties of abstract argumentation semantics. A correction and extension to dynamics of argumentation systems: a division-based method. Artif. Intell. **212**, 104–115 (2014)
5. Baumann, R.: Splitting an argumentation framework. In: Delgrande, J.P., Faber, W. (eds.) LPNMR 2011. LNCS (LNAI), vol. 6645, pp. 40–53. Springer, Heidelberg (2011). doi:10.1007/978-3-642-20895-9_6
6. Baumann, R.: Normal and strong expansion equivalence for argumentation frameworks. Artif. Intell. **193**, 18–44 (2012)
7. Baumann, R.: Context-free and context-sensitive kernels: update and deletion equivalence in abstract argumentation. In: Proceedings of European Conference on Artificial Intelligence (ECAI), pp. 63–68 (2014)
8. Baumann, R., Brewka, G.: Expanding argumentation frameworks: enforcing and monotonicity results. In: Proceedings of International Conference Computational Models of Argument (COMMA), pp. 75–86 (2010)
9. Baumann, R., Brewka, G., Dvořák, W., Woltran, S.: Parameterized splitting: a simple modification-based approach. In: Erdem, E., Lee, J., Lierler, Y., Pearce, D. (eds.) Correct Reasoning. LNCS, vol. 7265, pp. 57–71. Springer, Heidelberg (2012). doi:10.1007/978-3-642-30743-0_5
10. Bench-Capon, T.J.M., Dunne, P.E.: Argumentation in artificial intelligence. Artif. Intell. **171**(1015), 619–641 (2007). argumentation in Artificial Intelligence
11. Bisquert, P., Cayrol, C., de Saint-Cyr, F.D., Lagasquie-Schiex, M.: Characterizing change in abstract argumentation systems. Trends Belief Revision Argumentation Dyn. **48**, 75–102 (2013)
12. Boella, G., Kaci, S., Torre, L.: Dynamics in argumentation with single extensions: abstraction principles and the grounded extension. In: Sossai, C., Chemello, G. (eds.) ECSQARU 2009. LNCS (LNAI), vol. 5590, pp. 107–118. Springer, Heidelberg (2009). doi:10.1007/978-3-642-02906-6_11

13. Boella, G., Kaci, S., Torre, L.: Dynamics in argumentation with single extensions: attack refinement and the grounded extension (extended version). In: McBurney, P., Rahwan, I., Parsons, S., Maudet, N. (eds.) ArgMAS 2009. LNCS (LNAI), vol. 6057, pp. 150–159. Springer, Heidelberg (2010). doi:10.1007/978-3-642-12805-9_9

14. Calautti, M., Greco, S., Trubitsyna, I.: Detecting decidable classes of finitely ground logic programs with function symbols. In: Proceedings of International Symposium on Principles and Practice of Declarative Programming (PPDP), pp. 239–250 (2013)

15. Caminada, M.: Semi-stable semantics. In: Proceedings of International Conference on Computational Models of Argument (COMMA), pp. 121–130 (2006)

16. Caminada, M., Sá, S., Alcântara, J., Dvořák, W.: On the equivalence between logic programming semantics and argumentation semantics. Int. J. Approx. Reasoning **58**, 87–111 (2015)

17. Cayrol, C., de Saint-Cyr, F.D., Lagasquie-Schiex, M.: Revision of an argumentation system. In: Proceedings of International Conference on Principles of Knowledge Represent and Reasoning (KR), pp. 124–134 (2008)

18. Cayrol, C., de Saint-Cyr, F.D., Lagasquie-Schiex, M.: Change in abstract argumentation frameworks: adding an argument. J. Artif. Intell. Res. (JAIR) **38**, 49–84 (2010)

19. Charwat, G., Dvořák, W., Gaggl, S.A., Wallner, J.P., Woltran, S.: Methods for solving reasoning problems in abstract argumentation - a survey. Artif. Intell. **220**, 28–63 (2015)

20. Dung, P.M.: On the acceptability of arguments and its fundamental role in non-monotonic reasoning, logic programming and n-person games. Artif. Intell. **77**(2), 321–358 (1995)

21. Dung, P.M., Mancarella, P., Toni, F.: Computing ideal sceptical argumentation. Artif. Intell. **171**(10–15), 642–674 (2007)

22. Dunne, P.E.: The computational complexity of ideal semantics. Artif. Intell. **173**(18), 1559–1591 (2009)

23. Dunne, P.E., Wooldridge, M.: Complexity of abstract argumentation. In: Simari, G., Rahwan, I. (eds.) Argumentation in Artificial Intelligence, pp. 85–104. Springer, USA (2009)

24. Dvořák, W., Pichler, R., Woltran, S.: Towards fixed-parameter tractable algorithms for argumentation. In: Proceedings of International Conference on Principles of Knowledge Representation and Reasoning (KR) (2010)

25. Dvořák, W., Woltran, S.: Complexity of semi-stable and stage semantics in argumentation frameworks. Inform. Process. Lett. **110**(11), 425–430 (2010)

26. Eiter, T., Strass, H., Truszczyński, M., Woltran, S. (eds.): Advances in Knowledge Representation, Logic Programming, and Abstract Argumentation. LNCS (LNAI), vol. 9060. Springer, Cham (2015)

27. Falappa, M.A., García, A.J., Kern-Isberner, G., Simari, G.R.: On the evolving relation between belief revision and argumentation. Knowl. Eng. Rev. **26**(1), 35–43 (2011)

28. Fazzinga, B., Flesca, S., Parisi, F.: Efficiently estimating the probability of extensions in abstract argumentation. In: Proceedings of International Conference on Scalable Uncertainty Management (SUM), pp. 106–119 (2013)

29. Fazzinga, B., Flesca, S., Parisi, F.: On the complexity of probabilistic abstract argumentation. In: Proceedings of International Joint Conference on Artificial Intelligence (IJCAI), pp. 898–904 (2013)

30. Fazzinga, B., Flesca, S., Parisi, F.: On the complexity of probabilistic abstract argumentation frameworks. ACM Trans. Comput. Log. **16**(3), 22 (2015)

31. Fazzinga, B., Flesca, S., Parisi, F.: On efficiently estimating the probability of extensions in abstract argumentation frameworks. Int. J. Approx. Reasoning **69**, 106–132 (2016)
32. Fazzinga, B., Flesca, S., Parisi, F., Pietramala, A.: PARTY: a mobile system for efficiently assessing the probability of extensions in a debate. In: Chen, Q., Hameurlain, A., Toumani, F., Wagner, R., Decker, H. (eds.) DEXA 2015. LNCS, vol. 9261, pp. 220–235. Springer, Cham (2015). doi:10.1007/978-3-319-22849-5_16
33. Flesca, S., Furfaro, F., Parisi, F.: Preferred database repairs under aggregate constraints. In: Proceedings of First International Conference Scalable Uncertainty Management (SUM), pp. 215–229 (2007)
34. Flesca, S., Furfaro, F., Parisi, F.: Range-consistent answers of aggregate queries under aggregate constraints. In: Proceedings of International Conference Scalable Uncertainty Management (SUM), pp. 163–176 (2010)
35. Greco, S., Molinaro, C., Trubitsyna, I.: Logic programming with function symbols: checking termination of bottom-up evaluation through program adornments. TPLP **13**(4–5), 737–752 (2013)
36. Greco, S., Molinaro, C., Trubitsyna, I., Zumpano, E.: NP datalog: a logic language for expressing search and optimization problems. TPLP **10**(2), 125–166 (2010)
37. Greco, S., Parisi, F.: Efficient computation of deterministic extensions for dynamic abstract argumentation frameworks. In: Proceedings of European Conference on Artificial Intelligence (ECAI), pp. 1668–1669 (2016)
38. Greco, S., Parisi, F.: Incremental computation of deterministic extensions for dynamic argumentation frameworks. In: Michael, L., Kakas, A. (eds.) JELIA 2016. LNCS (LNAI), vol. 10021, pp. 288–304. Springer, Cham (2016). doi:10.1007/978-3-319-48758-8_19
39. Liao, B.S., Jin, L., Koons, R.C.: Dynamics of argumentation systems: a division-based method. Artif. Intell. **175**(11), 1790–1814 (2011)
40. Lifschitz, V., Turner, H.: Splitting a logic program. In: Proceedings of International Conference on Logic Programming (ICLP), pp. 23–37 (1994)
41. Martinez, M.V., Parisi, F., Pugliese, A., Simari, G.I., Subrahmanian, V.S.: Policy-based inconsistency management in relational databases. Int. J. Approx. Reasoning **55**(2), 501–528 (2014)
42. Modgil, S., Prakken, H.: Revisiting preferences and argumentation. In: Proceedings of International Joint Conference on Artificial Intelligence (IJCAI), pp. 1021–1026 (2011)
43. Oikarinen, E., Woltran, S.: Characterizing strong equivalence for argumentation frameworks. Artif. Intell. **175**(14–15), 1985–2009 (2011)
44. Pollock, J.L.: Perceiving and reasoning about a changing world. Comput. Intell. **14**(4), 498–562 (1998)
45. Rahwan, I., Simari, G.R.: Argumentation in Artificial Intelligence, 1st edn. Springer Publishing Company, Incorporated (2009)
46. Santos, E., Martins, J.P., Galhardas, H.: An argumentation-based approach to database repair. In: Proceedings of European Conference on Artificial Intelligence (ECAI), pp. 125–130 (2010)
47. Thimm, M.: Tweety: A comprehensive collection of java libraries for logical aspects of artificial intelligence and knowledge representation. In: Proceedings of International Conference on Principles of Knowledge Representation and Reasoning (KR) (2014)
48. Xu, Y., Cayrol, C.: The matrix approach for abstract argumentation frameworks. In: Black, E., Modgil, S., Oren, N. (eds.) TAFA 2015. LNCS (LNAI), vol. 9524, pp. 243–259. Springer, Cham (2015). doi:10.1007/978-3-319-28460-6_15

Conflicts Resolution with the SoDA Methodology

Nikolaos I. Spanoudakis[1][(✉)], Antonis C. Kakas[2], and Pavlos Moraitis[3]

[1] Applied Mathematics and Computers Laboratory,
Technical University of Crete, Chania, Greece
nikos@science.tuc.gr
[2] University of Cyprus, Nicosia, Cyprus
antonis@cs.ucy.ac.cy
[3] LIPADE, Paris Descartes University, Paris, France
pavlos@mi.parisdescartes.fr

Abstract. This paper studies the application of argumentation theory and methods from Artificial Intelligence to the problem of conflict resolution. It shows how the decision theories of each of the parties involved in a conflict can be captured and formalized within a framework of preference-based argumentation. In particular, it studies how the *SoDA* methodology and its support tool, *Gorgias-B* for developing argumentation software, facilitate the elucidation of each party's preferences over their available options for addressing the conflict, and, through this, the construction of appropriate argumentation theories corresponding to the decision theories of the parties involved. These argumentation theories are generated automatically and can be executed directly to find out the position of each party at any particular stage of the negotiation process. This connection between argumentation and conflict resolution is illustrated through a real-life example of conflict resolution between the US and China after a plane collision.

Keywords: Argumentation · Conflict resolution · Decision making · Software methodology · Software tool

1 Introduction

Argumentation is an important area of AI, with a wealth of theoretical work over the last twenty years (see e.g. [2,14]), addressing a variety of problems in AI and multi-agent systems. Several practical works exist, showing that argumentation is well suited for dealing with different kind of real life applications, such as finding interesting products in e-commerce [9], negotiating supply strategies [20], making credit assignments [13], managing waste-water discharges [1], deciding about an automatic freight process [4], improving the performance of transport systems in rural areas [19], emergency rescue [21], aggregating clinical evidence [10], smarter electricity [12], delivering clinical decision support services [6], evaluating debates

© Springer International Publishing AG 2017
R. Aydoğan et al. (Eds.): COREDEMA 2016, LNAI 10238, pp. 82–99, 2017.
DOI: 10.1007/978-3-319-57285-7_6

on the social networks [18]. An interesting general study on the use of argumentation techniques for multi-agent systems can be found in [3].

Recently, we proposed the *SoDA* methodology, along with an argumentation tool called *Gorgias-B* [17], for modeling and developing application software, whose outputted source code is an argumentation theory for the problem at hand. *SoDA* helps developers structure their application knowledge at several levels. The first level serves for enumerating the different possible actions or decisions that can be considered under some satisfied conditions, while each higher level serves for resolving conflicts at the previous level, taking into account default and contextual knowledge. Conflict resolution at the higher levels is based on the definition of dynamic priority relations among conflicting decision policies of the previous level. The aim is to provide argumentation-based software solutions that are flexible to partial and conflicting information and that can be modularly developed.

In this paper, our aim is to show how *SoDA* and *Gorgias-B* can be used for dealing with conflict resolution problems. According to [8], a conflict has two or more decision makers, each of them having his/her own objectives. A possible resolution of a conflict depends on the strategic interactions of the decision makers during the evolution of the dispute. To apply conflict analysis to a particular problem we need the following information for developing a conflict model: (a) the decision makers who are participating in the conflict, (b) the options corresponding to the course of action available to each decision maker, and, (c) the preferences expressing the relative importance of options as viewed by each decision maker. *SoDA* and *Gorgias-B* allow to take into consideration all the above requirements.

In the following we will briefly present *SoDA* and then we will use a real world use case, namely the United States-China plane collision negotiation scenario as it is presented in [16], to show SoDA's applicability for conflict resolution and analysis problems. We will present how the modeled theories based on the assumptions made in [16] of both USA and China have been implemented with *Gorgias-B* in order to generate the solution that had been mutually accepted.

2   Basics of Argumentation

In this section we review the basic theory of argumentation which we will use to model conflict resolution problems. The theory will be presented from a general point of view of applying argumentation to real-life (decision) problems.

In [11] a preference-based argumentation framework was proposed for representing multi-agent application problems via argumentation theories composed of different levels. **Object level arguments** represent the possible decisions or actions in a specific application domain and **first-level priority arguments** express preferences on the object level arguments in order to resolve possible conflicts. Then **higher-order priority arguments** are also used to resolve potential conflicts between priority arguments of the previous level.

Formally, an **argumentation theory** is a pair $(\mathcal{T}, \mathcal{P})$ whose sentences are formulae in the background monotonic logic, $(\mathcal{L}, \vdash)$, of the form $L \leftarrow L_1, \ldots, L_n,$

where $L, L_1, \ldots, L_n$ are positive or negative ground literals. The derivability relation, $\vdash$, is given simply by the inference rule of modus ponens. The head literal L can also be empty. Rules in $\mathcal{T}$ represent the **object level arguments**, or denials when the head is empty. Rules in $\mathcal{P}$ represent **priority arguments** where the head L of these rules has the general form, $L = h\_p(rule1, rule2)$, where $rule1$ and $rule2$ are atoms naming two rules and h_p refers to an (irreflexive) *higher priority* relation amongst the rules of the theory.

The semantics of an argumentation theory are defined via the abstract argumentation framework $< Args, Att >$ associated to any given theory $(\mathcal{T}, \mathcal{P})$. The **arguments** in $Args$ are given by the composite subsets, (T, P), of the given theory, where $T \subseteq \mathcal{T}$ and $P \subseteq \mathcal{P}$. An argument (T, P) **supports** its conclusions, of either a literal, L, or a priority (ground) atom, $h\_p(r, r')$, where r and r' are the names of two rules in the theory, when $T \vdash L$ or $T \cup P \vdash h\_p(r, r')$.

The **attack relation**, Att, allows an argument, (T, P), to attack another argument, (T', P'), when (i) these arguments derive contrary conclusions (i.e. derive L and $\neg L$, or $h\_p(r, r')$ and $h\_p(r', r)$) and (ii) (T, P) makes the rules of its counter proof at least "as strong" as the rules of the proof of the argument (T', P') that is attacked. The detailed formal definition of the attacking relation can be found in [11]. The **admissibility** of (sets of) arguments, Δ, is defined in the usual way [5], i.e. that Δ does not attack itself and that it attacks back any argument that attacks it.

It is important to note that typically for an argument (T, P) to be *admissible* its object level part, T, has to have along with it priority arguments, P (from $\mathcal{P}$), in order to make itself at least "as strong" as its opposing counter-arguments. This need for priority rules can repeat itself when the initially chosen ones can themselves be attacked by opposing priority rules. In that case the priority rules have to be made themselves at least "as strong" as their opposing priority ones.

2.1   An Argumentation Framework for Conflict Resolution Problems

We will now further specialize this general argumentation framework to facilitate its use for conflict resolution problems. Following [8], a conflict has two or more decision makers, each of whom has his/her own objectives. A possible resolution of a conflict depends on the strategic interactions of the decision makers during the evolution of the dispute. As mentioned in the introduction, to apply conflict analysis to a particular problem we need the following information for developing a conflict model: (a) decision makers who are participating in the conflict, (b) options corresponding to the course of action available to each decision maker and (c) preferences expressing the relative importance of options as viewed by each decision maker.

For modeling such problems with argumentation, we separate the language $\mathcal{L}$ of the theory into two ontological categories: **Options** and **Beliefs**, where the first refers to the properties that we are primarily interested, i.e. the solutions of the application problem, and the second refers to properties of the application problem environment. Beliefs can be decomposed, although not necessary, into *Defeasible and Non-Defeasible* beliefs and some of the defeasible beliefs can be designated as **abducible** beliefs, so that they can be hypothesized when needed. Furthermore, apart from the incompatibility relation that we have through negation, we can also have a **complementary** or **conflict** relation between the different options of the application.

In an argumentation theory representing an application problem, we can separate the object level statements, T, into two parts, $T = T^O \cup B$, where T^O is the subset of rules that provide arguments for the various options, i.e. rules whose head refers to an option predicate, and B, called the **background theory**, is the subset of rules whose heads are belief predicates.

Definition 1. *An* **application (argumentation) theory,** T*, is an argumentation theory* (T, P) *where its object level rules are separated into rules for options and rules for beliefs and its priority rules part is partitioned into a finite set of levels,* $T = (T^O \cup B, P_1 \ldots P_n)$*, such that all the rules in* P_1 *are priority rules with head* $h\_p(r_1, r_2)$ *with* $r_1, r_2 \in T^O$ *and, for any* $1 < k \le n$*, all rules in* P_k *are priority rules with head* $h\_p(q_1, q_2)$ *s.t.* $q_1, q_2 \in P_{k-1}$*.*

In general, the different levels in the priority rules relate to the granularity or **specificity** of the **context** in which we want to consider our application problem. Belief predicates are used to describe the various external problem environments, called **application scenarios**, under which we want to solve our problem. For simplicity, we are assuming that belief predicates are non-defeasible and hence their rules in the background theory are not prioritized.

When we are solving an application problem, we consider specific cases of application scenarios. Solutions to problems are then given through the admissible arguments of the given application argumentation theory extended with the application scenario of interest.

Definition 2. *Let* T *be an application argumentation theory and* S *an application scenario. Then a ground literal,* L*, is* **credulously supported** *by* T *under* S *iff there exists an admissible argument in* T'*, obtained from* T *by extending its background theory by* S*, that derives* L*. We say that* L *is* **sceptically supported** *by* T *under* S *iff it is credulously supported by* T *under* S *and all complements of* L *are not credulously supported by* T *under* S*. When the literal* L *refers to an option predicate then we will also say that* L *is a* **credulous solution** *or* **sceptical solution** *under* S*.*

Given the above theoretical notions of argumentation the link with conflict resolution problems rests on being able to capture the decision making process of the decision makers in the conflict in terms of argumentation theories expressing the options and, importantly, the preferences of the decision maker according to the high-level **values** that each decision maker has at the time of the conflict. These values may change as the resolution process unfolds. The main challenge in this, is, indeed, to be able to capture the high-level preferences of the decision makers, expressed in a natural manner by the decision makers (who are generally non-computing experts), in an executable argumentation theory. This theory should automate the preference-based decision making of the parties through the argumentative reasoning in them. Hence, the challenge is to cognitively and transparently extract the various options and preferences of the decision makers into rules and priorities, of the form given above, in an argumentation theory that automates the decision making.

3   The *SoDA* methodology

We will now present *SoDA*, a general software methodology for developing application software whose outputted source code is an argumentation theory for the problem at hand. This methodology defines a high level process requiring from the developer to consider questions about the requirements of the problem at various scenarios without the need to consider the underlying software code that will be generated. Software is thus developed in a principled way with high-level declarative executable code.

Software development processes can be defined in a standard way by using the SPEM (Software Process Engineering Metamodel) 2.0 language[1]. A Software Process can be defined as a series of tasks (or activities) that produce Work Products (WPs). Work products can be textual models, which can be completely free (free text) or follow some specifications or grammar (a structured work product).

When drawing software processes in SPEM, each process contains yellow coloured tasks (or activities) connected with arrows showing flow of control. A black dot shows where the process starts and a black dot in a circle where it ends. A small black orthogonal can be used to fork control to more than one paths (that can be followed in parallel) or merge previously forked control. An activity has input and output work products. An arrow from an activity to a work product means that the product is created (or updated) by the activity. An arrow from a work product to an activity means that the product is an input to the activity.

Figure 1 presents the *SoDA* process. Let us explain the different tasks (T) and their input and output work products (WP):

T1: This task defines the different **options** of the application problem, given in predicate format with all the relevant parameters. The **conflict relation** between options is also defined here. For example, the option to deny access or to give partial access to a file is conflicting with the option to give full access. All this information is written in work product one (WP1).

T2: The second task is a knowledge engineering task required to identify the knowledge needed in order to describe the different application environments which can arise in the application problem domain. This knowledge is written in WP2 in the form of various **belief predicates**. WP2 also contains predicates that are used to type all object parameters of the problem

---

[1] SPEM is a standard for defining software processes, http://www.omg.org/spec/SPEM/2.0/.

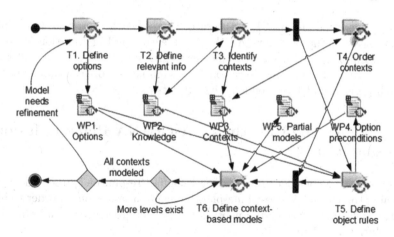

Fig. 1. The *SoDA* process

that appear in the option and belief predicates. Moreover, we define any background interrelationships that might exist amongst the belief predicates generating the **background theory**[2], which are also inserted into WP2.

T3: This task aims to separate the information in WP2 into two types: information that always exists for all instances of the problem and information that is **circumstantial**, which may be present in all instances of the problem. Circumstantial predicates are removed from WP2 and inserted in WP3. The next two tasks can be executed in parallel (T4 and T5).

T4: This task aims to sort the circumstantial information (predicates or groups of predicates) from the more general to the more specific application **contexts** in levels, starting from level one (more general contexts). Independent contexts (i.e. when the one is not a refinement of the other) can appear at the same level.

T5: The four previous tasks were preparatory. This task begins the process of capturing the application requirements. It aims to define for each option, O_i, the different problem environments, i.e. the sets of **preconditions**, C_i, in terms of non-circumstantial predicates appearing in WP2, where the **option is possible**. Its output, WP4, contains all such sets of preconditions. Care must be taken to ensure that the parameters of the options are typed in the preconditions. It is possible for options, to be always possible, in which case they have the (only) precondition, $\{true\}$.

T6: This final task iteratively defines sequences of increasingly more specific **partial models or scenarios** of the world (stored in WP5) and considers how options might win over others. This starts with information from WP4

---

[2] For simplicity we will assume that the background theory is monotonic, i.e. contains strict information that is not defeasible. Otherwise, the same process needs to be followed for the defeasible belief predicates in analogy with the process for the option predicates that we are describing here.

to precondition the world and iterates getting each time contextual information from the next level in WP3. At each **level** of iteration it defines which option is stronger over another under the more specific contextual information. In the final iteration, the winning options (if they exist) for each partial model are defined without extra information.

4   Applying *SoDA* for the USA-CHINA Plane Collision Negotiation

In this section we consider an example of conflict resolution, presented in [16], concerning the United States-China plane collision negotiation, in order to illustrate the suitability of our argumentation based approach for conflict analysis and resolution problems.

This conflict problem is described in [16] as follows, quoting directly from this paper:

On April 1, 2000 an American surveillance plane and a Chinese fighter plane collided about 70 miles off the coast of China. China considers its airspace to extend 200 miles off its coast; international agreements specify 12 miles. The Chinese pilot parachuted out of his aircraft but was presumed dead; his body was not found. The U.S. plane made as emergency landing at a Chinese military airfield on the island of Hainan without receiving China's permission. China thus had possession of the U.S. plane and crew. China said that the U.S. was responsible for the crash and should "apologize" and call off future surveillance flights. The U.S. expressed "regret" mentioning specifically regret that the Chinese pilot had died, but declared it had no apology to give as the fault lay with the Chinese pilot. After a while, the U.S. used the words "sorry" and then "very sorry" that can convey more emotion in referring to the loss of the Chinese pilot and the landing at the Chinese airfield without permission, but China still insisted on an apology.

So USA and China disagreed on the control action that should express the reconciliation statement. For satisfying the common goal "saving face", the pair "apology/dao qian" that was asked by China was rejected by USA while the pair "regret/yihan" that could be accepted by USA was rejected by China. Then, to these two alternatives the author in [16] added two other alternatives namely "regret/bao qian" and "apology/bao qian". He supported these two options by explaining that:

A situation merits that a party A apologize to a party B for specific actions would appear to involve: (1) standards or norms and (2) departures from standards caused by actions of party A resulting in negative effects to party B. Because of disagreement about standards, departures, actions, causes and negative effects, any USA reconciliation statement, as expressed in both English and Chinese, had to be flexible enough for each side to interpret the statement as acceptable, i.e. for China the statement serving as a U.S. apology and for the USA as not constituting apology, a vacuous apology from the U.S.

The author explained in [16] how his suggestions reached the U.S. authorities. Subsequently, on April 11, an agreement between the U.S. and China was announced (for more details the reader can refer to [16]). In the agreement, the English version of the U.S. statement used the word "regret" (China droped its demand for apology), while the Chinese version of the U.S. statement used the word "bao qian" (expressing apology).

We will now use *SoDA* to model this conflict reconciliation problem by representing the possible decision policies of both USA and China as argumentation theories. In the following, we will use the above explanation of the author in order to model the USA and China argumentation theories that should capture this conflicting situation and its resolution. For this reason, we will first use the predicate *goal(saving_face)* for representing the common goal "saving face" of two parties. Then, we will use the predicate *violation_of_norms* for representing the presumed by China violation of its airspace by the USA pilot, as China considers that its airspace is extended to 200 miles off its coast. Finally, we will use the predicate *disagreement_on_violation* for representing the disagreement between USA and China on this Chinese consideration as international agreements specify 12 miles as the official airspace off a country's coast. We consider that these predicates represent the shared knowledge by both parties.

During the first task, T1, we identify the different options available in WP1. For the USA decision theory we have the three **options**:

propose(*regret_yihan*)
propose(*regret_bao qian*)
propose(*apology_bao qian*)

In task T2, we identify scenario information which is needed for the options to be enabled for possible consideration, and, during T3, we identify relevant circumstantial information and sort it in levels (from general to specific). In our example, WP2 can be considered empty, i.e. all three options are enabled from the start and constitute possible options, while WP3 would contain:

Level 1: goal(*saving_face*), *violation_of_norms*
Level 2: *disagreement_on_violation* (or *violation_in_special_circumstances*)

Note that these contexts are ranked from the more general to the most specific. For a more specific context to be valid, the previous level context must also be valid. Otherwise, they are independent contexts appearing at the same level. For example, if there is a *violation_of_norms* (level 1 context), there **may** be a *disagreement_on_violation* (level 2, more specific, context). The *goal* (*saving_face*) and *violation_of_norms* are independent contexts (thus are ranked at the same level).

In the next task, T5, we define, based on WP2, the different object level arguments that support each option by specifying the (eventual) preconditions from WP2 that must be satisfied for the option to be possible for consideration. Thus, in the case of the USA theory, as WP2 is empty, we have the following object level arguments for the three options:

Option1: propose(regret_yihan) : true
Option2: propose(regret_bao qian) : true
Option3: propose(apology_bao qian) : true

Then, in WP5 we consider partial models as possible world models showing the various possibilities for the options as the model/world is extended with new (contextual) information according to the refinement levels in WP3. In these models we specify which of the (enabled) options can be possible, i.e. are (possibly) preferred over the other options. Note that these models are non-monotonic in the sense that as we refine the scenario conditions options may be dropped, i.e. options lose their preference over others.

In our example, following the analysis of [16], we have:

M1: {goal(saving_face)} : propose(regret_yihan); propose(regret_bao qian)
M2: {violation_of_norms} : propose(apology_bao qian)
M3: {goal(saving_face), violation_of_norms, disagreement_on_violation} : propose(regret_bao qian)

These express the following preferences on the options, from the USA point of view:

M1: Generally, prefer options that would serve the goal of "saving face".
M2: If we (USA) violate some norms then we would prefer options that are not "face saving", i.e. of apologizing as we (USA) have violated international standards.
M3: If we (USA) consider that there is no departure from the international standards, then we would prefer options that serve the goal of "saving face".

We will now consider how we can capture, through the *SoDA* methodology, the decision theory for China, following again the analysis of [16]. China has three possible options corresponding to possibly accepting the three proposals of USA. These are:

accept *(regret_yihan)*
accept *(regret_bao qian)*
accept *(apology_bao qian)*

As with the case of USA, we can consider that all these options are enabled, i.e. WP2 is empty, meaning that the object-level arguments for each of these options do not need any preconditions.

Hence for China the different options are the following:

Option1: accept(regret_yihan) : true
Option2: accept(regret_bao qian) : true
Option3: accept(apology_bao qian) : true

Then, considering the application scenarios we identify in WP3 relevant circumstantial information and sort it in levels (from general to specific). Based on this we identify partial models that express the preferred options as the scenarios are made more specific. Following the analysis in [16] we may assume that China has the following preferences:

M1: Generally, prefer options that would serve the goal of "saving face" for China.
M2: If the other party (USA) violates some norms then we (China) would prefer options that are "face saving" in China i.e. the other party (USA) apologizing in China and in USA.
M3: If there is a disagreement on the violation of norms, we (China) can also accept the weaker option of USA expressing regret in USA but apologizing in China.

Then based on this the partial models generated in WP5 for the China theory are as follows:

M1: $\{goal(saving\_face)\}$: *accept(apology_bao qian); accept(regret_bao qian)*
M2: $\{violation\_of\_norms\}$: *accept(apology_bao qian)*
M3: $\{goal(saving\_face), violation\_of\_norms, disagreement\_on\_violation\}$: *accept (regret_bao qian); accept(apology_bao qian)*

Note here that the condition $goal(saving\_face)$ is different from the analogous condition in the USA theory, referring now to China saving face. The other two conditions can be taken as being common to both theories.

4.1 Argumentation Theories for USA and China

The specification for our real world case scenario modeled with the *SoDA* methodology, as analyzed above, is automatically translated into the following argumentation theories. Note that we restrict the attention here to the two options that according to [16] have been mainly considered for the final decision, namely *propose(regret_bao qian)* and *propose(apology_bao qian)*.

For USA we have the argumentation theory:

$r_{1\_1} : propose(regret\_baoqian) \leftarrow true$
$r_{2\_1} : propose(apology\_baoqian) \leftarrow true$
$pr^1_{12\_1} : h\_p(r_{1\_1}, r_{2\_1}) \leftarrow goal(saving\_face)$
$pr^1_{21\_1} : h\_p(r_{2\_1}, r_{1\_1}) \leftarrow violation\_of\_norms$
$pr^2_{12\_1} : h\_p(pr^1_{12\_1}, pr^1_{21\_1}) \leftarrow disagreement\_on\_violation$

and for China we have the argumentation theory[3]:

$r_{1\_1} : accept(regret\_baoqian)) \leftarrow true$

$r_{2\_1} : accept(apology\_baoqian) \leftarrow true$

$pr^1_{21\_1} : h\_p(r_{2\_1}, r_{1\_1}) \leftarrow violation\_of\_norms$

$pr^1_{12\_1} : h\_p(r_{1\_1}, r_{2\_1}) \leftarrow violation\_of\_norms, disagreement\_on\_violation$

Then, under these two argumentation theories, as decision theories for the respective parties of USA and China in the final (negotiation) scenario where all conditions of, $\{goal^{USA}(saving\_face), goal^{China}(saving\_face),$ $violation\_of\_norms, disagreement\_on\_violation\}$, hold, we get that the option $propose(regret\_baoqian)$ is sceptically entailed by the USA theory and $accept(regret\_baoqian)$ is credulously entailed by the China theory. Therefore, a resolution of the conflict can be reached with the action $regret\_baoqian$.

4.2 Conflict Resolution in Argumentation

We will now discuss how the treatment of the above case study example points towards a general way to capture conflict resolution problems within the preference based argumentation framework on which the *SoDA* argumentation software methodology is based. This is a preliminary investigation which merits further study, as we will discuss in the concluding section.

We will be concerned mainly with the conceptualization of the high-level general structure of the problem as followed by most approaches to conflict resolution (see e.g. [7,15]). In the standard conceptualization of the problem we have a situation in which each one of two parties has a set of options or actions that it can carry out and wants to decide which option to adopt. The problem of conflict resolution, as a decision problem for the two parties involved, can be abstracted to have the following general form.

Definition 3 (Conflict Resolution Problem). *A conflict resolution problem consists of two parties, each of which has a decision theory D_1 and D_2 for selecting options from the set of (contradictory) problem options, $\{p_1, p_2, m_1, ..., m_k\}$, in any given state of the environment in which the problem is situated. Initially, option p_1 is the preferred option under D_1 for the first party and option p_2 is the preferred option under D_2 for the second (other) party. None of the other options, m_i is preferred by either party in the initial state of the problem environment. The task is to find an option m amongst all possible options such that this is preferred under both D_1 and D_2 in possibly a new state of the problem environment.*

---

[3] Note that the condition $goal(saving\_face)$ does not appear in this fragment of the China theory as this condition only plays a role in the default preference of the all the options over the first option of $accept(regret\_yihan)$ which we are not considered in this fragment.

For simplicity of presentation, we will assume that there is only one middle position "m". In practice, there will be several middle options coming about as the process of resolution unfolds.

We see that the important ontological aspect of this definition is to capture the notion of **preferred option** under the decision theory of a party. This notion needs to be sensitive to the changing information in the problem environment as the negotiation process unfolds. We will now examine how argumentation can provide this kind of preference notion in a natural way.

In our example above $p_1 = regret\_yihan$ is the preferred option for USA, $p_2 = apology\_baoqian$ is the preferred option for China, and $m = regret\_baoqian$ is a possible middle position, on which they eventually resolve the conflict.

There are three central aspects of the general structure of problem of conflict resolution that we need to consider in a formalization of the problem in argumentation. These are:

– Capture the preferences that each party has for the various options based on the goals and/or desired values that each option (currently) serves for each party.
– Capture the special circumstances, normally arising through a negotiation process, that can affect or even overturn the general value-based preferences of a party.
– Formalize the notion of a **solution** to a conflict resolution problem in terms of the semantic notions of argumentation.

Let us consider these in turn. For the first aspect we note that we can associate to each option a value under some **valuation function** for each party. The valuation function could be based on a dominant value that the party is interested in, as in the case above, where for both the USA and China there is a dominant value of "saving face". As analyzed in [16], USA and China assign value 1 or 0 to the various options of the problem according to the degree that the option "saves face" for their country. Hence, the option $p_1 = regret\_yihan$ has value 1 for USA but value 0 for China, whereas the option $p_2 = apology\_baoqian$ has value 0 for USA and 1 for China.

The default preferences are then easily captured by preferring options whose valuation is higher over others whoe valuation is lower. This will provide to the argumentation theory first-level priority rules of the schematic form:

$$pr^1_{ij\_1} : h\_p(r_{i\_1}, r_{j\_1}) \leftarrow value(O_i, V_i), value(O_j, V_j), V_i \sqsupset V_j$$

where the valuation function, $value(Option, Value)$, and the order relation, $\sqsupset$, on the possible values, are defined (non-defeasibly) in the associated background theory of each party. Note that values do not need to be arithmetic and the order relation could in general be a partial multi-criteria one.

In the USA-China case example described above, we can see these default priority rules in a compiled form where, for example in the USA theory, the priority rule:

$$pr^1_{12\_1} : h\_p(r_{1\_1}, r_{2\_1}) \leftarrow goal(saving\_face)$$

is a compiled case of the general schema above as the condition $goal(saving\_face)$ captures the higher value, 1, given to the preferred option of $regret\_baoqian$.

The second aspect of formalizing conflict resolution through argumentation concerns the ability of the argumentation theory to capture exceptional circumstances of the problem environment, i.e. exceptional states, where the default value-based preferences are changed, possibly overturned. The argumentation framework adopted in this paper is well suited for such exceptions to default preferences (see [11]) by having its priority rules being conditional and by allowing higher-order priority rules, i.e. priorities over priorities, amounting to allowing statements that make the preferences vary as the information that we have about the problem case at hand changes.

We can see a case of this in the USA argumentation theory above with the following two priority rules in its theory:

$$pr^1_{21\_1} : h\_p(r_{2\_1}, r_{1\_1}) \leftarrow violation\_of\_norms$$
$$pr^2_{12\_1} : h\_p(pr^1_{12\_1}, pr^1_{21\_1}) \leftarrow disagreement\_on\_violation$$

where the first of these says that under its condition the option p_2 of apologizing is (possibly) preferred over the regret option, p_1, thus mitigating the default valued based preference which is in the opposite way (note that this alone does not overturn completely the default preference the other way but simply that it allows the apologizing option to be acceptable by the party). Then the second of these rules, which is a higher-order priority rule, has the effect of overturning this possibility and preferring the saving face option p_1, when $disagreement\_on\_violation$ also holds in the problem's environment.

The third aspect of formally capturing what is meant by a resolution or a solution to a conflict resolution problem in the argumentation formulation of the problem is given by the following definition.

Definition 4 (Conflict Resolution Solution(S)). *Let a conflict resolution problem between two parties D_1 and D_2 be given with options $\{p_1, p_2, m\}$. Then a **satisfactory resolution** of the problem, is reached in a state S of the problem environment when both argumentation theories, $D_1 \cup S$ and $D_2 \cup S$, corresponding to the two parties, credulously support the same option from the given set. We say that an **ideal resolution** is reached when $D_1 \cup S$ and $D_2 \cup S$, sceptically support the same option.*

In the example above, the resolution reached via the $m = regret\_baoqian$ middle option is a satisfactory resolution, but not an ideal one, as this option is only credulously supported by the China theory.

Note that the above definition allows for the solution of the conflict to be reached via any of the three options. In practice, it will be the middle option that would be reached as the common option decided by both parties. But, it is possible that in some cases the reconciliation can come from an original position of one of the parties, i.e. when one party eventually manages to convince the other party of its position.

5   Solving the USA-China Conflict with *Gorgias-B*

Herein we demonstrate the usage of the *Gorgias-B* tool[4] for developing the USA-China plane collision conflict decision policy for the USA. *Gorgias-B* supports the *SoDA* methodology and automatically generates the source code in the form of an application argumentation theory in the *Gorgias* framework.

When the user starts a new project in the *Gorgias-B* tool, a dialog prompts the user to enter the application options (see the *Options View* in Fig. 2). The user inserts the option predicates and their conflicts (corresponding to WP1 of the *SoDA* methodology). The user can also insert background knowledge in similar views (WP2 and WP3). From the *Options View*, with the "Add arguments for options" button the user can edit preconditions (WP4) for options in the *Argument View* (Fig. 2). This is how the user is building the (object-level) arguments for the various options.

The *Argue View* appears as soon as the user clicks the "Resolve conflicts" button. Here the user selects among scenarios with conflicting options more specialized cases (if they exist) where an option is preferred over another. When such specialized cases exist for both conflicting options, they are combined to a

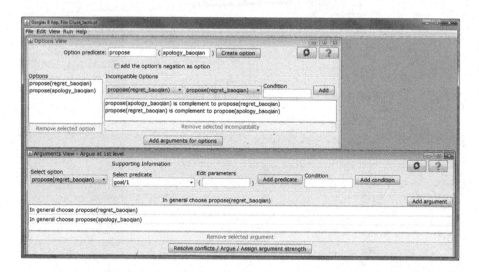

Fig. 2. A *Gorgias-B* screenshot showing the options view on top of the arguments view

---

[4] *Gorgias-B* is a Java application with a Graphical User Interface (GUI) that is freely downloadable from its web-site and can execute in a computer with the minimum requirements of a Windows OS, SWI-Prolog version 7.0 or later, and Java version 1.7 or later. Download it from http://gorgiasb.tuc.gr.

new more specific scenario and the user can then repeat the same process in the next level, which is always visible at the top of the dialog window.

In Fig. 3 we show the argue view at the second level, where we define two models, one that prefers *propose(regret_baoqian)* when *goal(saving_face)* and one that prefers *propose(apology_baoqian)* when *violation_of_norms*. Figure 4 shows the third level of arguing. Here, the scenario is the combination of *goal(saving_face)* and *violation_of_norms*. In this scenario we add the preference for *propose(regret_baoqian)* provided that *disagreement_on_violation*.

Finally, the decision maker can test the scenarios in the "Execute" View. He/she can instantiate as many facts as needed and then either search for specific options, or select the "Explore all options" button to see which of the options can be valid. In the case shown in Fig. 5 we see that when *goal(saving_face)*, *violation_of_norms* and *disagreement_on_violation*, the only possible option (supported by *Argument #1*), a skeptical result, is *propose(regret_baoqian)*.

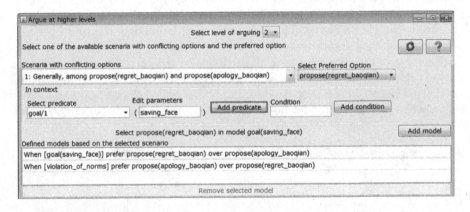

Fig. 3. An instance of the Argue view: Second level

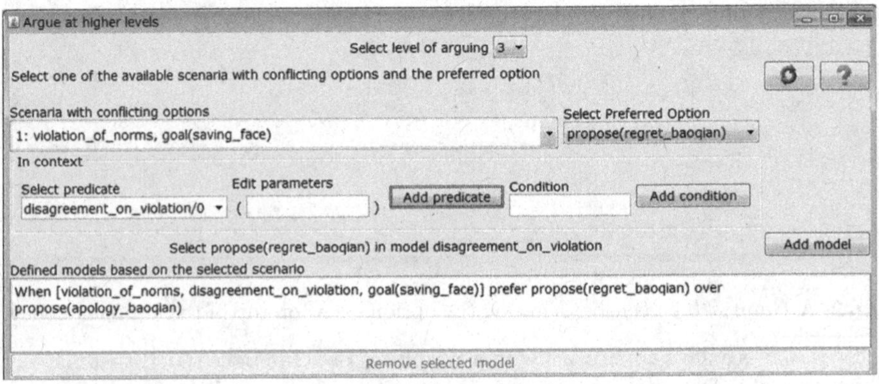

Fig. 4. Another instance of the Argue view: Third level

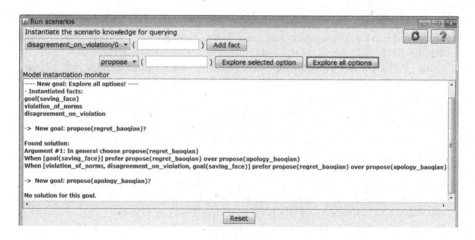

Fig. 5. The execution of a scenario for USA

6   Conclusions

We have presented an application of argumentation theory and methods from Artificial Intelligence to the problem of conflict resolution. We showed that the *SoDA* methodology, which we have briefly presented herein, helps to build in a natural way argumentation theories that can represent the decision policies of the parties involved in a conflict. We have also shown that its associated tool, namely *Gorgias-B*, allows the implementation of these theories in a transparent way, thus automating and simulating the decisions that the involved parties could/should made during the conflict resolution process.

In our future work, we aim to use techniques from the Natural Language Processing area to remove the requirement that users must be familiar with first-order logic in order to formulate their decision theories. A more natural way that allows the users to express their preferences in some structured form of natural language or graphical form will be examined. Visualizing the scenarios, contexts and options available will help us develop cognitive systems based on user decision policies. This, in turn, will help us study multi-party negotiations and how our systems can support the process of negotiation and the development of the conditions that would lead to the resolution of a given conflict.

References

1. Aulinas, M., Tolchinsky, P., Turon, C., Poch, M., Cortés, U.: Argumentation-based framework for industrial wastewater discharges management. Eng. Appl. AI **25**(2), 317–325 (2012). http://dx.doi.org/10.1016/j.engappai.2011.09.016
2. Bench-Capon, T.J.M., Dunne, P.E.: Argumentation in artificial intelligence. Artif. Intell. **171**(10–15), 619–641 (2007). http://dx.doi.org/10.1016/j.artint.2007.05.001
3. Carrera, Á., Iglesias, C.A.: A systematic review of argumentation techniques for multi-agent systems research. Artif. Intell. Rev. **44**(4), 509–535 (2015). http://dx.doi.org/10.1007/s10462-015-9435-9

4. Chow, H.K.H., Siu, W., Chan, C., Chan, H.C.B.: An argumentation-oriented multi-agent system for automating the freight planning process. Expert Syst. Appl. **40**(10), 3858–3871 (2013). http://dx.doi.org/10.1016/j.eswa.2012.12.042

5. Dung, P.M.: On the acceptability of arguments and its fundamental role in non-monotonic reasoning, logic programming and n-person games. Artif. Intell. **77**, 321–357 (1995)

6. Fox, J., Glasspool, D., Patkar, V., Austin, M., Black, L., South, M., Robertson, D., Vincent, C.: Delivering clinical decision support services: there is nothing as practical as a good theory. J. Biomed. Inform. **43**(5), 831–843 (2010). http://dx.doi.org/10.1016/j.jbi.2010.06.002

7. Fraser, N.M., Garcia, F.: Conflict analysis of the NAFTA negotiations. Group Decis. Negot. **3**(4), 373–391 (1994). http://dx.doi.org/10.1007/BF01414412

8. Fraser, N., Hipel, K.: Conflict analysis: models and resolutions. North-Holland series in system science and engineering, North-Holland (1984)

9. Huang, S., Lin, C.: The search for potentially interesting products in an e-marketplace: an agent-to-agent argumentation approach. Expert Syst. Appl. **37**(6), 4468–4478 (2010). http://dx.doi.org/10.1016/j.eswa.2009.12.064

10. Hunter, A., Williams, M.: Aggregation of clinical evidence using argumentation: a tutorial introduction. In: Foundations of Biomedical Knowledge Representation - Methods and Applications, pp. 317–337 (2015). http://dx.doi.org/10.1007/978-3-319-28007-3_20

11. Kakas, A.C., Moraitis, P.: Argumentation based decision making for autonomous agents. In: Proceedings of the Second International Joint Conference on Autonomous Agents & Multiagent Systems, AAMAS 2003, Melbourne, Australia, pp. 883–890 (2003). http://doi.acm.org/10.1145/860575.860717

12. Makriyiannis, M., Lung, T., Craven, R., Toni, F., Kelly, J.: Smarter electricity and argumentation theory. In: Hatzilygeroudis, I., Palade, V., Prentzas, J. (eds.) Combinations of Intelligent Methods and Applications. SIST, vol. 46, pp. 79–95. Springer, Cham (2016). doi:10.1007/978-3-319-26860-6_5

13. Pashaei, K., Taghiyareh, F., Badie, K.: A negotiation-based genetic framework for multi-agent credit assignment. In: Müller, J.P., Weyrich, M., Bazzan, A.L.C. (eds.) MATES 2014. LNCS (LNAI), vol. 8732, pp. 72–89. Springer, Cham (2014). doi:10.1007/978-3-319-11584-9_6

14. Rahwan, I., Simari, G.R.: Argumentation in Artificial Intelligence, 1st edn. Springer Publishing Company, Incorporated (2009)

15. Shakun, M.F.: Modeling and supporting task-oriented group processes: purposeful complex adaptive systems and evolutionary systems design. Group Decis. Negot. **5**(4), 305–317 (1996). http://dx.doi.org/10.1007/BF00553905

16. Shakun, M.F.: United States-China plane collision negotiation. Group Decis. Negot. **12**(6), 477–480 (2003). http://dx.doi.org/10.1023/B:GRUP.0000004348.68980.4d

17. Spanoudakis, N.I., Kakas, A.C., Moraitis, P.: Applications of argumentation: the SoDA methodology. In: 22nd European Conference on Artificial Intelligence (ECAI 2016), The Hague, Holland, 29 August–2 September (2016)

18. Toni, F., Torroni, P.: Bottom-up argumentation. In: Modgil, S., Oren, N., Toni, F. (eds.) TAFA 2011. LNCS (LNAI), vol. 7132, pp. 249–262. Springer, Heidelberg (2012). doi:10.1007/978-3-642-29184-5_16

19. Velaga, N.R., Rotstein, N.D., Oren, N., Nelson, J.D., Norman, T.J., Wright, S.: Development of an integrated flexible transport systems platform for rural areas using argumentation theory. Res. Transp. Bus. Manag. **3**, 62–70 (2012). http://www.sciencedirect.com/science/article/pii/S2210539512000090, flexible Transport Services

20. Wang, G., Wong, T.N., Wang, X.H.: A negotiation protocol to support agent argumentation and ontology interoperability in mas-based virtual enterprises. In: Seventh International Conference on Information Technology: New Generations, ITNG 2010, Las Vegas, Nevada, USA, 12–14 April 2010, pp. 448–453 (2010). http://dx.doi.org/10.1109/ITNG.2010.39

21. Zhang, W., Liang, Y., Ji, S., Tian, Q.: Argumentation agent based fire emergency rescue project making. In: 2012 IEEE Symposium on Robotics and Applications (ISRA), pp. 892–895, June 2012

A Multi-agent Argumentation Framework to Support Collective Reasoning

Jordi Ganzer-Ripoll[1]([⊠]), Maite López-Sánchez[1],
and Juan Antonio Rodriguez-Aguilar[2]

[1] University of Barcelona, Barcelona, Spain
`jordi891@gmail.com`, `maite@maia.ub.es`
[2] Artificial Intelligence Research Institute (IIIA-CSIC), Bellaterra, Spain
`jar@iiia.csic.es`

Abstract. Argumentative debates are a powerful tool for resolving conflicts and reaching agreements in open environments such as on-line communities. Here we introduce an argumentation framework to structure argumentative debates. Our framework represents the arguments issued by the participants involved in a debate, the (attack and defence) relationships between them, as well as participants' opinions on them. Furthermore, we tackle the problem of computing a collective decision from participants' opinions. With this aim, we design an aggregation function that satisfies valuable social-choice properties.

1 Introduction

As argued in [10,12], argumentative debates are a powerful tool for reaching agreements in open environments such as on-line communities. Nowadays, this is particularly true in our society due to the increasing interest and deployment of e-participation and e-governance ICT-systems that involve citizens in governance [16]. Not surprisingly some European cities are opening their policy making to citizens (e.g. Reykjavík [2], Barcelona [1]). Moreover, the need for argumentative debates has also been deemed as necessary for open innovation systems [13]. On-line debates are usually organised as threads of arguments and counter-arguments that users issue to convince others so that debates eventually converge to agreements. Users are allowed to express their opinions on arguments by rating them (e.g. [12]). There are two main issues in the management of large-scale on-line debates. First, as highlighted by [10,12], there is simply too much noise when many individuals participate in a discussion, and hence there is the need for *structuring* it to keep the focus. Second, the opinions on arguments issued by users must be aggregated to achieve a collective decision about the topic under discussion [4]. In this paper we try to make headway on these two issues.

Recently, argumentation has become one of the key approaches to rational interaction in artificial intelligence [5,15]. Here, we propose to follow an

Funded by Collectiveware TIN2015-66863-C2-1-R (MINECO/FEDER) and 2014 SGR 118.

R. Aydoğan et al. (Eds.): COREDEMA 2016, LNAI 10238, pp. 100–117, 2017.
DOI: 10.1007/978-3-319-57285-7_7

argumentation-based approach that allows agents to issue arguments in favour or against a *topic* under discussion as well as about other agents' arguments. Furthermore, we will consider that agents express their opinions about each other's arguments and the topic itself.

Within our multi-agent framework, we face the following collective decision problem: *given a set of agents, each with an individual opinion about a given set of arguments related to a topic, how can agents reach a collective decision on the topic under discussion?* To solve this problem, we propose a social choice function that aggregates agents' opinions to infer the overall opinion about the topic under discussion. Our aggregation function is based on combining opinions and exploiting dependencies between arguments to produce an aggregated opinion. Moreover, and most importantly, our aggregation function guarantees the resulting aggregated opinion to be *coherent*, i.e., it is free of contradictions. In more detail, here we make the following contributions:

- A novel multi-agent argumenation framework, the so-called *target-oriented discussion framework*, to support discussions about the acceptance of a target proposal. Besides the usual attack relationship between arguments, our framework allows agents to express explicit defence relationships between arguments. Furthermore, it introduces a mechanism for assessing whether individual opinions about the arguments are reasonable (coherent) or not. Formally, this is captured through the notion of *coherent labelling*, which can be regarded as a relaxed version of the notion of complete labelling in [4] to provide further flexibility to express opinions.
- A novel aggregation function that combines agents' opinions in our multi-agent argumentation framework to assess the collective decision reached by the agents about the topic under discussion. Interestingly, our aggregation function guarantees the *coherent collective rationality* of the outcome. Besides collective rationality, we show that our aggregation function satisfies further valuable social-choice theoretic properties for the argumentation domain.

Organisation. Sections 2 and 3 characterise and formalise our multi-agent argumentation framework; Sect. 4 details both our decision problem and the desired properties of an aggregation function; Sect. 5 introduces our aggregation function and studies its social-choice properties; and Sect. 6 draws conclusions and plans future research.

2   Characterising a Target-Oriented Discussion Framework

From a general perspective, we envision a setting where some individuals discuss collectively about a given issue or topic (the so-called *target*) with the aim of reaching a consensus on it. Discussion is articulated by means of arguments in favour or against this topic. Thus, we consider an argumentation scenario where participants issue their opinions by labelling such arguments. For explanatory purposes, below we consider that this topic under discussion may well correspond to a norm. Henceforth, we will refer to this setting as a target-oriented argumentation framework (see Sect. 3 for a formal definition). Within this target-oriented argumentation framework, two argument relationships (attack and defence) can be established so that arguments are defined as being in favour of (or against) other arguments. Both relationships are binary, directed and mutually exclusive, and the target is an argument that deserves special attention since it is the only one not defending nor attacking any other argument. Additionally, participants can show that they like or dislike some (not necessarily all) existing arguments. In order to do so, participants assign labels to each argument indicating whether they accept it; reject it; or they abstain from deciding whether to accept or reject it. Thus, participants can also explicitly indicate that they are uncertain about whether they like or dislike an argument. Moreover, we consider that this uncertainty may also capture the fact that a participant may skip providing an opinion (i.e., label) on an argument, which seems to be a suitable feature when dealing with human agents.

Overall, the problem we tackle is that of aggregating all the legitimate and subjective participant's opinions (i.e., labellings) into a single collective one. That will allow us to asses whether the group of participants: accepts the topic under discussion; rejects it; or there is not enough support in favour or against the given target.

However, considering human participants prevents us from requiring rationality, since contradictions or inconsistencies may occur when expressing opinions. In fact, we aim at designing an aggregation function that guarantees some desirable properties so that the outcome does represent the consensus on the topic under discussion. From these properties we highlight that of *coherent labelling*, which intuitively characterises whether an individual exhibits non-contradictory opinions (i.e., labelling). The next section introduces this concept formally and subsequent sections study how our aggregation function results in a single aggregated coherent labelling which also satisfies further desirable properties. Next, we introduce a simple example that will allow us to illustrate some of the presented concepts along the paper.

Example 1 (Flatmates' discussion). *Consider three flatmates (Alan, Bart, and Cathy) discussing about norm (N): "Flatmates take fixed turns for dishwashing at 10 p.m." and issuing the following arguments: $a_1 =$ "10 p.m. is too late and cannot be changed"; $a_2 =$ "Schedule is too rigid"; and $a_3 =$ "Fair distribution". Notice that: arguments a_1 and a_2 attack N whereas a_3 defends it; and a_1 is in favour of a_2. Once all arguments and their relations are clear, flatmates express their opinions by accepting, rejecting (or not opining about) each argument: (1) Alan (Ag_1) gets up early 4 days per week, and so (as first row in Table 1 shows) he rejects norm N and accepts arguments a_1 and a_2. Nevertheless, he acknowledges and acccepts argument a_3. (2) Bart (Ag_2) has spare time at night and is clearly pro norm N. Second row in Table 1 shows he accepts N and a_3, and rejects a_1 and a_2. Finally, (3) Cathy (Ag_3) is keen on routines so she rejects a_2 and accepts N, a_1, and a_3 (see third row in Table 1).*

Therefore, the question that arises is how to aggregate all these opinions so that a consensus is reached over the acceptance (or not) of this dish-washing norm.

3   The Target-Oriented Discussion Framework

The flatmates' discussion illustrates the main elements of our argumentation framework. Within such framework, the norm constitutes the target of a multi-agent argumentation scenario where: (i) a number of arguments are issued; and (ii) participating agents express their opinions about those arguments as well as about the norm under discussion. Additionally, we characterise *coherent* opinions as those not incurring in contradictions. The purpose of this section is to formally capture all these core elements of our argumentation framework. Thus, Sect. 3.1 introduces the *target-oriented discussion framework*, Sect. 3.2 characterises the formal structure of an agent's opinion, and Sect. 3.3 characterises our notion of *coherent* opinion.

Table 1. Flatmates' opinions in the discussion on the dish-washing norm.

3.1   Formalising Our Argumentation Framework

Our purpose is to provide an argumentation framework that allows one to capture both attack and defence relationships between arguments, as done in bipolar argumentation frameworks [3,8].[1] The motivation for including defence relationships is based on recent studies in large-scale argumentation frameworks involving humans (e.g. [12,13]). There, humans naturally handle both attack and defence relationships between arguments. Our notion of *discussion framework* aims at offering such expressiveness.

---

[1] Nevertheless, there are notable differences with bipolar argumentation frameworks. First, bipolar argumentation does not consider labellings (different opinions on arguments), nor their aggregation. Second, bipolar argumentation focuses on studying the structure between arguments and groups of arguments, whereas we focus on computing a collective decision from differing opinions about arguments. Third, arguments in bipolar argumentation can be regarded as objective facts, while in our case, arguments can be subjective facts on which individuals can differ. Thus, our argumentation framework is less restrictive to include humans in the loop.

Definition 1. *A discussion framework is a triple $DF = \langle \mathcal{A}, \mapsto, \Vdash \rangle$, where $\mathcal{A}$ is a finite set of arguments, and $\mapsto \subseteq \mathcal{A} \times \mathcal{A}$ and $\Vdash \subseteq \mathcal{A} \times \mathcal{A}$ stand for attack and defence relationships that are disjoint, namely $\mapsto \cap \Vdash = \emptyset$. We say that an argument $b \in A$ attacks another argument $a \in A$ iff $b \mapsto a$, and that b defends a iff $b \Vdash a$.*

A discussion framework can be depicted as a graph whose nodes stand for arguments and whose edges represent either attack or defence relationships between arguments. Figure 1 shows our graphical representation of attack and defence relationships.

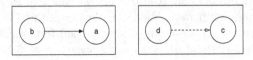

Fig. 1. Representation of an attack relationship $b \mapsto a$ and a defence relationship $d \Vdash c$.

Each argument in a discussion framework can be indirectly related to other arguments through a chain of attack and defence relationships. Given an argument, we capture its indirect relationships with other arguments through the notion of *descendant*.

Definition 2. *Let $DF = \langle \mathcal{A}, \mapsto, \Vdash \rangle$ be a discussion framework and $a \in A$ one of its arguments. We say that an argument $b \in \mathcal{A}$ is a descendant of a if there is a finite subset of arguments $\{c_1, \cdots, c_r\} \subseteq \mathcal{A}$ such that $b = c_1$, $c_1 R_1 c_2$, $\cdots, c_{r-1} R_{r-1} c_r$, $c_r = a$ and $R_i \in \{\mapsto, \Vdash\}$ for all $1 \leq i < r$.*

Now we are ready to define our argumentation framework, the so-called *target-oriented discussion framework*, which considers that there is a target argument (e.g. a norm or a proposal) under discussion.

Definition 3. *A target-oriented discussion framework $TODF = \langle \mathcal{A}, \mapsto, \Vdash, \tau \rangle$ is a discussion framework satisfying the following properties: (i) for every argument $a \in \mathcal{A}$, a is not a descendant of itself; and (ii) there is an argument $\tau \in \mathcal{A}$, called the target, such that for all $a \in \mathcal{A} \setminus \{\tau\}$, a is a descendant of τ.*

Observation 1. *From the previous definitions we infer some properties that help us further characterise a target-oriented discussion framework:*

1. *No reflexivity. No argument can either attack or defend itself. Formally, $\forall a \in \mathcal{A}$, $a \not\mapsto a$ and $a \not\Vdash a$.*
2. *No reciprocity. If an argument a attacks another argument b, then a cannot be attacked nor defended back by b, namely $\forall a, b \in \mathcal{A}$, if $a \mapsto b$ then $b \not\mapsto a$ and $b \not\Vdash a$. Analogously, if an argument a defends another argument b, a cannot be defended nor attacked by b, namely $\forall a, b \in \mathcal{A}$, if $a \Vdash b$ then $b \not\Vdash a$ and $b \not\mapsto a$.*

3. No target contribution. *The target neither attacks nor defends any other argument, namely for all $a \in \mathcal{A} \setminus \{\tau\}$, $\tau \not\mapsto a$ and $\tau \not\Vdash a$. This distinguishes the special role of the target as the center of discussion to which attacks and supports are directly or indirectly pointed.*

The next result follows from Definition 2 and the Observation 1.

Proposition 4. *Let $TODF = \langle \mathcal{A}, \mapsto, \Vdash, \tau \rangle$ be a target-oriented discussion framework and $E =\mapsto \cup \Vdash$. The graph associated to a $TODF$, $G = \langle \mathcal{A}, E \rangle$, is a directed acyclic graph, where $\mathcal{A}$ is the set of nodes and E the edge relationship.*

Proof. Straightforward from Definition 2 and Observation 1.

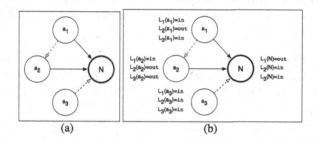

(a)   (b)

Fig. 2. Flatmates example: (a) associated graph to $TODF$; (b) $TODF$ together with labellings.

Example 2 (Flatmates' example formalization). *Figure 2(a) depicts the flatmates' target-oriented discussion framework. The nodes in the graph represent the set of arguments $\mathcal{A} = \{N, a_1, a_2, a_3\}$ in the example of Sect. 2, where N is the dish-washing norm, and a_1, a_2, a_3 are the rest of arguments. Thus, N, the norm under discussion, is taken to be τ in our $TODF$. As to edges, they represent both the attack and defence relationships: $a_1 \mapsto N$, $a_2 \mapsto N$ and $a_1 \Vdash a_2$, $a_3 \Vdash N$ respectively.*

3.2   Argument Labellings

Given a target-oriented argumentation framework shared by agents, now we focus on how these encode their opinions (argument evaluations). Here we consider that each agent's opinion over our argumentation framework corresponds to a *labelling* [6,7]. Furtheremore, we adhere to the labelling-based semantics proposed by Caminada in [6,7], which gives a labelling per argument. By means of argument labellings, each agent can support an argument (by labelling it as *in*), reject it (by labelling it as *out*), or abstain from deciding whether to accept it or reject it (by labelling it as *undec*). Besides expressing uncertainty regading the assessment of an argument, the *undec* label stands for the absence of an opinion. This is important in large-scale argumentation frameworks involving humans. As observed in [12], we cannot expect that humans express their opinions about all the arguments involved in a discussion, since they tend to focus on the arguments of their interest. Formally:

Definition 5 (Argument labelling). *Let $TODF = \langle \mathcal{A}, \mapsto, \Vdash, \tau \rangle$ be a target-oriented discussion framework. An argument labelling for $TODF$ is a function $L : \mathcal{A} \longrightarrow \{\mathtt{in}, \mathtt{out}, \mathtt{undec}\}$ that maps each argument of $\mathcal{A}$ to one out of the following labels:* $\mathtt{in}$ *(accepted),* $\mathtt{out}$ *(rejected), or* $\mathtt{undec}$ *(undecidable).*

We note as $Ag = \{ag_1, \ldots, ag_n\}$ the set of agents taking part in a $TODF$, and as L_i the labelling encoding the opinion of agent $ag_i \in Ag$. We will put together the opinions of all the agents participating in an argumentation as follows.

Definition 6 (Labelling profile). *Let $L_1, \ldots, L_n$ be argument labellings of the agents in Ag, where L_i is the argument labelling of agent ag_i. A labelling profile is a tuple $\mathcal{L} = (L_1, \ldots, L_n)$.*

Example 3 (Flatmates' opinions). *Figure 2(b) graphically depicts Alan's, Barbara's, and Charles' labellings (noted as L_1, L_2, L_3 respectively), each one appearing next to the corresponding arguments in the $TODF$'s graphical representation in Fig. 2(a).*

3.3 Coherent Argument Labellings

As noted in [4], there are multiple reasonable ways in which an agent may evaluate an argument structure through a labelling. There, authors introduce the notion of *complete* labelling[2]. Here we argue that the conditions required by a complete labelling are very restrictive. Instead, we will consider alternative, more relaxed conditions for an argument labelling (an opinion) to be reasonable. With this aim, for each argument a we will compare the labelling over the argument, what we consider to be its *direct opinion*, with the aggregated labellings over its children or immediate descendants, namely, its *indirect opinion*.

Considering the example in Fig. 2(b), if we take any argument, such as for instance N, we consider its associated labels as the direct opinion, whereas we think of the labels associated to its immediate descendants a_1, a_2, and a_3 as its indirect opinion. Analogously, the direct opinion on argument a_2 corresponds to its associated labels, whereas the labels associated to a_1, its single immediate descendant, constitute its indirect opinion.

Thus, informally, we will say that the labelling of an argument is coherent if its direct opinion is in line with its indirect opinion. This will occur when the *majority* of arguments in the indirect opinion of an argument agree with the labelling of the argument. In what follows, we formalise our notion of coherent labelling.

---

[2] A complete labelling requires that: an argument is labelled *in* iff all its defeaters are labelled *out*; and an argument is labelled *out* iff at least one of its defeaters is accepted.

First, given an argument a we will define its set of attacking arguments $A(a) = \{b \in \mathcal{A}|b \mapsto a\}$; and its set of defending arguments $D(a) = \{c \in \mathcal{A}|c \Vdash a\}$. Thus, the labelling of the arguments in $A(a) \cup D(a)$ compose the indirect opinion on a.

Given an argument labelling L and a set of arguments $S \subseteq A$, we can quantify the number of accepted arguments in S as $\mathtt{in}_L(S) = |\{b \in S\ |L(b) = \mathtt{in}\}|$. Analogously, we can also quantify the number of rejected arguments in S as $\mathtt{out}_L(S) = |\{b \in S\ |L(b) = \mathtt{out}\}|$. Thus, given an argument a, we can readily quantify its accepted and rejected defending arguments as $\mathtt{in}_L(D(a))$ and $\mathtt{out}_L(D(a))$ respectively. Moreover, we can also quantify its accepted and rejected attacking arguments as $\mathtt{in}_L(A(a))$ and $\mathtt{out}_L(A(a))$ respectively. Now we are ready to measure the *positive* and *negative support* contained in the indirect opinion of a given argument as follows.

Definition 7 (Positive support). *Let $a \in \mathcal{A}$ be an argument and L a labelling on $\mathcal{A}$. We define the* positive (pro) *support of a as: $Pro_L(a) = \mathtt{in}_L(D(a)) + \mathtt{out}_L(A(a))$. If $Pro_L(a) = |A(a) \cup D(a)|$ we say that a receives* full positive *support from L.*

Definition 8 (Negative support). *Let $a \in \mathcal{A}$ be an argument and L a labelling on $\mathcal{A}$. We define the* negative (con) *support of a as: $Con_L(a) = \mathtt{in}_L(A(a)) + \mathtt{out}_L(D(a))$. If $Con_L(a) = |A(a) \cup D(a)|$ we say that a receives* full negative support *from L.*

Notice that the positive support of an argument combines the strength of its accepted defending arguments with the weakness of its rejected attacking arguments in the argument's indirect opinion. As a dual concept, the negative support combines accepted attacking arguments with rejected defending arguments.

We now introduce our notion of coherence by combining the positive and negative support of an argument. We say that a labelling is coherent if the following conditions hold for each argument: (1) if an argument is labelled accepted (in) then it cannot have more negative than positive support (the majority of its indirect opinion supports the argument); and (2) if an argument is labelled rejected (out) then it cannot have more positive than negative support (the majority of its indirect opinion rejects the argument).

Definition 9 (Coherence). *Given a $TODF = \langle \mathcal{A}, \mapsto, \Vdash, \tau \rangle$, a coherent labelling is a total function $L : \mathcal{A} \to \{\mathtt{in}, \mathtt{out}, \mathtt{undec}\}$ such that for all $a \in \mathcal{A}$ with $A(a) \cup D(a) \neq \emptyset$: (1) if $L(a) = \mathtt{in}$ then $Pro_L(a) \geq Con_L(a)$; and (2) if $L(a) = \mathtt{out}$ then $Pro_L(a) \leq Con_L(a)$.*

Finally, we offer a more refined version of coherence based on the difference between positive and negative supports.

Definition 10 (c-Coherence). *Let $TODF = \langle \mathcal{A}, \mapsto, \Vdash, \tau \rangle$ be a target-oriented discussion framework. A c-coherent labelling for some $c \in \mathbb{N}$ is a total function $L : \mathcal{A} \to \{\mathtt{in}, \mathtt{out}, \mathtt{undec}\}$ such that for all $a \in \mathcal{A}$ with $A(a) \cup D(a) \neq \emptyset$: (i) if $L(a) = \mathtt{in}$*

then $Pro_L(a) > Con_L(a)+c$; (ii) if $L(a) = $ out   then $Pro_L(a)+c < Con_L(a)$; and (iii) if $L(a) = $ undec then $|Pro_L(a) - Con_L(a)| \leq c$.

Let $TODF$ be a target oriented discussion framework. We will note the class of all the argument labellings of $TODF$ as $\mathbf{L}(TODF)$, the subclass of coherent argument labellings as $Coh(TODF)$, and the subclass of c-coherent argument labellings as $Coh_c(TODF)$ for some $c \in \mathbb{N}$.

Example 4. *Again, considering our example, and its labellings from Fig. 2(b) (L_1, L_2, L_3 in $\mathbf{L}(TODF)$), we note that just L_1, L_2 belong to the subclass of its coherent argument labellings $Coh(TODF)$. Moreover, L_1 and L_2 are 0-coherent.*

4   The Aggregation Problem

Recall that our aim is to have multiple agents jointly decide whether to accept a target (e.g. a norm) or not. In Sect. 4.1 we pose such problem as a *judgement aggregation* [14] problem in the context of argumentation: a set of agents collectively decide how to label a target-oriented argumentation framework, and such collective labelling provides a label for the target. Since there are many ways of aggregating labellings, following [4], Sect. 4.2 states that such aggregation must guarantee that the outcome is *fair*.

4.1   Collective Labelling

First, a discussion problem will encompass a target-oriented discussion framework together with a set of agents' individual labellings.

Definition 11 (Labelling discussion problem). *Let $Ag = \{ag_1, \cdots, ag_n\}$ be a finite non-empty set of agents, and $TODF = \langle \mathcal{A}, \mapsto, \Vdash, \tau \rangle$ be a target-oriented discussion framework. A labelling discussion problem is a pair $\mathcal{LDP} = \langle Ag, TODF \rangle$.*

Given an $\mathcal{LDP}$, our aim is to find how to aggregate the individuals' labellings into a single labelling that captures the opinion of the collective.

Definition 12 (Aggregation function). *An aggregation function for a labelling discussion problem $\mathcal{LDP} = \langle Ag, TODF \rangle$ is a function $F : \mathbf{L}(TODF)^n \longrightarrow \mathbf{L}(TODF)$.*

Plainly, an aggregation function F takes a labelling profile representing all agents' opinions and yields a single labelling computed from the individual labellings. Such aggregation function is key to assessing the collective decision over the target.

Definition 13 (Decision over a target). *Let $\mathcal{LDP} = \langle Ag, TODF \rangle$ be a labelling discussion problem, $\mathcal{L}$ a labelling profile, and F an aggregation function for the $\mathcal{LDP}$. The decision over the target of the $TODF$ is the label $F(\mathcal{L})(\tau)$.*

4.2   Desirable Properties of an Aggregation Function

The literature on Social Choice theory has already identified fair ways of aggregating votes. These can be translated into formal properties that an aggregation function is required to satisfy [9]. Based on [4], here we formally state the desirable properties for an aggregation function that allows to assess the decision over the target of a target-oriented discussion framework. First, notice that an aggregation function may not compute over every labelling profile, so we start by referring the domain properties of an aggregate function.

Exhaustive Domain (ED). F can take as input all labelling profiles, i.e., all $\mathcal{L} \in \mathbf{L}(TODF)^n$.

Coherent Domain (CD). F can take as input all the coherent labelling profiles, $\mathcal{L} \in Coh(TODF)^n$.

Furthermore, it is natural to require that aggregation outcomes are also coherent, namely, that the aggregation results in *collective coherence*.

Collective coherence (CC). $F(\mathcal{L}) \in Coh(TODF)$ for all $\mathcal{L} \in \mathbf{L}(TODF)^n$.

Collective coherence is our most desired property. Notice that if an aggregation function does not produce a coherent labelling, there is at least some argument whose collective label (direct opinion) is in contradiction with its indirect opinion. Thus, the resulting aggregation would not be reliable.

Notice also that the agents involved in a discussion expect that their opinions are as important as others'. This idea is captured by the anonymity property, where all opinions are equally significant.

Anonymity (A). If $\mathcal{L} = (L_1, \cdots, L_n)$ is a labelling profile and σ is a permutation over Ag then: if $\mathcal{L}' = (L_{\sigma(1)}, \cdots, L_{\sigma(n)})$ then $F(\mathcal{L}) = F(\mathcal{L}')$.

A weaker version of anonymity, non-dictatorship, states that no agent can decide over the others, like a dictator. Notice that, this directly follows from anonymity.

Non-Dictatorship (ND). There is no agent $ag_i \in Ag$ such that, for every labelling profile $\mathcal{L}$ we have $F(\mathcal{L}) = L_i$.

Regarding unanimity, we shall consider two main notions of unanimity: direct and endorsed. On the one hand, we formulate the *direct unanimity* property to capture the following requirement: if all the agents agree (share the opinion) on one argument, then the aggregate opinion must reflect such agreement.

Direct Unanimity (DU). Let $l \in \{\mathtt{in}, \mathtt{undec}, \mathtt{out}\}$. For each $a \in \mathcal{A}$ such that $L_i(a) = l$ for all $ag_i \in Ag$, then $F(\mathcal{L})(a) = l$.

Endorsed unanimity is a variant of direct unanimity: for each argument, if all the agents agree on the indirect opinion of an argument (be it to give it full positive support or full negative support), this cannot contradict the aggregated opinion on the argument.

Endorsed Unanimity (EU). Let $\mathcal{L}$ be a labelling profile. For each $a \in A$: (i) if a receives full positive support for all $L_i \in \mathcal{L}$ then $F(\mathcal{L})(a) = \text{in}$; and (ii) if a receives full negative support for all $L_i \in \mathcal{L}$ then $F(\mathcal{L})(a) = \text{out}$.

As an additional variant of unanimity, we consider supportiveness: the aggregated opinion on an argument cannot be set to a label $l \in \{\text{in}, \text{out}, \text{undec}\}$ unless at least one agent labels the argument with l.

Supportiveness (S). Let $\mathcal{L}$ be a labelling profile. For all $a \in A$, there exists some agent $ag_i \in Ag$ such that $F(\mathcal{L})(a) = L_i(a)$.

Finally, we state a novel notion of monotonicity, the so-called *familiar monotonicity*, which considers the opinions of an argument's descendants. Intuitively, our notion of familiar monotonicity captures the following principle: if the support for an argument increases, the collective labelling of the argument should remain the same, but provided that the opinions on the argument's descendants do not change. The latter condition is necessary because changes in the opinions about the descendants of the argument may affect the support on the argument. In other words, our notion of monotonicity, unlike the notion of monotonicity presented in [4], is aware of the dependencies between arguments.

We also formulate a weaker version of familiar monotonicity that only applies to in and out.

Familiar Monotonicity (FM). Let $a \in \mathcal{A}$ be an argument and two labelling profiles $\mathcal{L} = (L_1, \cdots, L_i, \cdots, L_{i+k}, \cdots, L_n)$, $\mathcal{L}' = (L_1, \cdots, L_i', \cdots, L_{i+k}', \cdots, L_n)$ such that $F(\mathcal{L})(a) = l \in \{\text{in}, \text{out}, \text{undec}\}$, agents $ag_i, \ldots, ag_{i+k}$ only differing on their labellings of a (namely, for all b descendant of a, $L_j(b) = L_j'(b)$ for every $j \in \{i, \cdots, i+k\}$) and $L(a)_j \neq L'(a)_j = l$ for $j \in \{i, \cdots, i+k\}$, if $F(\mathcal{L})(a) = l$ then $F(\mathcal{L}')(a) = l$.

The next property establishes the same idea considering only the cases where the previous aggregate opinion is either in or out, not undec.

in/out-Familiar Monotonicity (i/o-FM). Let $a \in \mathcal{A}$ be an argument and two labelling profiles $\mathcal{L}$ and $\mathcal{L}'$ satisfying the previous hypothesis of the familiar monotonicity property adding that $F(\mathcal{L})(a) = l \neq \text{undec}$. Then, if $F(\mathcal{L})(a) = l$ then $F(\mathcal{L}')(a) = l$.

Some other properties that are desirable in other multi-agent argumentation contexts (e.g. [4]) are not desirable here. In particular, systematicity and independence are not desirable because we want to exploit dependence relationships between arguments.

5   The Coherent Aggregation Function

Next we define an aggregation function to compute the collective labelling, and hence the decision over a target, for a labelling discussion problem. Section 5.1 introduces our function, while Sect. 5.2 analyses the satisfaction of the properties in Sect. 4.2.

5.1   Defining the Coherent Aggregation Function

First, we introduce notation to quantify the direct positive and negative support of an argument. Let $\mathcal{L} = (L_1, \cdots, L_n)$ be a labelling profile and a an argument. We note the *direct positive support* of a as $\text{in}_{\mathcal{L}}(a) = |\{ag_i \in Ag \,|L_i(a) = \text{in}\}|$; and its *direct negative support* as $\text{out}_{\mathcal{L}}(a) = |\{ag_i \in Ag \,|L_i(a) = \text{out}\}|$. Next, we define our chosen aggregation function: the *coherent aggregation function*. The main purpose of this function is to compute a coherent aggregated labelling, and hence fulfil the collective coherence property. Notice that we consider that the most important desirable property for an aggregation function is to yield a rational outcome that is free of contradiction.

Definition 14 (Coherent aggregation function). *Let $\mathcal{L}$ be a labelling profile. For each argument a the coherent function over $\mathcal{L}$ is defined as:*

$$
CF(\mathcal{L})(a) = \begin{cases} \text{in}, & IO(\mathcal{L})(a) + DO(\mathcal{L})(a) > 0 \\ \text{out}, & IO(\mathcal{L})(a) + DO(\mathcal{L})(a) < 0 \\ \text{undec}, & IO(\mathcal{L})(a) + DO(\mathcal{L})(a) = 0 \end{cases}
$$

where the functions IO (indirect opinion) and DO (direct opinion) are defined as:

$$
IO(\mathcal{L})(a) = \begin{cases} 1, & Pro_{CF(\mathcal{L})}(a) > Con_{CF(\mathcal{L})}(a) \\ 0, & Pro_{CF(\mathcal{L})}(a) = Con_{CF(\mathcal{L})}(a) \\ -1, & Pro_{CF(\mathcal{L})}(a) < Con_{CF(\mathcal{L})}(a) \end{cases}
$$

$$
DO(\mathcal{L})(a) = \begin{cases} 1, & \text{in}_{\mathcal{L}}(a) > \text{out}_{\mathcal{L}}(a) \\ 0, & \text{in}_{\mathcal{L}}(a) = \text{out}_{\mathcal{L}}(a) \\ -1, & \text{in}_{\mathcal{L}}(a) < \text{out}_{\mathcal{L}}(a) \end{cases}
$$

Example 5 (Flatmates' discussion). *Back to our example involving a flatmates' discussion, we use the coherent aggregation function to obtain the aggregated opinion of the provided labellings (see Fig. 2(b)). Figure 3 shows the results of the aggregation and the decision over the target as produced by CF. We observe that the flatmates collectively accept arguments a_1 and a_3, whereas argument a_2 becomes undecidable. Finally, the decision over the norm is to accept it.*

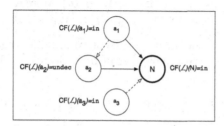

Fig. 3. Flatmates example: aggregated labellings (and decision over target N) computed by *CF*.

5.2   Analysing the Coherent Aggregation Function

Below we analyse the desired properties from Sect. 4.2 that our aggregation function CF fulfils.

The first two results about domain properties follow from CF's definition.

Proposition 15. *CF satisfies the exhaustive domain property.*

Corollary 16. *CF satisfies the coherent domain property.*

Proof. It is clear that CF is defined for all labelling profiles, and hence it is also defined for every coherent labelling $\mathcal{L} \in Coh(TODF)^n$.

Notice that, since CF is defined for all labelling profiles, it is also defined for labelling profiles in $Coh_c(TODF)^n$, namely for labelling profiles whose argument labellings are c-coherent. Now recall that we designed our CF function to satisfy the collective coherence property. Thus, the following property naturally follows.

Proposition 17. *CF satisfies the collective coherence property.*

Proof. Let a be an argument such that $CF(\mathcal{L})(a) = \mathsf{in}$. From Definition 14 we know that $IO(\mathcal{L})(a) + DO(\mathcal{L})(a) > 0$. Thus, there are three possibilities: (i) $DO(\mathcal{L})(a) = 1$ and $IO(\mathcal{L})(a) = 1$; (ii) $DO(\mathcal{L})(a) = 1$ and $IO(\mathcal{L})(a) = 0$; or (iii) $IO(\mathcal{L})(a) = 0$ and $DO(\mathcal{L})(a) = 1$. Since $IO(\mathcal{L})(a) \geq 0$ in all cases, this implies that $Pro_{CF(\mathcal{L})}(a) \geq Con_{CF(\mathcal{L})}(a)$, and hence CF satisfies the coherence property. The proof goes analogously for the case $CF(\mathcal{L})(a) = \mathsf{out}$.

Now we turn our attention into the anonymity property and its weaker version: the non-dictatorship property.

Proposition 18. *CF satisfies the anonymity property.*

Proof. Let $\mathcal{L} = (L_1, \cdots, L_n)$ be a labelling profile and σ a permutation over Ag such that $\mathcal{L}' = (L_{\sigma(1)}, \cdots, L_{\sigma(n)})$. Since CF only uses the number of elements, there is no dependency on the identities of the agents' labellings. We only have to check that $DO(\mathcal{L}) = DO(\mathcal{L}')$ because functions IO, Pro, and Con only depend on $CF(\mathcal{L})$, and hence in turn they will not depend either on the identities of the agents' labellings. This amounts to checking whether $\mathsf{in}_{\mathcal{L}}(a) = \mathsf{in}_{\sigma(\mathcal{L})}(a)$ and $\mathsf{out}_{\mathcal{L}}(a) = \mathsf{out}_{\sigma(\mathcal{L})}(a)$ hold. Indeed, on the one hand $\mathsf{in}_{\mathcal{L}}(a) = |\{ag_i \in Ag \,|\, L_i(a) = \mathsf{in}\}| = |\{\sigma(ag_i) \in Ag \,|\, L_{\sigma(i)}(a) = \mathsf{in}\}| = \mathsf{in}_{\sigma(\mathcal{L})}(a)$. Moreover, $\mathsf{out}_{\mathcal{L}}(a) = |\{ag_i \in Ag \,|\, L_i(a) = \mathsf{out}\}| = |\{\sigma(ag_i) \in Ag \,|\, L_{\sigma(i)}(a) = \mathsf{out}\}| = \mathsf{out}_{\sigma(\mathcal{L})}(a)$.

Since CF satisfies anonymity, the identity of which agent submits which labelling is irrelevant. Furthermore, recall from Sect. 4.2 that non-dictatorship follows.

Corollary 19. *CF satisfies the non-dictatorship property.*

Next, we focus on unanimity properties. First, we will show that CF fulfils the endorsed unanimity property. With this aim, we will introduce an additional hypothesis based on the following lemma.

Lemma 1. *Let $TODF$ be a target-oriented discussion framework, $\mathcal{L}$ a 0-coherent labelling profile ($\mathcal{L} \in Coh_0(TODF)^n$), a an argument in $\mathcal{A}$, and m the number of immediate descendants of a ($m = |A(a) \cup D(a)|$). If $Pro_{L_i}(a) = m$ for all $i \in \{1, \cdots, n\}$ then $in_{\mathcal{L}}(a) = n$; and if $Con_{L_i}(a) = m$ for all $i \in \{1, \cdots, n\}$ then $out_{\mathcal{L}}(a) = n$.*

Proof. We next prove that if $Pro_{L_i}(a) = m$ then $L_i(a) = in$, for all $i \in \{1, \cdots, n\}$. Thus, all the agents label argument a as in, i.e., $in_{\mathcal{L}}(a) = n$. Since we assume that each L_i is 0-coherent, a's label can be neither out, because $Pro_{L_i}(a) \nleq Con_{L_i}(a)$, nor $undec$, because $Pro_{L_i}(a) \neq Con_{L_i}(a)$. Thus, the only option is that a is labelled as in. The proof runs analogously when considering the case $Con_{L_i}(a) = m$. $\square$

Plainly, the lemma says that, when assuming 0-coherence, if the indirect opinion on an argument is unanimous, the direct opinion on the argument will also be unanimous. Using this lemma we can prove the following result.

Proposition 20. *Let $\mathcal{L} = (L_1, \cdots, L_n)$ be a labelling profile. If every L_i, $i \in \{1, \cdots, n\}$, satisfies the 0-coherence property, then CF satisfies the endorsed unanimity property.*

Proof. We focus on the case for which if each argument a receives full positive support for all $L_i \in \mathcal{L}$, namely $Pro_{L_i}(a) = m$ for every i, then $CF(\mathcal{L})(a) = in$. First of all, we will analyse the aggregated indirect opinion on a given argument a. Let b be a defending argument of a, namely $b \in D(a)$. Since $Pro_{L_i}(a) = m$ for all i, $L_i(b) = in$. Since we do not know the labellings of the immediate descendants of b, we can assume that $DO(\mathcal{L})(b) = 1$, and therefore either $CF(\mathcal{L})(b) = undec$ or $CF(\mathcal{L})(b) = in$. Following a similar reasoning, we observe that if $b \in A(a)$, then either $CF(\mathcal{L})(b) = undec$ or $CF(\mathcal{L})(b) = out$. Therefore, we have that $IO(\mathcal{L})(a) \geq 0$. Because $Pro_{L_i}(a) = m$ and L_i is 0-coherent for every agent ag_i, we have that $n = in_{\mathcal{L}}(a) > out_{\mathcal{L}}(a) = 0$ by Lemma 1, and hence $DO(\mathcal{L})(a) = 1$. Since $IO(\mathcal{L})(a) \geq 0$, we finally have that $CF(\mathcal{L})(a) = in$. Analogously, we can also prove that $CF(\mathcal{L})(a) = out$ if $Con_{L_i}(a) = m$ for every $ag_i \in Ag$. $\square$

Notice however that CF does not satisfy the other two unanimity properties presented in Sect. 4.2, namely direct unanimity and supportiveness.

Proposition 21. *Neither direct unanimity nor supportiveness are satisfied by CF.*

Proof. Figure 4(a) graphically represents a $TODF$ that will serve to illustrate our proposition. Our $TODF$ contains a target argument $\tau = a$, which is defended by five other arguments $\{a_1, a_2, a_3, a_4, a_5\}$. The $TODF$ involves the argument labellings of three agents, noted as L_1, L_2, and L_3: (1) agent 1 accepts (labels with in) arguments a, a_1, a_2, and a_3, and refuses (labels with out) arguments a_4 and a_5; (2) Agent 2 accepts arguments a, a_1, a_2, and a_4, and rejects arguments a_3, and a_5; and agent 3 accepts arguments a, a_1, a_2, and a_5, and rejects arguments a_3, and a_4.

Notice that the three agents agree on accepting the target ($L_1(a) =$ in, $L_2(a) =$ in, and $L_3(a) =$ in), and hence there is unanimous opinion on a.

Figure 4(b) depicts the resulting labelling when computing the CF function for this $TODF$ over the labelling profile $\mathcal{L} = (L_1, L_2, L_3)$. Since arguments a_1 and a_2 are collectively accepted ($CF(\mathcal{L})(a_1) =$ in, $CF(\mathcal{L})(a_2) =$ in) and arguments a_3, a_4, and a_5 are rejected ($CF(\mathcal{L})(a_3) =$ out, $CF(\mathcal{L})(a_4) =$ out, $CF(\mathcal{L})(a_5) =$ out), the target is neither accepted nor rejected ($CF(\mathcal{L})(a) =$ undec). Thus, although the three agents agree on accepting a, the collective decision obtained by CF is undec. Therefore, CF does not satisfy direct unanimity.

As to supportiveness, it does not hold either. Observe that although the aggregate label of a is undec, no agent has labelled argument a as undec.

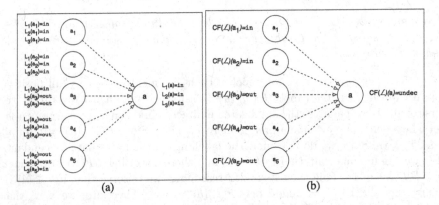

(a)   (b)

Fig. 4. Counterexamples to illustrate lack of: (a) direct unanimity and supportiveness (argument labellings); (b) direct unanimity and supportiveness (result of the coherent aggregation function).

Finally, we study CF's monotonicity. Although familiar monotonicity does not hold for CF, its weaker version, in/out-familiar, does hold.

Proposition 22. *CF does not satisfy the familiar monotonicity property.*

Proof. Our proof only requires a simple $TODF$ with a target argument a and two labelling profiles with two argument labellings. Let $\mathcal{L} = (L_1, L_2)$ and $\mathcal{L}' = (L_1, L_2')$ where $L_1(a) =$ in, $L_2(a) =$ out and $L_2'(a) =$ undec. These two labelling profiles satisfy the hypothesis required by the familiar monotonicity property. Nonetheless, notice now that the aggregate labellings on the target obtained for each labelling are: $CF_{\mathcal{L}}(a) = \texttt{undec}$ and $CF_{\mathcal{L}'}(a) = \texttt{in}$. Since $CF_{\mathcal{L}}(a) \neq CF_{\mathcal{L}'}(a)$, familiar monotonicity does not hold.

Proposition 23. *CF satisfies the* in/out*-familiar monotonicity property.*

Proof. Let $\mathcal{L}, \mathcal{L}'$ be two labelling profiles satisfying the hypothesis required by the in/out-familiar monotonicity property on the argument a, and whose collective label on a for $\mathcal{L}$ is $CF(\mathcal{L})(a) = l = \texttt{in}$. Since $L_j(b) = L'_j(b)$ for all b descendant of a, we know that $IO(\mathcal{L})(a) = IO(\mathcal{L}')(a)$ because IO only depends on the descendants. Since $CF(\mathcal{L})(a) = \texttt{in}$, we have that $DO(\mathcal{L})(a) \geq 0$. Now, because $\texttt{in}_{\mathcal{L}}(a) \leq \texttt{in}_{\mathcal{L}'}(a)$ and $\texttt{out}_{\mathcal{L}}(a) \geq \texttt{out}_{\mathcal{L}'}(a)$, we know that $DO(\mathcal{L}')(a) \geq DO(\mathcal{L})(a) \geq 0$. From this follows that $DO(\mathcal{L}')(a) + IO(\mathcal{L})(a) \geq DO(\mathcal{L}')(a) + IO(\mathcal{L})(a) = 1$, and hence $CF(\mathcal{L}')(a) = \texttt{in}$. We can analogously check the case $CF(\mathcal{L})(a) = \texttt{out}$. $\square$

Analysis. First, notice that CF satisfies a significant number of the desirable properties identified in Sect. 4.2 for *any* sort of labelling profiles. This means that CF does not constrain at all an agent's labelling, and hence even can cope with the inconsistencies of agents' opinions. This is not the case though for endorsed unanimty. This property is constrained to labellings that are 0-coherent. Second, properties such as direct unanimity and supportiveness, which are not satisfied by CF, assume that aggregation is computed independently for each argument. In other words, they serve to analyse the behaviour of an aggregation function in a single argument. Since in this paper we pursue to exploit dependencies between arguments within a discussion, such properties prevent us from making a more informed decision about the discussion target.

5.3   Computing the Decision over a Target

Given a target-oriented discussion framework $TODF = \langle \mathcal{A}, \mapsto, \Vdash, \tau \rangle$ shared by the agents in Ag, a labelling profile $\mathcal{L}$, and our coherent aggregation function CF, we now consider how to compute the collective label assigned to the target τ, namely $CF(\mathcal{L})(\tau)$. Such computation is based on the following observation:

Since the graph associated to a target-oriented discussion framework $TODF$ is a directed acyclic graph (DAG), we can embed the computation of the collective label of each argument in $\mathcal{A}$ within its the traversal. of its associated graph. Such a graph traversal could be performed by its topological sorting [11]. Therefore, the running time required to compute $CF(\mathcal{L})(\tau)$ is linear in the number of arguments plus the number of edges, asymptotically, namely $O(|\mathcal{A}| + |\mapsto| + |\Vdash|)$. Algorithm 1 shows the pseudo-code of function COMPUTETARGETDECISION, which returns the collective label of target τ for an input graph G_{TODF} and a labelling profile $\mathcal{L}$.

Algorithm 1. Algorithm to compute the collective label of a target

---

1: **function** COMPUTETARGETDECISION($G_{TODF}, \mathcal{L}, \tau$)
2:     $ToVisit \leftarrow \{a \in A | A(a) \cup D(a) = \emptyset\}$ ▷ Arguments with neither attacks nor defences (no descendants)
3:     **while** $ToVisit \neq \emptyset$ **do**
4:         remove an argument b from $ToVisit$
5:         compute $CF(\mathcal{L})(b)$
6:         **for** each node c with an edge $(b, c) \in G_{TODF}$ **do**
7:             remove edge (b, c) from graph G_{TODF}
8:             **if** c has no other incoming edges **then**
9:                 insert c into $ToVisit$
10:    **return** $CF(\mathcal{L})(\tau)$ ▷ Return collective label for target τ

---

6   Conclusions and Future Work

Along this paper we have formalised the problem of taking a collective decision over a target. We claim this problem can be tackled within a target oriented decision framework, and we have tailored it for humans, due to the increasing interest on e-participation, e-governance and open innovation systems. Within this framework, we have also proposed a coherent aggregation function that combines participants' opinions and has proven to satisfy valuable social choice properties without any additional assumption (with the exception of endorsed unanimity, which just requires the labelling profile to be 0-coherent). When considering humans, we hypothesise that the larger the number of people, the less the number of undecidable labels will result from combining their opinions, and thus, the less unlikely will be the occurrence of an undecidable outcome (i.e., a target collective decision).

Finally, notice that although our argumentation framework shares the use of attack and defense relations with bipolar argumentation frameworks [3,8], there are notable differences. First, bipolar argumentation does not consider labellings (different opinions on arguments), neither their aggregation. Second, bipolar argumentation focuses on studying the structure between arguments and groups of arguments, whereas we focus on computing a collective decision from differing opinions about arguments. Third, arguments in bipolar argumentation can be regarded as objective facts, while in our case, arguments can be subjective facts on which individuals can differ. Thus, our argumentation framework pursues to be less restrictive to include humans in the loop.

As to future work, we plan to consider alternative semantics for arguments' pros and cons that diminish the relevance associated to the rejection of arguments. Furthermore, we plan to extend our TODF to allow loops, and hence ease rebuttal, a common feature of argumentation systems. Finally, we plan to provide more fine-grained means of computing argument support.

References

1. City of Barcelona participation portal (2016). https://decidim.barcelona
2. City of Reykjavík participation portal (2016). http://reykjavik.is/en/participation
3. Amgoud, L., Cayrol, C., Lagasquie-Schiex, M.-C., Livet, P.: On bipolarity in argumentation frameworks. Int. J. Intell. Syst. **23**(10), 1062–1093 (2008)
4. Awad, E., Booth, R., Tohmé, F., Rahwan, I.: Judgement aggregation in multi-agent argumentation. J. Logic Comput. **27**(1), 227–259 (2017)
5. Bench-Capon, T.J.M., Dunne, P.E.: Argumentation in artificial intelligence. Artif. Intell. **171**(10–15), 619–641 (2007)
6. Caminada, M.: On the issue of reinstatement in argumentation. In: Fisher, M., Hoek, W., Konev, B., Lisitsa, A. (eds.) JELIA 2006. LNCS (LNAI), vol. 4160, pp. 111–123. Springer, Heidelberg (2006). doi:10.1007/11853886_11
7. Caminada, M.W.A., Dov, M.G.: A logical account of formal argumentation. Studia Logica **93**(2–3), 109–145 (2009)
8. Cayrol, C., Lagasquie-Schiex, M.C.: On the acceptability of arguments in bipolar argumentation frameworks. In: Godo, L. (ed.) ECSQARU 2005. LNCS (LNAI), vol. 3571, pp. 378–389. Springer, Heidelberg (2005). doi:10.1007/11518655_33
9. Dietrich, F.: A generalised model of judgment aggregation. Soc. Choice Welfare **28**(4), 529–565 (2007)
10. Gabbriellini, S., Torroni, P.: Microdebates: structuring debates without a structuring tool1. AI Commun. **29**(1), 31–51 (2015)
11. Kahn, A.B.: Topological sorting of large networks. Commun. ACM **5**(11), 558–562 (1962)
12. Klein, M.: Enabling large-scale deliberation using attention-mediation metrics. Comput. Support. Coop. Work (CSCW) **21**(4–5), 449–473 (2012)
13. Klein, M., Convertino, G.: A roadmap for open innovation systems. J. Soc. Media Organ. **2**(1), 1 (2015)
14. List, C., Pettit, P.: Aggregating sets of judgments: an impossibility result. Econ. Philos. **18**(01), 89–110 (2002)
15. Rahwan, I., Simari, G.R., Benthem, J.: Argumentation in Artificial Intelligence, vol. 47. Springer, USA (2009)
16. Weerakkody, V., Reddick, C.G.: Public sector transformation through e-government: experiences from Europe and North America. Routledge (2012)

Human-Computer Agent Negotiation Using Cross Culture Reliability Models

Galit Haim[(✉)], Dor Nisim, and Marian Tsatkin

The College of Management Academic Studies, Rishon Lezion, Israel
haimgalit1@gmail.com, nisimdor@gmail.com, marian.ts91@gmail.com

Abstract. People's cultural background has been shown to affect the way they reach agreements in negotiation and how they fulfill these agreements. This paper presents a novel methodology that can be used as a good infrastructure to design a computer-agent for negotiating with people from different cultures. Our setting involved data from different agents and human versus human data that were based on an alternating-offer protocol that allowed parties to choose the extent to which they kept each of their agreements during the negotiation. A challenge to develop this methodology for such setting is to create cross culture models automatically that will predict how people reciprocate their actions over time, despite the scarcity of prior data on different cultures. Our methodology addresses this challenge by using a Leave-One-Out algorithm named CCMA, which is described in Sect. 5, with classical machine learning algorithms to predict the extent to which people fulfill agreements. Our methodology based its strategy on a data from different agents that used the same negotiation scenario in different cultures. This methodology used data in three countries: Lebanon, the U.S.A and Israel, in which people are known to vary widely in their negotiation behaviour. Our methodology was able to find the accurate models that should be used when designing a computer-agent in the negotiation scenario.

1 Introduction

Negotiation is a tool widely used by humans to resolve disputes in settings as diverse as business transactions, diplomacy and personal relationships. Many tasks in day-to-day life require negotiation. Negotiation can be as simple and ordinary as haggling over a price in the market, through deciding what show to watch on TV, booking a trip [21], bargaining over certain issues [1,5,6,15], in e-commerce [17,19] and it can also involve tasks in which millions of lives are at stake, such as resource allocation [4], countries' disputes [13] and dismantling of nuclear weapons.

Building an automated computer negotiation agent that can perform as one of the parties in the negotiation, or even both, by making rational choices and decisions is an important task. Computer agents can negotiate on behalf of individual people or organizations(e.g., bidders in on-line auctions [2,14]); they can act as training tools for people to practice and evaluate different negotiation strategies in a lab setting prior to embarking on negotiation in the real

© Springer International Publishing AG 2017
R. Aydoğan et al. (Eds.): COREDEMA 2016, LNAI 10238, pp. 118–133, 2017.
DOI: 10.1007/978-3-319-57285-7_8

world (e.g., agents for negotiating in a simulated diplomatic crisis [16]), or work autonomously to reach agreements for which they are responsible (e.g., computer games, systems for natural disaster relief [18,22]). Using such an agent may help reach agreements that are the best for all sides involved, and which might not have been accepted without the existence of the agent.

Culture is a key determinant of the way people interact and reach agreements in different social settings. It is thus important to understand the decision-making strategies that people of different cultures deploy when computer systems are among the members of the groups in which they work and to determine their response to different kinds of decision-making behavior of others [7].

There is a body of work in the psychological and social sciences that investigate cross cultural behavior among human negotiators [9,10]. However, there is scant computational models of human negotiation behavior that reason about cultural differences. In this paper, we investigate, the hypothesis that explicitly representing behavioral traits which vary across cross cultures will improve the ability of computer agents to predict human negotiation behaviour, and in turn, improve the performance of computer agents when negotiating with people. To evaluate this hypothesis, Haim et al. [12] collected data on human negotiation behavior from three different countries, including Israel, Lebanon and the U.S.A. This data was collected from different computer-agents that used an identical negotiation scenario in each country that required that people complete a task by engaging in bilateral negotiation rounds. The negotiation protocol included alternating take-it-or-leave-it offers for the exchange of resources. Participants were free to choose the extent to which they fulfilled their commitments. Such settings characterize the real-world applications discussed above, where participants make commitments to purchase items or carry out tasks, and they can choose whether and how to fulfill such commitments. These decisions affect their future interactions with the other participants. For example, a seller who is late in delivering an item or does not deliver it at all, may be negatively reciprocated by the buyer in a future transaction.

Haim et al. [12] developed a specific model for each country and for each game configuration for all the prediction models that were used in their agent. For example, when their agent played with an Israeli human player, it used specific models that were trained on the data that was collected from human versus human and human versus another agent from Israel. Similarly, when their agent played with a human player from U.S.A, it used models from U.S.A and so on.

The challenge of this paper is to improve the models that were used in the previous agents. In order to address this challenge we will examine the notion of using data from various cultures to train a future agent. The process of choosing the best model is determined upon the data set and machine learning algorithm that the model will be based upon. In this paper, we present a methodology that finds the best prediction model for a given culture automatically. The results from using that methodology will later contribute to the construction of an agent which addresses various cultures.

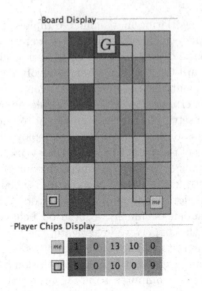

2   The Colored Trails Negotiation Scenario

In this section we present the Colored Trails negotiation scenario that was used in all the given data. The used CT configuration consisted of a game played on a 7×5 board of colored squares with a set of chips. One square on the board was designated as the goal square. Each player's icon was initially located in one of the non-goal positions, eight steps away from the goal square. To move to an adjacent square a player needed to surrender a chip in the color of that square. Each player was issued 24 colored chips at the onset of the game.

At the onset of the game, one of the players was given the role of proposer, while the other was given the role of the responder. The interaction proceeded in a recurring sequence of phases. In the communication the proposer could make an offer to the responder, who could accept or reject the offer. In the transfer phase, both players could choose chips to transfer to each other. The transfer action was done simultaneously, such that neither player could see what the other player transferred until the end of the phase. In particular, players were not required to fulfill their commitments to an agreement reached in the communication phase. A player could choose to transfer more chips than it agreed to, or any subset of the chips it agreed to, including transferring no chips at all. In the movement phase, players could manually move their icons on the board across one square by surrendering a chip in the color of that square. At the end of the movement phase, a new communication phase began. The players alternated their roles, such that the previous proposer was designated as a responder, and vice verse. These phases repeated until the game ended. Note that players had full view of the board and each others chips, and thus they had complete knowledge of the game situation at all times during the negotiation process.

2.1 Game Termination and Scoring

The game ends when one of the following conditions holds: (1) at least one of the participants reached the goal square; or (2) at least one of the participants remained dormant and did not move for three movement phases. When the game ends, both participants are automatically moved as close as possible to the goal square, and their score is computed as follows:

- 100 bonus points are awarded for reaching the goal square,
- 5 bonus points for any chip left in a player's possession,
- a 10 point penalty is imposed for each square left in the path from a player's final position to the goal square.

These parameters were chosen so that reaching the goal would be considered by far the most important component, but if a player could not reach the goal, it was preferable to get as close to the goal as possible. Note that the score in CT depends not only on whether a player can reach the goal square, but also on the number of chips the player has in its possession at the end of the game.

3 The Cultural Sensitive Data

In this paper, we used four sources of data to train and test our methodology. These sources were taken from the collected data within the paper of Haim et al. [12]. The four sources of data are described as follows:

3.1 The Human Versus Human Data

In the U.S.A and in Israel, we used the 112 collected data of game instances of people playing other people in the identical CT negotiation scenario.

3.2 The Purb Agent

Purb is the Personality Utility and Rule Based agent developed by Gal et al. [11], that modelled other participants in terms of two behavioural traits: helpfulness, and reliability. The helpfulness measure of a participant represented the extent to which the participant shared resources with its negotiation partner through initiating and agreeing to proposals. The reliability of a participant is the degree to which the participant kept commitments to its negotiation partner. Purb's decision-making paradigm was a set of rules that narrowed the search space of possible actions to be considered by the agent's utility function. These rules depended on aspects relating to the state of the game (e.g., the number of chips each agent had, whether a participant can independently reach the goal). At each step of the game, the agent used its social utility function to choose the best action from the set of possible actions that were constrained by the rules. The rules were designed such that the Purb agent begins by acting reliably, and adapts over time to the individual measure of cooperativeness that is exhibited by its negotiation partner. The collected data from Purb includes 222 game instances consisting of people playing the Purb agent.

3.3   The Nasty Agent

In Lebanon, Haim et al. [12] built a model of a human based on data collected, and found that the probability of the human to fulfill the agreement is very high regardless of the agents' behavior. Therefore, in order to enrich the model with another behavior, in Lebanon, Haim et al. [12] collected 64 additional games in which people played against a NASTY agent, which was a variant of the PURB agent used by Haim et al. [11], but programmed to be significantly less reliable when fulfilling its agreement. Consequently, Haim et al. were able to collect data on peoples reactions to more diverse negotiation behavior in the game. It was not necessary to run the Nasty agent in Israel or in the USA, since we already had a diversity of data in these countries.

3.4   The PAL Agent

PAL is the Personality Adaptive Learning agent developed by Haim et al. [12]. It used machine learning strategy to take his decision actions in the negotiation game. The PAL agent was based on learning and adaptation. This agent used predictive models of human negotiation behaviour, to predict the extent to which a person was reliable in the negotiation (also named as Transfer model), i.e., whether the person fulfill the agreement within the negotiation or not.

PAL used a specific model for each country and for each game configuration for all the prediction models. For example, when PAL played a co-dependent board configuration with an Israeli human player, it used the models that were trained on the data of the co-dependent board configuration that were collected from human versus human and human versus the Purb agent from Israel.

To evaluate PAL they recruited 157 subjects from the three countries. These subjects played identical CT negotiation scenario of human negotiation behaviour under laboratory conditions in different countries.

4   Cross Cultures Features Set

In this paper, we reconsidered the prediction-model question and investigate the possibility of using all the data available hitherto with additional feature sets, to determine automatically the type of data that is useful when building prediction models of people from different cultures in the CT game.

Haim et al. [12] used some features in order to build a specific model for a specific CT configuration a specific country. These features do not reflect the behavior of a human in previous rounds of the game. Therefore, we combine new features set with the old ones, that will include the behavior of a human in previous rounds. The features that Haim et al. [12] used in their paper are the baseline for our feature set.

4.1 The Baseline Features

- The current round n.
- The current score for a player round n.
- The resulting score of a player given proposal at round n.
- The score-base-reliability of a player at round n.
- The weighted score-base-reliability of a player.
- The generosity of a player at round n.
- The dependency role of a player at round n, task independent or task dependent. Task dependent means one player needs the chips of the other player in order to reach the goal. Task independent means one player can reach the goal without any help of the other player.
- Missing chips: this feature includes the total number of chips a player needs to reach its goal given its position on the board at round n.

4.2 The New Cross Cultures Feature Set

The new features that we used in our paper in addition to the baseline features are as follows:

- *Country*: this parameter indicates what is the source of the data: ISRAEL, LEBANON or U.S.A.
- *data type*: this parameter indicates what is the type of the data. The options are:
  - **HvsH:** relates to games in which both players are human. HvsH games were played only in Israel and the U.S.A.
  - **HvsPurb:** relates to games that were played with the Purb agent.
  - **HvsNasty:** relates to games that were played with the Nasty agent. HvsNasty games were played only in Lebanon in order to see the way people in Lebanon play with an agent that is not always reliable. This was done in order to increase the data in Lebanon and to see different behavior of the Lebanese people. This agent was not running in Israel neither in the U.S.A since this kind of data and human behavior were already given in the HvsH games.
  - **HvsPAL:** relates to those games that were played with the PAL agent.
- *board type*: this parameter indicates the board type data. The options are:
  - **BOTH-DD:** refers to games in which an agent played with a human in a co-dependent board, i.e., both players depends on each other in reaching the goal.
  - **GUI-TI:** refers to games in which an agent played with a human in a dependent board, but the human player was the task-independent, i.e., the human had all the chips needed to reach the goal while the agent did not have the chips to reach the goal.
  - **AGENT-TI:** refers to games in which an agent played with a human in a dependent board, but the agent player was the task-independent, i.e., the agent had all the chips needed to reach the goal while the human did not have the chips to reach the goal.

- **TI-TD:** refers to human versus human games in which one side was task-independent and the other human player was task-dependent.
- *dormant*: for each player in the game, this parameter indicates the number of consecutive rounds the player did not move.
- *isFirstProposal*: indicates whether the proposal is the first proposal in the game.
- *firstAcceptedProposal*: indicates whether the proposal is the first proposal in the game that was accepted.
- *originalDependency*: indicates the task dependency of each player at the beginning of the game, which was one of the options: task-dependent or task-independent.
- *resultingDependency*: indicates the task dependency of each player at round n+1 assuming the offer is fulfilled. The options are: task-dependent or task-independent.
- *prevFullTransfer*: for each player, this parameter indicates whether the previous proposal in round n−1 the player fulfilled the agreement or not.
- *prevPartialTransfer*: for each player, this parameter indicates whether the previous proposal in round n−1 the player at least partially fulfilled the agreement or not.
- *sentOnceFullTransfer*: for each player, this parameter indicates whether at least one of the previous proposals within the game, the player fulfilled the agreement.
- *sentOncePartialTransfer*: for each player, this parameter indicates whether at least in one of the previous proposals within the game, the player partially fulfilled the agreement or not.

5   The CCMA

The purpose of our research is to create a novel methodology that will automate the process of building a learning model from available data using machine learning algorithms. The machine learning algorithms will be chosen automatically, out of four potential algorithms, by comparing the performance on the available data. In this section we present the CCMA, i.e., Cross Culture Methodology Algorithm. The CCMA evaluates and compares learning algorithms using the Leave-One-Out strategy. The reason for using the Leave-One-Out technique is to examine a model's prediction accuracy based on a single game instance. The more game instances a model is tested upon, the more reliable a model's predication accuracy is. The Leave-One-Out strategy first partitions the data into k instances. Subsequently k iterations of training and validation are performed such that nearly all the data except for a single instance is used for training and the model is tested on that single instance. According to the paper by Efron [3] the accuracy that is obtained from using this strategy is known to be almost unbiased. In the CCMA we have selected four algorithms to use in order to determine models for predication: J48, RepTree, Naive Bayes and Multilayer Perceptron (Sigmoid). The reason for using only four algorithms is due to the fact that there are many machine learning algorithms, and the process of running the CCMA has its overhead, and thus only four common algorithms were chosen. Moreover, the reason for not choosing a single algorithm is due the fact that each algorithm builds a different model. Thus in some situations one algorithm is preferable than the other based on the prediction accuracy. These algorithms are known as machine learning algorithms that can give a probability of predication [8,20,24]. The J48 algorithm is used to generate a decision tree. The decision tree can be used for classification, and for this reason, J48 is often referred to as a statistical classifier. According to *"Top 10 algorithms in data mining"* paper [23] The J48 algorithm was ranked the first. The RepTree algorithm is a fast decision tree learner. It builds a decision/regression tree using information gain/variance and prunes it using reduced-error pruning (with back-fitting). The Naive Bayes is an algorithm from a family of simple probabilistic classifiers based on applying Bayes' theorem with strong (naive) independence assumptions between the features. The Sigmoid algorithm is a feed-forward artificial neural network model that maps sets of input data into a set of appropriate outputs. In order to build the aforementioned learning models we used the Weka framework, which is a toolkit containing machine learning algorithms for data mining tasks.[1]

5.1   Implementation

As opposed to manually determine learning models for prediction, based on trial and error, the CCMA automates the process of building a learning model from available data using a machine learning algorithm that will yield the best predication. Before describing the CCMA methodology, we make the following definitions. The *Source set*, denoted S, composed of game instances, as described in Sect. 3, will be used to test a given model. Let S_i denote the current game instance used for testing. The *Integrated set*, denoted T, composed of game instances, as described in Sect. 3, will be used to build the learning model. The *local set* for game instance i, denoted L_i, is a data set composed from the *Source set*, excluding S_i, as defined below.

$$L_i = (S \backslash \{S_i\}) \tag{1}$$

The *local model* for game instance i, denoted L_i^{mod}, is a model based on the *local set* for game instance i, L_i, with a given algorithm.

The *cross culture set* for game instance i, denoted C_i, is a data set composed from the *local set*, L_i and the *Integrated set*, as defined below.

$$C_i = L_i \cup T \tag{2}$$

The *cross culture model* for game instance i, denoted C_i^{mod}, is a model based upon the *cross culture set* for game instance i, C_i, with a given algorithm.

The *cross culture algorithm*, denoted C^{alg}, is the algorithm that will yield the best prediction when based upon the *cross culture model*.

---

[1] http://www.cs.waikato.ac.nz/ml/weka/.

The *local algorithm*, denoted L^{alg}, is the algorithm that will yield the best prediction when based upon the *local model*.

The *local average*, denoted $L_{avg}[alg]$, is the averaged prediction for the *local model* based upon the *alg* algorithm.

The *cross culture average*, denoted $C_{avg}[alg]$, is the averaged prediction for the *cross culture model* based upon the *alg* algorithm.

CCMA(S, T)

1. for each *alg* do
   (a) for S_i in S
       i. $L_i = S \backslash \{S_i\}$
       ii. $C_i = L_i \cup T$
       iii. $L_i^{mod} = $ buildModel(alg, L_i)
       iv. $C_i^{mod} = $ buildModel(alg, C_i)
       v. $L_{avg}[alg]$ += checkPrediction(alg, L_i^{mod}, S_i)
       vi. $C_{avg}[alg]$ += checkPrediction(alg, C_i^{mod}, S_i)
2. $L^{alg} = \max_{alg}\{L_{avg}[alg]\}$
3. $C^{alg} = \max_{alg}\{C_{avg}[alg]\}$
4. return L^{alg}, C^{alg}

Following is a detailed explanation to the CCMA:

1. The algorithm is executing a Leave-One-Out strategy on the *Source set*. In the process, the algorithm will isolate a single instance of a game S_i from the *Source set* that will be defined as the test instance(**CCMA: (a)**).
2. The algorithm creates the *local set* for the current game instance by removing the S_i instance from the *Source set*(**CCMA: i.**).
3. The algorithm creates the *cross culture set* for the current game instance by combining the *local set* with the *Integrated set*(**CCMA: ii.**).
4. The CCMA will create the *local model* using the Weka framework based on the *local set* and the current algorithm *alg*(**CCMA: iii.**).
5. The CCMA will create the *cross culture model* using the Weka framework based on the *cross culture data set* and the current algorithm *alg*(**CCMA: iv.**).
6. Using The Weka framework, we will predict the test set, s_i with the *local model* and add the predication to the *local average* (**CCMA: v.**).
7. Using The Weka framework, we will predict the test set, s_i with the *cross culture model* and add the predication to the *cross culture average* (**CCMA: vi.**).
8. The *local algorithm* is set to be the algorithm with the highest prediction average in the *local average* (**CCMA: 2.**).
9. The *cross culture algorithm* is set to be the algorithm with the highest prediction average in the *cross culture average* (**CCMA: 3.**).

5.2 CCMA Results

The CCMA examines two sets of data: *Source set* and *Integrated set*. In order to automate the process upon various data sets, we have defined 122 combinations upon which to execute the CCMA. Before examining the results, we will present the following definitions. Each data set is associated with the country from which the game instances were created. As described in Sect. 3, we have focused on three countries:

- **Israel** will be referred in the data sets as *IL*
- **Lebanon** will be referred in the data sets as *LEB*
- **United States** will be referred in the data sets as *USA*

The data sets from each country is divided as well into various board configurations:

- **Human versus Human** will be referred in the data sets as *HvH*
- **Human versus Purb** will be referred in the data sets as *Purb*
- **Human versus Pal** will be referred in the data sets as *Pal*
- **Human versus Nasty** will be referred in the data sets as *Nst*

It is important to note that when different board configurations are combined into a data set within the same country, a '+' sign will be used. In addition to the data sets from the three countries we have created combined data sets which are composed from various countries:

- **AllHAllPr** All the Human vs. Human games in both Israel and the U.S.A together with all the Human vs. Purb games in all culture.
- **AllPr** All the Human vs. Purb games from all the culture.
- **Purb_USA_IL** All the Human vs. Purb games in both Israel and the U.S.A together
- **AllPl+Nst** All the Human vs. Pal games from all the culture together with the Human vs. Nasty games.
- **AllPr+Nst** All the Human vs. Purb games from all the culture together with the Human vs. Nasty games.

For example the data set of Human versus Purb in Israel is defined as *IL_Purb*, and all the Human versus Pal games instances in addition to the Human versus Nasty played in Lebanon is defined as *AllPl+Nst* Table 1 shows the results which had better prediction when considering the *Integrated set* as part of the learning model using the CCMA.

6 Cross Culture Analysis

We have executed the CCMA upon data sets regarding the transfer model, as described in Sect. 3.4. The Transfer model predicts the extent to which a person was reliable in the negotiation. Each row contains the following columns:

– **Source** the *Source data set*.
– **Results** a brief description of results using the *local model* as learning model (as described in Sect. 5). Contains the following info:
  • **Algorithm** the selected algorithm for the *local model*, as described in Sect. 5.
  • **Accuracy** the accuracy (Accuracy) of the transfer model based on the *local model*.
  • **Frequency** the frequency selection of the chosen algorithm.
– **Integrated** the *Integrated data set*.
– **Algorithm** the selected algorithm for the *cross culture model*, as described in Sect. 5.
– **Accuracy** the accuracy (Accuracy) of the transfer model based on the *cross culture model*.
– **Frequency** the frequency selection of the chosen algorithm.

Table 1 reports performance for each of the *Source data set* and for each *Integrated data set*. To fully understand the reports, we will examine *line 22*. In *line 22* the *Source data set* is LEB_Pal, i.e. all the Human vs. Pal games played in Lebanon. In the *Results* info we can see that the Sigmoid had the best predication in 28 instances out of 47 when using the *local model*, with an average accuracy of 82.02. In addition, we can see that the *Integrated set* was Purb_USA_IL, i.e. all the Human vs. Purb games in both Israel and the U.S.A together. In the *Algorithm* column, we can see that the Sigmoid had the best predication in 23 instances out of 47 when using the *cross culture model*, with an average accuracy of 90.58. In order to find a common learning model for various culture, we will examine each data type (such as HvH, Pal, Purb) and it is recommended learning model.

6.1   HvsH Data-Type Analysis

Regarding the HvsH data-type, i.e., IL_HvH and USA_HvH (Lebanon is not included since no human versus human games were played), we can see that when each one of them is used as *Source set*, the recommended *Integrated set* is either USA_Purb or IL_Pal. When observing lines 10–12 in Table 1, using only the IL_HvH as the *Source set* for the learning model, we have a prediction accuracy of 70.64 with the J48 algorithm that was chosen with a frequency of 48/57. However, using USA_Purb as the *Integrated set* (line 11), we have a prediction accuracy of 71.17 with the Naive algorithm that was chosen with a frequency of 56/57. When using IL_Pal as the *Integrated set* (line 12), we have a prediction accuracy of 70.78 with the Naive algorithm that was chosen with a frequency of 44/57. When observing lines 24–29, using only the USA_HvH as the *Source set* for the learning model, we have a prediction accuracy of 60.10 with the J48 algorithm that was chosen with a frequency of 44/57. However, using USA_Purb as the *Integrated set* (line 24), we have a prediction accuracy of 68.14 with the J48 algorithm that was chosen with a frequency of 30/57. When using IL_Pal as the *Integrated set* (line 27), we have a prediction accuracy of 61.46 with the

Table 1. Performance comparison for each *Source data set* and *Integrated data set*

Source	Results	Integrated	Algorithm	Accuracy	Frequency	Line
AllPl+Nst	Algorithm: J48 Accuracy: 70.80 Frequency: 130/195	IL_HvH	J48	75.26	96/195	1
		AllPr	RepTree	73.05	167/195	2
		USA_Purb	J48	72.76	189/195	3
		USA_HvH	RepTree	72.69	152/195	4
		AllHAllPr	J48	71.77	154/195	5
		LEB_Purb	RepTree	71.28	166/195	6
AllPr	Algorithm: J48 Accuracy: 85.71 Frequency: 172/173	LEB_Pal	RepTree	87.27	73/173	7
AllPr+Nst	Algorithm: RepTree Accuracy: 79.19 Frequency: 176/227	LEB_Pal	RepTree	83.27	127/227	8
Purb_USA_IL	Algorithm: J48 Accuracy: 72.07 Frequency: 66/94	USA_HvH	J48	73.75	44/94	9
IL_HvH	Algorithm: J48 Accuracy: 70.64 Frequency: 48/57	LEB_PAL+Purb	Naive	74.07	17/57	10
		USA_Purb	Naive	71.17	56/57	11
		IL_Pal	Naive	70.78	44/57	12
IL_Purb	Algorithm: Sigmoid Accuracy: 76.61 Frequency: 31/40	LEB_Nst+Purb	J48	76.89	32/40	13
		LEB_Purb	J48	76.86	39/40	14
LEB_Nst+Pal	Algorithm: RepTree Accuracy: 77.52 Frequency: 76/101	IL_HvH	J48	77.96	98/101	15
LEB_Nst+Purb	Algorithm: J48 Accuracy: 82.78 Frequency: 106/133	IL_HvH	J48	88.56	55/133	16
		LEB_Pal	J48	85.08	100/133	17
		USA_HvH	RepTree	84.49	108/133	18
		IL_Pal	Sigmoid	84.36	65/133	19
		IL_Purb	RepTree	83.76	127/133	20
		USA_Purb	J48	83.48	110/133	21
LEB_Pal	Algorithm: Sigmoid Accuracy: 82.02 Frequency: 28/47	Purb_USA_IL	Sigmoid	90.58	23/47	22
		USA_HvH	J48	86.09	32/47	23
USA_HvH	Algorithm: J48 Accuracy: 60.10 Frequency: 44/57	USA_Purb	J48	68.14	30/57	24
		Purb_USA_IL	J48	64.93	42/57	25
		AllPl+Nst	Navie	63.19	39/57	26
		IL_Pal	Sigmoid	61.46	48/57	27
		USA_Pal	Sigmoid	60.97	23/57	28
		IL_HvH	Sigmoid	60.75	45/57	29
USA_Pal	Algorithm: Sigmoid Accuracy: 68.96 Frequency: 18/42	AllPr	Sigmoid	70.51	18/42	30
USA_Purb	Algorithm: J48 Accuracy: 74.12 Frequency: 38/54	LEB_Nst+Purb	J48	75.63	52/54	31
		LEB_Pal	RepTree	75.27	23/54	32

Sigmoid algorithm that was chosen with a frequency of 48/57. Although we have found a common *Integrated data set* for the HvsH data-types, we see that the algorithms composing the models are different. As a result, a specific model will be defined for each HvsH data-type per country.

6.2   Purb Data-Type Analysis

Regarding the Purb data-type, when the LEB_Purb is set as the *Source set*, we can see that there is not any *Integrated data set* that can contribute to the model's prediction accuracy (since there is not a line regarding the LEB_Purb as *Source set*). However, when the IL_Purb or the USA_Purb are defined as the *Source data set*, the recommended *Integrated set* is LEB_Nst+Purb. Observing lines 13–14, when using only the IL_Purb as the *Source set* for the learning model, we have a prediction accuracy of 76.61 with the Sigmoid algorithm that was chosen with a frequency of 31/40. However, using LEB_Nst+Purb as the *Integrated set* (line 13), we have a prediction accuracy of 76.89 with the J48 algorithm that was chosen with a frequency of 32/40. Observing lines 31–32, when using only the USA_Purb as the *Source set* for the learning model, we have a prediction accuracy of 74.12 with the J48 algorithm that was chosen with a frequency of 38/54. However, using LEB_Nst+Purb as the *Integrated set* (line 31), we have a prediction accuracy of 75.63 with the J48 algorithm, that was chosen with a frequency of 52/54. In conclusion, we have found a common *Integrated data set* for the Purb data type and using only the J48 algorithm for the learning model, we can conclude that the LEB_Nst+Purb data is a common model for Israel and U.S.A Purb games.

When the LEB_Nst+Purb is set as *Source set* the recommended *Integrated set* is LEB_Purb. Observing lines 16–21, when using only the LEB_Nst+Purb as the *Source set* for the learning model, we have a prediction accuracy of 82.78 with the J48 algorithm that was chosen with a frequency of 106/133. However, using IL_HvH as the *Integrated set* (line 16), we have a prediction accuracy of 88.56 with the J48 algorithm that was chosen with a frequency of 55/133. In conclusion, we have found that using a different culture data set can improve another's learning model and result a better prediction accuracy.

6.3   Pal Data-Type Analysis

Regarding the Pal data-type, when the IL_Pal is set as the *Source set*, there is not any *Integrated data set* that can contribute to the model's prediction accuracy (since there is not a line regarding the IL_Pal as *Source set*). However, when considering LEB_Pal and the USA_Pal as *Source sets*, the Purb_USA_IL and the AllPr respectively as *Integrated data set* are recommended. Observing lines 22–23, when using only the LEB_Pal as the *Source set* for the learning model, we have a prediction accuracy of 82.02 with the Sigmoid algorithm that was chosen with a frequency of 28/47. However, using Purb_USA_IL as the *Integrated set* (line 22), we have a prediction accuracy of 90.58 with the Sigmoid algorithm that was chosen with a frequency of 23/47. Observing line 30, when using only the USA_Pal as the *Source set* for the learning model, we have a prediction accuracy of 68.96 with the Sigmoid algorithm that was chosen with a frequency of 18/42. However, using AllPr as the *Integrated set*, we have a prediction accuracy of 70.51 with the Sigmoid algorithm that was chosen with a frequency of 18/42. In conclusion, we have found that using a different culture data set and a different data types can improve another's learning model and result a better prediction accuracy.

6.4   Combined Data-Type Analysis

Regarding the data sets that were combined of multiple data sets from different culture, we can see that when the AllPr or the AllPr+Nst are used as *Source set* the recommended *Integrated set* is LEB_Pal. I.e. the Nasty (Human versus Nasty agent) games did not affect the selection of LEB_Pal as the recommended *Integrated set*. Observing line 7, when using only the AllPr as the *Source set* for the learning model, we have a prediction accuracy of 85.71 with the J48 algorithm that was chosen with a frequency of 172/173. However, using LEB_Pal as the *Integrated set*, we have a prediction accuracy of 87.27 with the RepTree algorithm that was chosen with a frequency of 73/173. Observing line 8, when using only the AllPr+Nst as the *Source set* for the learning model, we have a prediction accuracy of 79.19 with the RepTree algorithm that was chosen with a frequency of 176/227. However, using LEB_Pal as the *Integrated set*, we have a prediction accuracy of 83.27 with the RepTree algorithm that was chosen with a frequency of 127/227. In conclusion, we can see that the LEB_Pal can be used as the *Integrated set*, based on the RepTree algorithm, regardless of whether the Nasty games are included in the *Source set*.

In addition, we can see that when the ALLPl+Nst is used as *Source set* the recommended *Integrated set* is IL_HvH. Observing lines 1–6, when using only the ALLPl+Nst as the *Source set* for the learning model, we have a prediction accuracy of 70.80 with the J48 algorithm that was chosen with a frequency of 130/195. However, using IL_HvH as the *Integrated set*, we have a prediction accuracy of 75.26 with the J48 algorithm that was chosen with a frequency of 96/195. In conclusion, we have found that using a different culture data set can improve another's learning model and result a better prediction accuracy.

7   Conclusions and Future Work

In this section, we present guidelines for the type of data, from different cultures, that is useful in building prediction models. We were looking for a generic rule that would be beneficial for all the countries. After using the CCMA to automate the process of selecting the data set to use for the learning model, and the machine learning algorithm to use, the conclusions are that for the transfer model, when the test set is composed of HvH (Human versus Human) games, the recommended data set to integrate for the learning model is the USA_Purb. However, each culture will have a specific model based on the recommended algorithm mentioned in Sect. 6.1.

When the test set is composed of Purb (Human versus Purb) games, the games played in Israel and U.S.A will be tested on a common model created from the LEB_Nst+Purb data set and the J48 algorithm. Whereas the games played in Lebanon will be tested on a different model created from the IL_HvH data set and the J48, proving that a different culture data set can improve another's learning model and result a better prediction accuracy.

When the test set is composed of Pal (Human versus Pal) games, we can see that when IL_Pal is tested, there is no *Integrated set* that can improve the model's prediction. However, when considering LEB_Pal and USA_Pal as Source sets, the Purb_USA_IL with the Sigmoid algorithm and the AllPr with the Sigmoid algorithm respectively are the recommended models to use.

And lastly, when all the Purb games are played, the Nasty (Human versus Nasty agent) games have no effect on the prediction accuracy of the learning model that is based on LEB_Pal as the *Integrated set* with the RepTree algorithm, that is recommended for the AllPr games. And when testing all the games of Human vs. Pal, a learning model that is based on IL_HvH and the J48 algorithm has the best prediction accuracy.

Our future work will focus on building a new cultural sensitive agent which will first examine the models and algorithms which had the best accuracy prediction per culture. Upon the results we will determine which test set was the closest to simulating the human behaviour.

Acknowledgments. We wish to express our gratitude to the Research Fund of the Research Authority of the College of Management Academic Studies, Rishon Lezion, Israel, for the financial support provided for this research.

References

1. Dagan, N., Volij, O., Winter, E., et al.: The time-preference nash solution. Technical report, Citeseer (2001)
2. Das, R., Hanson, J.E., Kephart, J.O., Tesauro, G.: Agent-human interactions in the continuous double auction. In: International Joint Conference on Artificial Intelligence, vol. 17, pp. 1169–1178. Lawrence Erlbaum Associates Ltd. (2001)
3. Efron, B.: Estimating the error rate of a prediction rule: improvement on cross-validation. J. Am. Stat. Assoc. **78**(382), 316–331 (1983)
4. Faratin, P., Sierra, C., Jennings, N.R.: Using similarity criteria to make issue trade-offs in automated negotiations. Artif. Intell. **142**(2), 205–237 (2002)
5. Fatima, S.S., Wooldridge, M., Jennings, N.R.: Optimal negotiation strategies for agents with incomplete information. In: Meyer, J.-J.C., Tambe, M. (eds.) ATAL 2001. LNCS (LNAI), vol. 2333, pp. 377–392. Springer, Heidelberg (2002). doi:10.1007/3-540-45448-9_28
6. Fatima, S.S., Wooldridge, M., Jennings, N.R.: An agenda-based framework for multi-issue negotiation. Artif. Intell. **152**(1), 1–45 (2004)
7. Gal, Y., Kraus, S., Gelfand, M., Khashan, H., Salmon, E.: Negotiating with people across cultures using an adaptive agent. ACM Trans. Intell. Syst. Technol. **3**(1), 8 (2012)
8. Gardner, M.W., Dorling, S.R.: Artificial neural networks (the multilayer perceptron)–a review of applications in the atmospheric sciences. Atmos. Environ. **32**(14), 2627–2636 (1998)

9. Gelfand, M.J., Brett, J.M.: The Handbook of Negotiation and Culture. Stanford University Press, Stanford (2004)
10. Gelfand, M.J., Christakopoulou, S.: Culture and negotiator cognition: judgment accuracy and negotiation processes in individualistic and collectivistic cultures. Organ. Behav. Hum. Decis. Process. **79**(3), 248–269 (1999)
11. Haim, G., Gal, Y., Kraus, S., Blumberg, Y.: Learning human negotiation behavior across cultures. In: Second International Working Conference on Human Factors and Computational Models in Negotiation (HuCom 2010) (2010)
12. Haim, G., Gal, Y.K., Gelfand, M., Kraus, S.: A cultural sensitive agent for human-computer negotiation. In: Proceedings of the 11th International Conference on Autonomous Agents and Multiagent Systems, vol. 1, pp. 451–458. International Foundation for Autonomous Agents and Multiagent Systems (2012)
13. Hoz-Weiss, P., Kraus, S., Wilkenfeld, J., Andersen, D.R., Pate, A.: An automated agent for bilateral negotiations with humans. In: Proceedings of AAAI/IAAI, vol. 2, pp. 1000–1001 (2002)
14. Kamar, E., Horvitz, E., Meek, C.: Mobile opportunistic commerce: mechanisms, architecture, and application. In: Proceedings of the 7th International Joint Conference on Autonomous Agents and Multiagent Systems, vol. 2, pp. 1087–1094. International Foundation for Autonomous Agents and Multiagent Systems (2008)
15. Lin, R.J., Chou, S.T.: Bilateral multi-issue negotiations in a dynamic environment. In: Proceedings of the AAMAS Workshop on Agent Mediated Electronic Commerce (AMEC-2003) (2003)
16. Lin, R., Oshrat, Y., Kraus, S.: Investigating the benefits of automated negotiations in enhancing people's negotiation skills. In: Proceedings of The 8th International Conference on Autonomous Agents and Multiagent Systems, vol. 1, pp. 345–352. International Foundation for Autonomous Agents and Multiagent Systems (2009)
17. Mudgal, C., Vassileva, J.: Bilateral negotiation with incomplete and uncertain information: a decision-theoretic approach using a model of the opponent. In: Klusch, M., Kerschberg, L. (eds.) CIA 2000. LNCS (LNAI), vol. 1860, pp. 107–118. Springer, Heidelberg (2000). doi:10.1007/978-3-540-45012-2_11
18. Murphy, R.R.: Human-robot interaction in rescue robotics. IEEE Trans. Syst. Man Cybern. Part C Appl. Rev. **34**(2), 138–153 (2004)
19. Oprea, M.: An adaptive negotiation model for agent-based electronic commerce (2002)
20. Patil, T.R., Sherekar, S.S.: Performance analysis of naive bayes and J48 classification algorithm for data classification. Int. J. Comput. Sci. Appl. **6**(2), 256–261 (2013)
21. Rahwan, I., McBurney, P., Sonenberg, L.: Towards a theory of negotiation strategy (a preliminary report). In: Proceedings of the 5th Workshop on Game Theoretic and Decision Theoretic Agents (GTDT-2003), pp. 73–80. Citeseer (2003)
22. Schurr, N., Tambe, M.: Using multi-agent teams to improve the training of incident commanders. In: Pěchouček, M., Thompson, S.G., Voos, H. (eds.) Defence Industry Applications of Autonomous Agents and Multi-Agent Systems. Whitestein Series in Software Agent Technologies and Autonomic Computing, pp. 151–166. Springer, Heidelberg (2008)
23. Xindong, W., Kumar, V., Quinlan, J.R., Ghosh, J., Yang, Q., Motoda, H., McLachlan, G.J., Ng, A., Liu, B., Philip, S.Y., et al.: Top 10 algorithms in data mining. Knowl. Inf. Syst. **14**(1), 1–37 (2008)
24. Zhao, Y., Zhang, Y.: Comparison of decision tree methods for finding active objects. Adv. Space Res. **41**(12), 1955–1959 (2008)

A Multi-agent System for Group Decision Support Based on Conflict Resolution Styles

Silvia Rossi[1]([✉]), Claudia Di Napoli[2], Francesco Barile[3], and Luca Liguori[1]

[1] Dipartimento di Ingegneria Elettrica e delle Tecnologie dell'Informazione,
Università degli Studi di Napoli Federico II, Naples, Italy
silvia.rossi@unina.it
[2] Istituto di Calcolo e Reti ad Alte Prestazioni, CNR, Naples, Italy
claudia.dinapoli@cnr.it
[3] Dipartimento di Matematica e Applicazioni,
Università degli Studi di Napoli Federico II, Naples, Italy
francesco.barile@unina.it

Abstract. With the pervasive use of social networks supporting digital communities, the problem of finding a solution to a given problem shared by a group of users that meets the requirements/preferences of its members is gaining great interest in several research domains. Software systems supporting the decision-making process taking place when building "group solution" would greatly enhance the potentiality of these digital communities. In the present work, a Group Decision Support System is proposed to help a group of users to find a set of tourist attractions, selected among a huge set of possible alternatives, that meets the preferences of each individual. The proposed system relies on an automatic negotiation mechanism to incrementally build a single recommendation for the whole group, according to the individual lists of preferred attractions of each member. Negotiation occurs among software agents that simulate different conflict resolution styles of the real users they respectively represent. Experimental results show the effectiveness of the system also when dealing with real end users preferences.

Keywords: Automated negotiation · Group decision support systems · Thomas Kilmann Conflict resolution styles

1 Introduction

With the wide diffusion of social networks and online social group systems, the problem of providing automatic support to come to shared decisions is getting more and more attention [16]. Usually, the process to reach a decision shared among members of a group is very complex, and it includes several stages such as to generate and organize different ideas, to set priorities and to resolve possible conflicts. The variety of stages and the necessity to iterate them several times to reach a consensus makes the process very time-consuming requiring several meetings among the group members.

© Springer International Publishing AG 2017
R. Aydoğan et al. (Eds.): COREDEMA 2016, LNAI 10238, pp. 134–148, 2017.
DOI: 10.1007/978-3-319-57285-7_9

Decision Support Systems (DSS) are information systems that interact with individuals to support them in their decision-making activities by computing a set of recommendations among which users may select the one they consider more appropriate [9]. A subcategory of DSS is the *Group Decision Support Systems* (GDSS), used when decisions involve not a single user, but a group of people [12]. A crucial aspect in GDDS is how to reach a consensus in a group and how to measure individual satisfaction of its members once a decision is suggested [8].

The problem addressed in this work is to find a set of tourist attractions, referred to as Points of Interest (POI), for a group of users, according to the preferences of each member of the group, taking into account that the individual preferences can be inconsistent with the others, or even conflicting [17]. Of course, according to the number of members in the group and the number of preferences specified by them, the solution space may grow exponentially, so preventing the possibility to produce all possible solutions in a polynomial time. In addition, to come to a shared solution as close as possible to the user' preferences, users should interactively take part in each step of the process to build the solution.

In the present work, a GDSS designed to recommend a set of POI to a group of users is proposed. Each member of the group is represented by a software agent and the process of coming to a shared decision is modeled as an iterative automated negotiation among agents [4]. If negotiation is successful, it leads to an agreement representing the shared solution. Individual preferences are explicitly specified by end users, and they are used by the corresponding agents in the negotiation phase. During negotiation, agents have different behaviors to respond to conflicting situations modeled according to the widely used Thomas-Kilmann Conflict Mode [11]. In order to limit the solution search space during the negotiation process, two heuristic procedures are proposed. The proposed system has been evaluated through experimental tests in order to assess the impact of both the different conflict resolution styles of negotiating agents and the proposed heuristics on the process of finding a recommendation for the group. In addition, the system has been used by real users that provided, through online questionnaires, a measure of their level of satisfaction regarding the system usability and the quality of the received recommendations in relations with their preferences.

2   Related Works

The problem of defining the proper decision strategy is crucial in GDSS. In Choicla [18], for example, a decision support system is proposed that provides users with the possibility to choose among different decision strategies for independent decision tasks, so allowing to personalize the application to the user's preferences by providing different heuristic functions and trustworthiness levels to the group members. Another example is represented by the Social Dining system [7], that is an application helping users to find an agreed solution regarding the choice of a restaurant, with the peculiarity that recommendations are generated by collecting real data from social networks. The solution is obtained by aggregating the collected data using different strategies.

A different approach is proposed in [1], where negotiation among software agents, each one representing a group member, is used to merge the individual recommendations. However, differently from our case, they adopt different negotiation protocols according to the number of group members. In [6], a negotiation framework is proposed where agents are characterized by two profiles: a preference profile used to generate the individual recommendations, and a negotiation profile determining the agent behavior during the negotiation process, that can be self-interested, collaborative, and highly collaborative. This proposal was extended in [5], where different agents model different users, and a mediator agent manages the negotiation process. The approach is similar to the one presented in this work, but in our case agent profiles are based on real user profiles, as they result from questionnaires filled by the real users. In addition, in our approach the mediator agent is responsible for building the group recommendation according to the individual proposals of agents during negotiation, while in [5] the recommendation is jointly computed by the agents during negotiation relying on a more complex negotiation protocol. Also in [19] a negotiation approach is proposed, but differently from our work, there is not a mediator agent. Each agent uses a monotonic unilateral concession strategy, and it sends its proposal directly to the other agents, so one recommendation at a time is circulated during negotiation. An agent evaluates and accepts the proposal in case its utility value is the same as the agent's current proposal utility value. On the contrary, the proposal is rejected and a new proposal generated by an agent available to concede is selected for the next negotiation round so iterating the negotiation.

3   Conflict Management Style

The Conflict Management Style describes the human beings' strategies to resolve conflicts arising during negotiation. In literature, several models of conflict management have been proposed. In 1974, Kilmann and Thomas [11] identified five different categories of interpersonal conflict management styles. Such styles are identified with respect to two fundamental dimensions: *cooperation*, i.e., the extent to which the individual attempts to satisfy the other person's interests, and *assertiveness*, i.e., the extent to which the individual attempts to satisfy his/her own interests. These two dimensions are used to define five styles of dealing with conflicts, as follows:

- *Accommodating*: with this style a person prioritizes cooperation at the expense of assertiveness, putting aside her/his own goals and allowing the others to achieve their own;
- *Competitive*: this style relies on assertiveness, so a person tries to pursue its own interests;
- *Compromise*: this style models people that aim to build a solution meeting all parties preferences;
- *Collaborating*: this style models a collaborative approach that aims to resolve conflicts by making the involved parties working all together;

– *Avoiding*: with this style a person avoids conflicts by searching for a solution in a diplomatic way, i.e. going forward in the decision process until a solution is found, but withdrawing or postponing any threatening issue.

Here, the Thomas-Kilmann Conflict Mode Instrument (TKI), based on interviews consisting of questionnaires, is used to assess the conflict management style of real users. For each conflict management style a specific negotiation behavior is associated to the corresponding agent.

4   The Proposed Approach

The proposed Group Decision Support System relies on the design of a multi-agent system to help end-users to find, in a short time, a shared solution consisting in a set of a given number of tourist attractions, named *Points of Interest* (POI), to visit. The multi-agent system is composed of a set of agents, called *user agents*, each one acting on behalf of a group member, and of a special agent, called *mediator agent*, acting as a mediator that interacts with the others to build a recommendation for the group trying to minimize the users' intervention. At the end of the process, the end users would be requested to approve or not the recommendation proposed by the system.

A crucial step in the implementation of a GDSS is the definition of the decision-making strategy to use. For example, a voting mechanism could be deployed that provides an optimal solution in terms of decision speed allowing to avoid deadlocks problems. However, mathematical economist Kenneth Arrow proved in 1952 that there is no consistent method of making a fair choice among three or more choices with preferential voting [10], and one-shot mechanisms may not allow for the complete exploration of the solution space, whereas outcomes that satisfy also the minority of the users may exist. A second possibility is to design a consensus strategy, where group members try to reach an agreement on an outcome. This criterion usually requires a higher involvement of each group member in the decision-making process and longer computational times, but it ensures a good solution quality because a decision is based on the whole community consensus.

Here, we propose a consensus approach based on a negotiation mechanism where user agents try to reach an agreement on behalf of the corresponding group member users in an automatic way. Users are involved only in providing their preferences on items (to obtain reliable data), and in the final decision approval. Agents represent users with different behaviors in conflict resolution. It is assumed that there is a group U of n users, a set I of t POI, and a set R of evaluations (also called ratings), given by the individual users to some POI in the system. A user $u \in U$ assigns a rank $r_{u,i}$ to an item $i \in I$ with $r_{u,i} \in \{1, 2, 3, 4, 5\}$, so U_i is the set of users who evaluated the item i, and I_u is the set of items evaluated by the user u. A recommendation, i.e. a solution computed by the system, is a subset of the set I with dimension $m \leq t$, that represents a compromise among the individual users' preferences, i.e. a solution that maximizes the group satisfaction also guaranteeing a minimum utility value for each member of the group.

4.1   Group's Preferences

A key factor to implement an effective GDSS is to rely on reliable data [12]. In our domain, data are the lists of preferences/ratings on POI for each user (I_u). In this direction, we decided not to rely on any recommendation algorithm to estimate ratings, but to have the users explicitly expressing them. Whenever a user accesses the system, he/she is able to rate as many POI as he/she wants. This allows to guarantee the quality, attainability, and accuracy of the system data.

We define the POI list P_G for a specific group G as follows:

$$P_G = \bigcup_{u \in G} I_u$$

that represents the set of POI obtained from the aggregation of the individual preference lists of the different group members. The *mediator agent* is in charge of collecting and aggregating the users' preferences. The P_G set represents the initial solution space for the mediator agent. This space could change (e.g., increase) during the decision-making process.

In principle, in order for the mediator to search for a solution, each group member should evaluate all the POI that have been evaluated by the other members, but not by him/herself $(P_G \backslash I_u)$. This configuration (*complete knowledge*) allows to find optimal solutions.

However, each user should potentially be involved in a long process to provide all the needed information, so an upper bound to the number of POI to be rated could be set (*partial knowledge*). Typically, a reasonable upper bound is set to 20. In this case, in order to create the P_G set taking into account the users' preferences (i.e., the items they evaluated with the higher rates), the k-best rated POI for each user are selected from the corresponding I_u. Hence, the k value depends on the number of users in a group ($k = 20/n$). Subsequently, whenever the mediator requires additional information to proceed, additional ratings could be requested to the users. Of course, in the partial knowledge case, it is not guaranteed that an optimal solution is found.

4.2   Interaction Protocol

The proposed decision-making process is based on an alternation of a *Merging Ranks* step, performed by the mediator agent to aggregate preferences and compute a subset of POI to propose to the group, and a *Negotiation* step, where each user agent may accept the received proposal or reject it, and reply with an alternative proposal. In detail, such alternating protocol is composed of the following steps:

1. the mediator generates a suggested solution for the group according to the individual preference lists of each group member;
2. each user agent can accept/reject the received proposal;
   2.1 if the proposal is rejected, the user agent generates a counteroffer;
3. if the proposed solution is accepted by all user agents, it is proposed to the end users as a system recommendation;
   3.1 otherwise the mediator aggregates the received counteroffers generating a new solution for the group, and it starts a new negotiation round.

The negotiation process may be iterated for a number of rounds set by the mediator at the beginning of the negotiation. If all the allowed negotiation rounds take place without reaching an agreement, the process ends by proposing a solution to the end users composed of the best m POI in the mediator current POI domain.

4.3   The Mediator Agent Strategy

The mediator agent is responsible for building and sending proposals to the group members. Each proposal is a set of POI $P = \{p_1, ..., p_m\}$, that, if accepted by all members, becomes the group solution. In order to build a proposal, the mediator refers to the set of POI it is aware of, i.e. the set P_G that have been rated by all the users, known as the *Mediator Domain*. In order to build the first proposal, the mediator calculates a group rate $r_{G,j}$ for each POI j, as follows:

$$r_{G,j} = \sum_{u \in U} \frac{r_{u,j} \cdot p_j}{n}$$

that represents a weighted mean of the individual ratings where the weight $p_j \in [0, 1]$ is a measure of the popularity of j, with $p_j = 1$ if all the user in the group spontaneously assigned a rating to j (where spontaneously means that the rating is assigned without being explicitly required). In group recommendation literature different approaches to aggregate individual preferences are proposed and evaluated [15]; here, a simple weighted average is used, that is one of the most widely adopted approaches.

The first proposal is composed by selecting the m POI with the highest group rank. Once the first proposal is computed, the mediator sends it to all user agents that privately evaluate it according to their own utility functions.

In case the proposal is rejected, the mediator receives a number of counteroffers, each one composed of a possible new set of m POI ($O_i = \{p_{i_1}, ..., p_{i_m}\}$) from each user agent i that rejected the proposal. If a counteroffer contains POI that are not in the mediator domain P_G, the mediator asks the user agents to rate them (interacting with the real users). Then, the mediator generates a new proposal on the new domain P_G, by applying the same strategy used to build the first proposal. If the new proposal is different from the previous one, it is sent to the user agents; otherwise the mediator modifies it, according to the received counteroffers, by replacing the POI that in its previous solution was discharged by the highest number of user-agents (when the counteroffers were generated) with the one that had the highest number of new occurrences in the generated counteroffers.

4.4   The User Agent Strategy

Each user agent evaluates the proposal sent by the mediator according to its behavior in conflict resolution, assigned to the agent once the corresponding user filled the TKI questionnaire.

For each user agent, an individual *optimal value* (i.e., the value corresponding to the solution with the highest utility) and a *reservation value* are set. Given I_u the set of POI evaluated by the user u, and $I_u(m)$ the set of m POI with the highest rank for the user u, the optimal value, at time 0, is given by:

$$OPT_u(0) = \sum_{i \in I_u(m)} \frac{\tilde{r}_{u,i}}{m}$$

where $\tilde{r}_{u,i}$ is the rating the user u assigned to the POI i normalized in $[0,1]$. The reservation value is set to the half of $OPT_u(0)$ for all user agents, and it represents the minimum utility value up to which the user agent is willing to concede during the negotiation.

When a user agent receives an offer P^t from the mediator at negotiation round t, it evaluates the utility of the received offer as follows: $U_u(P^t) = \sum_{i \in P^t} \frac{\tilde{r}_{u,i}}{m}$. This value is compared with the agent utility value of the previous negotiation round $OPT_u(t-1)$. The decision strategy is implemented as follows:

1. if $U_u(P^t) \geq OPT_u(t-1)$, then the agent accepts the offer and sets $OPT_u(t) = U_u(P^t)$;
2. if $U_u(P^t) \geq OPT_u(t-1) - \Delta_u(t)$, then the agent accepts the offer by conceding in its utility of a value smaller or equal of $\Delta_u(t)$, and it sets $OPT_u(t) = U_u(P^t)$;
3. in all the other cases, the agent rejects the offer, and it makes a counteroffer either by randomly conceding in utility $(OPT_u(t) = OPT_u(t-1) - \Delta_u(t))$ or without conceding $(OPT_u(t) = OPT_u(t-1))$.

The utility concession value $\Delta_u(t)$, at time t, depends on the user conflict resolution style. In [14] the authors associated with each conflict resolution style of the TKI model different concession strategies depending on the negotiation round. Inspired by this work, we defined the agent concession strategies as follows:

- *Accommodating*, it concedes a constant utility value during all negotiation rounds, so being the most collaborative profile;
- *Competing*, it concedes low utility values at the beginning of the negotiation, while increasing the concession value at the end of negotiation to try to reach an agreement before a negotiation failure occurs;

- *Compromising*, it concedes high utility values at the beginning and at the end of the negotiation, while concedes a constant utility value in the intermediate rounds;
- *Collaborative*, it concedes a constant value throughout negotiation, but lower than the Accommodating one, since this behavioral style does not impact the negotiation [14];
- *Avoiding*, it is a passive style of conflict resolution, meaning that the agent would not negotiate in the first place, so, here a very low constant concession value is adopted.

The concession values for the different profiles were empirically derived from a set of experiments carried out adopting different conflict resolution styles and they are reported in Table 1, where the negotiation rounds are split in three negotiation steps, initial, intermediate and final, as proposed in [14].

Table 1. Concession strategies and Δ values.

	Initial rounds	Intermediate rounds	Final rounds
Accommodating	0.08	0.08	0.08
Competing	0.01	0.025	0.05
Compromising	0.06	0.025	0.06
Collaborative	0.07	0.07	0.07
Avoiding	0.01	0.01	0.01

The User Agent Counteroffer Generation. In case a user agent rejects a proposal, it has to generate a counteroffer whose utility value is calculated taking into account whether a concession takes place or not. Since there could be potentially many different POI combinations with the same utility value, the search space when computing a counteroffer can be too large. Hence, in order to compute a counteroffer, two different heuristic strategies to reduce the search space are defined, *Search in Domain* and *Reference Point*. Moreover, the mediator agent may communicate to the user agents which strategy to use according to the negotiation state, i.e., the number of rounds, or the number of agents that rejected its offer. The two heuristic strategies are illustrated in the next sections.

Search in Domain. With this heuristic, the user agent orders the items of the proposal P^t received by the mediator according to its own ranking, and it generates a counteroffer by modifying the proposal to obtain an admissible proposal (i.e., a proposal with the required utility) by making the less possible number of POI substitutions searching in its private domain.

Reference Point. In this strategy, the mediator sends a different proposal to each agent u that represents a *reference point* for the agent to build a counteroffer [3]. This means that the proposal is evaluated by considering the ratings of all the other agents except than u. Experimentally (see Sect. 5.1) it was evaluated that this strategy has a positive impact on the negotiation when there is only one agent conflicting with a given proposal that is admissible for the other members of the group. So, the conflicting agent is required to adapt its objectives to the reference point as much as possible, since it satisfies the majority of the group.

5   Experimental Results

In order to evaluate the proposed system performances in terms of the accepted recommendations generated, a first preliminary analysis was carried out on simulated data, i.e., by assigning random rating values to the POI extracted from the social network *Foursquare*. Two types of simulations were carried out in the cases of mediator *complete* and *partial knowledge* of POI ratings. Successively, the same experiments were executed in a pilot study, where a group of real end users were asked to use the system, so providing real data. After using the system, they filled a questionnaire concerning both the goodness of the recommendations provided by the system, and its usability.

5.1   Complete Knowledge

First, the performances of the heuristics for the generation of counteroffers, the *Search in Domain* and the *Reference Point*, were evaluated together with the negotiation success rate when the mediator has a *complete knowledge*, i.e. in the case it knows all the ratings for all the POI in the dataset. The generated recommendations were evaluated in different experimental setting by varying the number t of POI, from 20 to 1000, the group size n from 3 to 5 members, and the number m of POI in the solution from 1 to 5. The size of a group is kept within the chosen range because the focus of the present work is to test decision-making mechanisms for small groups that rely on mechanisms (e.g., interpersonal relationships and mutual influences) that are different with respect to the ones adopted for larger groups [13]. The group size determines the significant number of POI in the solution in the case of simulated experiments. In fact, from a preliminary experimental analysis, we derived that for cases with $m > n$ a solution is always found, so we set $m \leq n$.

Each algorithm was executed 100 times for each possible configuration, and for each execution, the users' behaviors, i.e. their conflict resolution styles, were randomly generated. The maximum number of allowed negotiation rounds was empirically set to 30.

The success rate for the first heuristic is 99%, against 77% of the second one. In Fig. 1(a), the average number of rounds to reach an agreement is plotted, varying the number of available POI, and discharging the cases of negotiation failures. As shown in Fig. 1(a), the Reference Point heuristic requires a greater

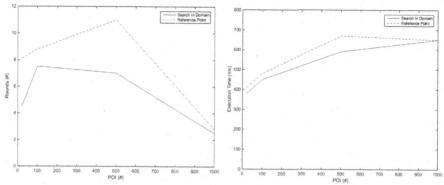

(a) Average number of rounds to reach an agreement.

(b) Average execution time to reach an agreement.

Fig. 1. Results in case of complete knowledge.

number of rounds to reach an agreement with respect to the Search in Domain case, reaching similar performances when the number of POI is greater than 1000. Therefore, the Reference Point does not represent a feasible solution for sets of POI that vary from 20 to 1000, by making more complicated for user agents to build counteroffers, so leading to failures in the negotiation process.

Moreover, by increasing the number of POI up to 500, the number of rounds necessary to reach an agreement increases, as expected, because of the increased dimension of the solution search space. On the contrary, by further increasing the number of POI, the number of rounds to reach an agreement decreases because the chances to generate acceptable counteroffers increase, so potentially reducing the number of conflicts.

The execution time of the Reference Point algorithm is slightly greater than the Search in Domain one, as reported in Fig. 1(b). Moreover, the trend of execution time differs from the one of negotiation rounds. In fact, while for a number of POI greater than 500, the number of rounds to reach an agreement starts to decrease, the average execution time increases. In this case, in fact, it is the time required to compute a counteroffer that impacts more on the execution time.

We also evaluated the performances of the two heuristics by varying the size of the group from 3 to 5 members. The success rate is very high, ranging from the 100%, for groups of 3, to 98% for groups of 5, in the case of complete knowledge for the mediator. As we expected, when the number of agents increases, the number of negotiation rounds necessary to reach a shared solution increases, reaching the value 7 when the number of POI varies from 250 to 500 (see Fig. 2(a)). Again, when the number of POI is more than 500, fewer negotiation rounds are necessary to find a solution (3 rounds). As shown in Fig. 2(b), when the number of POI and the number of agents increase, the execution time of both algorithms also increases, even though the execution time is more dependent on the number of POI than on the number of agents.

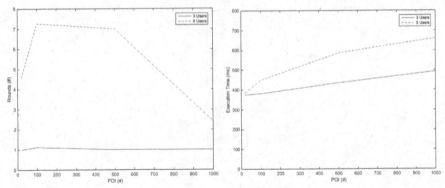

(a) Average number of rounds to reach an agreement.

(b) Average execution time to reach an agreement.

Fig. 2. Results in case of complete knowledge w.r.t. the number of users.

5.2   Partial Knowledge

In the second set of experiments the performance of the whole system using both heuristics, the Search in Domain one in the first rounds, and the Reference Point one in case of few conflicts, is analyzed with datasets varying from 20 to 1000 POI, the number of group's members varying from 3 to 5, and solutions with a number of POI varying from 1 to 4. The algorithm is executed 10 times for each setting, with a maximum number of 30 negotiation rounds. Also in this case, for each execution, the users' behaviors are randomly generated. The Partial Knowledge consists in setting the initial domain of the mediator with only the top-k POI (randomly generated), while the user agents have their own ratings on the complete dataset.

The success rate of the heuristics decreases by increasing the number of agents (98% with 3 agents, 92% with 4 agents, and 85% with 5 agents). The success rate in the case of partial knowledge is lower than the one obtained in the case of complete knowledge (from 99% to 91%), and the highest number of negotiation failures occurs in the case of a solution with 1 POI. As shown in Fig. 3(a), the average number of rounds necessary to find an agreement increases by increasing the number of agents (12.9 rounds with 3 agents and 13.5 rounds with 4 agents). Instead, for negotiations with 5 agents, the average number of rounds decreases (13.2 rounds) due to the highest number of negotiation failures. Accordingly, the negotiations among 4 agents require more rounds to find a solution, while the negotiations with 5 agents fail (when the algorithm fails, the number of rounds employed is not included in the computation of the average number of rounds).

The execution time of the negotiation algorithm, showed in Fig. 3(b), is lower than in the previous case since the combined use of the Reference Point and the Search in Domain heuristics improve the system performances when the number of POI is greater than 500.

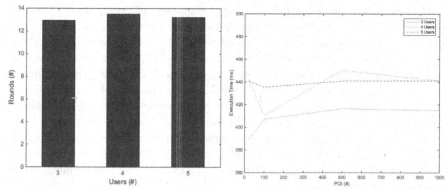

(a) Average number of rounds to reach an agreement.

(b) Average execution time to reach an agreement.

Fig. 3. Results in case of partial knowledge.

5.3   Pilot Study

In the last experiment, the system is evaluated in a realistic case study, with a group of users having to choose a set of restaurants with respect to the preferences of each group's member. The realized system is composed of a Web Application, showed in Fig. 4, and of an Automatic Negotiation Module, that represents the core of the system. The Web Application allows the users to interact with the system filling the TKI questionnaire, with providing the ratings for the POI, and indicating the group's composition. The Automatic Negotiation Module is developed using the Jade framework [2].

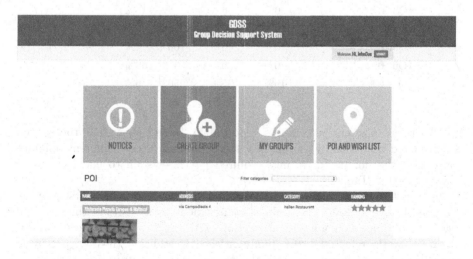

Fig. 4. The web application user interface.

We conducted the study on 10 groups, composed of 2 or 3 users. For each group, the required solution is composed of a number of restaurants varying from 1 and 3. The maximum number of rounds for each negotiation is set to 30. The used dataset contains 521 POI of the city of Naples, obtained using the Foursquare API. After using the system, we propose to each user a questionnaire containing 9 questions which aims to obtain an evaluation of the goodness of the recommendation and of the usability of the system. The questionnaire is composed of two sets of statements that the users are asked to rate with a score ranging from 1 to 5 (respectively, strongly disagree, disagree, neutral, agree, strongly agree). The first set concerns the evaluation of the user interaction with the system, while the second one concerns the evaluation of the quality of the proposed recommendations.

– System-User Interaction:
  Q1 The system is easy to use;
  Q2 Specific expertise is not required to use the system;
  Q3 The system does not require several user interaction steps;
  Q4 The number of required ratings is fair;
– Recommendations evaluation:
  Q5 The system produced a recommendation;
  Q6 The system produced a satisfying recommendation;
  Q7 The system allowed discovering new POI.

Table 2. Percentage of answers for each question.

	Strongly disagree	Disagree	Neutral	Agree	Strongly agree
Q1	0%	13%	0%	56%	31%
Q2	0%	0%	0%	69%	31%
Q3	0%	6%	6%	75%	13%
Q4	6%	19%	44%	31%	0%
Q5	0%	0%	0%	100%	0%
Q6	0%	0%	0%	31%	69%
Q7	0%	19%	25%	50%	6%

The users' answers percentages reported in Table 2 show that the system is considered user-friendly, rapid, easy to use and effortless. Different opinions concerning the number of ratings required by the system to end users were collected (Q4 in Table 2).

It should be noted that agents always find an agreement on the first solution proposed by the system. The evaluations assigned by the users to the provided recommendations show a great satisfaction, with the 70% of the users strongly satisfied, and the remainder 30% simply satisfied. In addition, the users positively replied to the question regarding if the system helped them in discovering new POI.

6   Conclusion

In this work, we propose a Group Decision Support System that uses an automatic negotiation mechanism among software agents representing members of a group of users, to provide the final decision for the group, i.e. a decision that meets the requirements/preferences of the members. There is an agent for each group's member that acts on his/her behalf during the negotiation, modelling his/her behavior in a conflict situation. The user's conflict resolution styles are obtained through the well-known Thomas Kilmann Instrument, a questionnaire filled by each user after the registration in the system. The negotiation is managed by a mediator agent that generates proposals of solutions, and it evaluates the counteroffers received by the other agents. It decides also the heuristics the user agents use in the generation of the new proposals.

We analyze the system by conducing two experiments with simulated data, and one real pilot study. The results show that the system provides high success rate in finding a solution with a number of negotiation rounds lower than 30, both in the case of complete knowledge and of partial knowledge. The pilot study reported satisfying results in terms of the negotiation success rate, and of the quality of the recommendations provided. These results are promising and suggest some possible way to extend the work. Firstly, it would be useful to try to automatize the steps where an interaction with the user is required, so users can avoid to fill the TKI questionnaires, and to provide lists of preferences. A way to automatically derive user profiling is to analyze the behavior of users on social networks. Another possibility is to avoid the interaction when the system requires explicit ratings for the POI during the negotiation, estimating these ratings with an individual recommendation system.

References

1. Bekkerman, P., Kraus, S., Ricci, F.: Applying cooperative negotiation methodology to group recommendation problem. In: Proceedings of Workshop on Recommender Systems in 17th European Conference on Artificial Intelligence, pp. 72–75 (2006)
2. Bellifemine, F.L., Caire, G., Greenwood, D.: Developing Multi-agent Systems with JADE, vol. 7. Wiley, London (2007)
3. Di Napoli, C., Di Nocera, D., Rossi, S.: Computing pareto optimal agreements in multi-issue negotiation for service composition. In: Proceedings of the 2015 International Conference on Autonomous Agents and Multiagent Systems, AAMAS 2015, pp. 1779–1780 (2015)
4. Di Napoli, C., Pisa, P., Rossi, S.: Towards a dynamic negotiation mechanism for qos-aware service markets. In: Pérez, J., et al. (eds.) Trends in Practical Applications of Agents and Multiagent Systems, Advances in Intelligent Systems and Computing, vol. 221, pp. 9–16. Springer, Cham (2013)
5. Garcia, I., Sebastia, L.: A negotiation framework for heterogeneous group recommendation. Expert Syst. Appl. **41**(4), 1245–1261 (2014)
6. Garcia, I., Sebastia, L., Onaindia, E.: A negotiation approach for group recommendation. In: Proceedings of the 2009 International Conference on Artificial Intelligence, Las Vegas Nevada, USA, pp. 919–925. CSREA Press (2009)

7. Gartrell, M., Alanezi, K., Tian, L., Han, R., Lv, Q., Mishra, S.: Socialdining: design and analysis of a group recommendation application in a mobile context (2014)

8. Ito, T., Shintani, T.: Persuasion among agents: an approach to implementing a group decision support system based on multi-agent negotiation. In: Proceedings of the 5th International Joint Conference on Artificial Intelligence (IJCAI97), pp. 592–597. Morgan Kaufmann (1997)

9. Keen, P.G., Morton, M.S.S.: Decision Support Systems: An Organizational Perspective, vol. 35. Addison-Wesley, Reading (1978)

10. Kenneth, O.M.: A set of independent necessary and sufficient conditions for simple majority decision. ECONOMETRICA **20**(4), 680–684 (1952)

11. Kilmann, R.H., Thomas, K.W.: Interpersonal conflict-handling behavior as reflections of jungian personality dimensions. Psychol. Rep. **37**(3), 971–980 (1975)

12. Laudon, J., Laudon, K.: Management Information Systems: Managing the Digital Firm, 10th edn. Prentice-Hall Inc., Upper Saddle River (2006)

13. Levine, J.M., Moreland, R.L.: Small Groups: Key Readings. Psychology Press, New York (2008)

14. Ludwig, S.A., Kersten, G.E., Huang, X.: Towards a behavioural agent-based assistant for e-negotiations. In: Proceedings of Montreal Conference on E-Technologies (2006)

15. Masthoff, J.: Group recommender systems: combining individual models. In: Ricci, F., Rokach, L., Shapira, B., Kantor, P.B. (eds.) Recommender Systems Handbook, pp. 677–702. Springer, USA (2011)

16. Rossi, S., Barile, F., Caso, A., Rossi, A.: Pre-trip ratings and social networks user behaviors for recommendations in touristic web portals. In: Monfort, V., Krempels, K.-H., Majchrzak, T.A., Turk, Ž. (eds.) WEBIST 2015. LNBIP, vol. 246, pp. 297–317. Springer, Cham (2016). doi:10.1007/978-3-319-30996-5_15

17. Rossi, S., Caso, A., Barile, F.: Combining users and items rankings for group decision support. In: Bajo, J., et al. (eds.) Trends in Practical Applications of Agents, Multi-Agent Systems and Sustainability. AISC, vol. 372, pp. 151–158. Springer, Cham (2015). doi:10.1007/978-3-319-19629-9_17

18. Stettinger, M., Felfernig, A.: Choicla: intelligent decision support for groups of users in the context of personnel decisions. In: Proceedings of the ACM RecSys 2014 IntRS Workshop, pp. 28–32 (2014)

19. Villavicencio, C., Schiaffino, S., Diaz-Pace, J.A., Monteserin, A., Demazeau, Y., Adam, C.: A MAS approach for group recommendation based on negotiation techniques. In: Demazeau, Y., Ito, T., Bajo, J., Escalona, M.J. (eds.) PAAMS 2016. LNCS (LNAI), vol. 9662, pp. 219–231. Springer, Cham (2016). doi:10.1007/978-3-319-39324-7_19

Author Index

Printed in the United States
By Bookmasters